STRATEGIC
BUSINESS
PLANNING

STRATEGIC

BUSINESS

PLANNING

A DYNAMIC SYSTEM
for improving performance & competitive advantage

2ND EDITION

CLIVE READING

KOGAN
PAGE

First published in 1993
Second edition, 2002

Kogan Page Limited
120 Pentonville Road
London N1 9JN
UK

British Library Cataloguing in Publication Data

A CIP record for this book is available from the British Library.

ISBN 0 7494 3807 X

Typeset by JS Typesetting Ltd, Wellingborough, Northants
Printed and bound in Great Britain by Biddles Ltd, Guildford and King's Lynn
www.biddles.co.uk

Contents

Introduction

Most senior executives think they know how to plan and implement strategy for their company or strategic unit. The difficulty they often have is that their approach is:

- ad hoc and developed in response to a particular situation;
- concentrated on limited functions or activities in the company;
- not an organized, comprehensive, process;
- not fully implemented.

The strategy they do develop is not robust and will change with even slight economic downturns or industry trends. Companies unable to hold to an agreed course, even over a period of three to five years, will never perform strongly. Robust strategy requires pursuing the most attractive strategic targets, focusing the resources of the business on them and aligning the organization, systems and technology to support their achievement.

Achieving focus in a company is not easy. Many members of the leadership team will have reached their position through being successful in one particular function, even though they may have worked in a number of different functions. They will tend to have a mindset formed of their earlier experiences. Bringing all this experience together to create a strategy can be a great strength, but it needs a unifying process to ensure there is ownership of the strategy in all members of the leadership team.

Fourteen years ago I developed the concept of strategic business planning, linking company purpose, business goals, strategy, performance targets and the action program in one framework. Having now worked with some 80 businesses in Europe, North America and Asia, many of them over a number of years, the success of the approach is proven. Over 700 top executives, 75 per cent of them chairmen or CEOs, have attended my one-day seminar. Many of those who have implemented the system have told me how effective they found it in developing highly competitive, sustainable strategies and, equally importantly, consensus and commitment within the leadership team and active endorsement from employees.

The approach is to ensure that the strategy is owned by the leadership team and the action program by executives and employees throughout the organization. This is the key to successful implementation.

The approach is not a fad, but a robust business process to improve the performance and competitive position of a company. If the leadership team want to try a new approach to business this can be incorporated into the system, but it will clearly be part of an overall strategy, not an isolated initiative. The Internet and the impact of e-commerce are all encompassed within the approach.

In a fast-changing world, strategy has to be capable of encompassing radical change, continuous improvement and the options in between. The part on strategic concepts, which has been developed mainly over the last three years, enables leadership teams to understand the cycle of strategy and develops ideas on how they can consider, decide and implement radical strategy as well as strategies for competing within the existing market/product/service arena.

All the top executives and leadership teams that I know are under time pressure; there is always more to do than the time to do it. Most of them work long hours in managing the business for today, winning new orders, keeping operations moving with continuous efficiency improvements and ensuring they meet the short-term expectations of their owners and Wall Street.

This approach uses their time effectively and sparingly. It can take no more than five days of their time over a period of two to four months to develop a robust strategy that will create new competitive advantage and focus the whole business on generating better returns for their intellectual, managerial, energy and resource inputs.

A clear strategy that is understood by employees, customers, investors and all stakeholders, and that has the universal support of the entire leadership team and board of directors, is essential to any successful enterprise, be it business or non-business. Strategic business planning will enable the leaders of companies to develop that strategy.

The book is structured in three parts. The first part concerns the development of the strategic business planning framework. It is this framework that ensures that the strategy that is developed is robust and involves the entire business. The second part outlines some strategic concepts that help to ensure that the strategy is ambitious and allows for the potential changes in the business environment. The third is concerned with how the strategy is developed, owned by the leadership team, cascaded through the organization and implemented.

PART ONE

The strategic business planning framework

Developing a strategy that will lead to sustainable competitive advantage and can be effectively implemented requires a clear strategic framework and a structured process.

This part describes the outline of a strategic framework that has proved highly successful in over 80 companies, from small businesses to large corporations. The process is usually developed using workshops for the leadership team. In this part there is occasional reference to workshops; this is simply to help the reader think how these areas could be developed. A fuller description of workshops is included in Part 3.

1

The purpose of strategic business planning

WHAT IS STRATEGIC BUSINESS PLANNING?

Strategic business planning (SBP) is the key to developing a business so that it runs effectively and efficiently. This may involve developing different products, services or markets. It may involve acquiring compatible companies or changing the whole nature of the business, such as when Richard Branson, the founder of the Virgin Group, decided that he wanted to diversify away from the music business into the airline business. It can incorporate any management concept, such as re-engineering, total quality or time based management. It is a process, not a management fad product, based on a proven strategic framework that is effective in setting direction and improving performance for businesses of all types and for divisions and departments within corporations. It incorporates the two fundamentals of strategy, deciding where you want to go and how to implement operational initiatives to take you there, coherently in one process.

Users of the process include companies with a single managing head and 50 employees to the largest multinational corporations. They use it every year as a means of constantly re-evaluating the strategy, modifying the direction if necessary and planning the next phase in its development.

The real value of SBP lies in the planning process: discussion, developing new understanding, new insights and generating new ideas for the business. It does not lie in developing a written plan. It has been suggested that the night before a business plan is published it should be burnt, because the process should be continuous, not a one-off exercise. The first time the executives use the process they set up a framework that should last for between three and five years, although it will be challenged at least every year. This framework makes it easier to develop the plan for each succeeding period, but the process of planning and making adjustments continues as long as the business survives.

The aim is for everyone in the business to think and manage strategically.

Strategic business planning is about setting a direction for the business, a direction to which everybody, executives and employees, can become committed. It ensures every part of the company is in harmony, moving towards a clear business purpose that will give it a competitive advantage and improve its performance.

THE CONFUSED COMPANY

One of the questions often asked of participants on management courses is 'what is good management?' The group will come up with a whole string of words: commitment, delegation, motivation, listening, and praise. Eventually someone offers the word 'leadership'. Leadership is enthusing people with where they are heading and motivating them to take the steps to move in that direction. In this sense this book and the entire SBP process is about leadership.

Next I ask them 'what is poor management?' Besides descriptions of the opposite of good management, such as poor communication, lack of honesty, criticism of employees, there is always one word that emerges: confusion. Poor management confuses. Every one of our client companies that had performed poorly was riddled with confusion. Middle managers were the most confused, the workforce was usually demoralized, and the thinking members of top management were depressed. They knew things were wrong, that the company ran by fire-fighting, that customer service was poor and complaints were not dealt with quickly, that staff left because they found their work unsatisfying. But they did not know how to remedy the situation.

Conceptually this kind of company can be represented as shown in Figure 1.1. Each department is looking in a different direction, and there is no overall focus to bring them together.

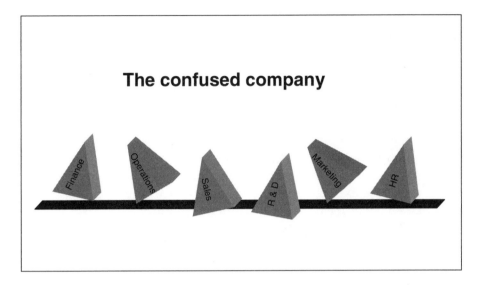

Figure 1.1 The confused company

I used to think the confused company was just an accident caused by lack of focus. Then some specific experiences indicated that it is often the result of deliberate intent. Sometimes it is caused by executives determined to have their own way even if they know that what they plan to do is not for the overall good of the business. Many such companies are intensely political organizations and to achieve anything requires what amounts to a coalition of executives to support it and make it work. Obtaining the support of a colleague for your plan implies giving him or her your support when needed for their plan. The overall needs of the company are lost sight of in this process of negotiated reciprocal support, yet executives using this approach are often the first to complain about lack of performance.

However, more often this push in different directions is caused inadvertently by executives trying to do something to improve the business. Their problem is that there are no clear guidelines on where the business is intended to go and therefore no clarity about the actions necessary to take it there. Not surprisingly, they all try to improve the business by doing what they perceive to be best for their particular function or division, rather than planning for the overall performance of the entire organization. They end up by taking different and often contradictory actions that are followed by recriminations among the executives and further disharmony.

This is rational considering that most departmental or functional managers have primarily developed through one function, say marketing, operations, finance, HR or IT. They have a perspective that maximizes the performance of that function. In operations it might be maximizing the utilization of operatives or resources, or cost minimization for manufacturing a product or delivering a service. It might include inventory reduction. For marketing it might be market share or mindshare achieved through advertising and promotions. In sales it might be maximizing revenue, which might involve high service levels and higher inventories as well as discounts for major customers. Finance might seek to maximize profit, cash flow or earnings per share. HR might be considering meeting recruitment requirements, relative pay scales and maintaining harmonious union relationships. For most CEOs growing the business will be their prime goal. Conceptually this is shown in Figure 1.2.

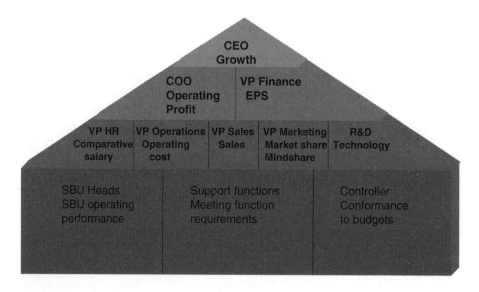

Figure 1.2 Mismatch of goals in a typical company

Even in corporations where there is a rational strategy, the way it is understood and interpreted by the board of directors, the president and vice presidents can be very different. The different strategic message they communicate down the line results in chaos at middle management and operating levels.

This type of organization seldom performs effectively or efficiently. To do so it has to be focused, united and absolutely clear on the goals to be achieved, the strategy for achieving them, the timescale, the resources required and the action program and implementation responsibilities.

What is being described here can sometimes appear to be the rule rather than the exception. Time and time again when one of my clients makes an acquisition and starts to understand the business they have purchased they are amazed at the confusion. The business may be profitable and even growing at a reasonable rate, but the waste of effort, the cost of delivery, the frustration and above all, the missed opportunities caused by poor leadership and management is staggering.

There are two concepts that executives and managers in confused companies do not understand. The first is quite simply to ensure that all parts of the company know and are working towards the same purpose. Understanding this is the first step to achieving it. The second step is to grasp that the business purpose is a unified, total, holistic concept for the whole business. It is not just a marketing, product development or sales strategy. It is the focus of everything that happens in the organization and depends on implementation throughout the whole organization for its success.

Throughout most of this book reference is made to working on an organization-wide basis. However, the approach will work effectively for divisions and subsidiaries that have autonomy to operate within boundaries specified by the corporate parent.

The approach is to think through the purpose of the division or department and decide what it contributes to the total organization that could not be obtained from another source within the organization or through outsourcing. By working through the five goals, the role and contribution of the unit (now and what it should be in the future) will become clearly understood. The strategy can then be developed to enable the division or department to make a more effective contribution to the entire enterprise.

THE FOCUSED COMPANY

Focus is what the strategic business planning process achieves. It enables an organization to operate as shown in Figure 1.3, by providing a forum and a structured process to resolve internal confusion and to channel energy and effort in a commonly agreed direction.

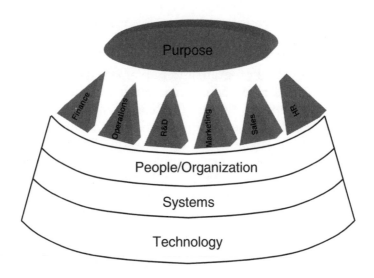

Figure 1.3 The focused company

The result is an organization where functions and departments are directing their efforts to achieve a common purpose. In addition, the way people, systems and technology are organized and resourced supports the functions in moving towards that common purpose.

Theory is fine, but how is it put into practice at the sharp end? My guarantee is that if you really apply and implement the process to develop the framework described in this book your business will come to resemble the focused company model.

Communicating a clear strategy to employees and ensuring they understand how their contribution is important for its success is the first requirement for creating a focused business. At a detailed level what is required is that everything in the company is aligned with the company purpose. This is shown in Figure 1.4. This is obviously not a complete list, but serves to indicate the range of issues that must be aligned to maximize company performance.

The second requirement paraphrases Peter Drucker and his 'Effectiveness is doing the right things, efficiency is doing things right' (Drucker, 1974). This encapsulates the overriding difference between high-performing and low-performing companies. (Drucker actually said 'Effectiveness is doing the right things. Efficiency concerns itself with the input of effort into all areas of activity.')

There is a well-known tenet in business called the 80/20 rule, or the Pareto principle. This states that 80 per cent of results come from 20

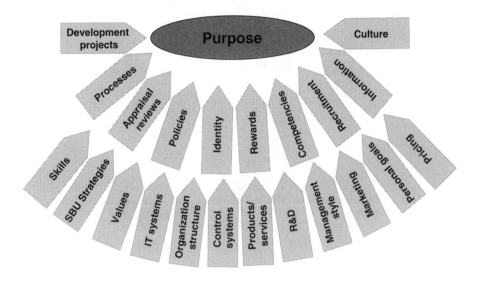

Figure 1.4 Company purpose

per cent of their possible causes: for example, 80 per cent of sales come from 20 per cent of customers, 80 per cent of problems come from 20 per cent of the product lines, and 80 per cent of stock value is in 20 per cent of stock items.

This can be extended to senior executives' decisions and actions: 80 per cent of a manager's impact comes from 20 per cent of his or her actions.

Actions or decisions with high impact are those that affect the company strategically, rather than those that merely concern its normal operating routine. They concern, for example, changing the business model, focusing on new market sectors, fundamental improvements in customer service, making critical investment decisions, obtaining a better return on research and development expenditure. Such actions or decisions affect the company's longer-term performance and enable it to achieve competitive advantage.

How this concept is applied to managers' decisions is illustrated in Figure 1.5.

Strategic decisions will be fewer in number than operational ones but will have a longer-term impact on the company. They are the domain of top executives and senior managers. Maintenance decisions are of a day-to-day, operational nature. They are critical to keeping the company running, but their impact is usually short-term. The nature of the SBP

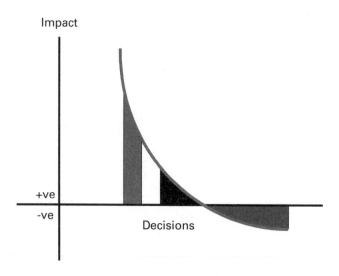

Figure 1.5 Decision impact

process is such that the executives will focus far more on strategic issues which address the future of the company and which will automatically increase the effectiveness of their contribution.

Some actions are negative: the production manager keeping the line busy with parts that are seldom required, the salesman offering discounts that mean selling at a loss and the engineers designing products with unnecessarily high tolerances on every dimension when there is no benefit to be gained from such accuracy. Such things usually come to the surface and can be stopped, although often a lot of money is wasted first.

The behavior that is really worrying, and that is endemic among some senior executives, is the kind that has either no real impact or only a marginal impact on the company. This kind of behavior ensures that decisions will be taken which maintain the status quo. It assumes yesterday will be replicated and does not prepare for tomorrow. Status quo maintenance decisions do not radically change anything. They do not dramatically reduce the delivery time of product to customer, or reduce costs, or improve quality, or add meaning to the job of the employee. They do not clarify fundamental misunderstandings, or create a culture that empowers people to make their own decisions. These maintenance decisions improve the operational efficiency of the organization and are essential, but they are the provinces of middle and junior managers and employees, who should be encouraged to produce all the 'one per cent' improvements an organization can implement. However, executives and managers who only take 'efficiency' or 'maintenance' decisions are not contributing to the development of the organization. They are not preparing it for tomorrow.

Senior managers who take only efficiency decisions do not understand their business role. They either lack the ability to make major decisions or work in a corporation where making major decisions is impossible for whatever reason.

The reason middle managers take ineffective decisions is that they are confused, lack confidence, are not empowered or have no direction; so they honestly do not know which actions will be effective or where the executives want the company to go.

SERVING THE CUSTOMER

The senior executives themselves are often the biggest problem. In some companies, when they are asked how many decisions they have made in the last week, they often say dozens, or even hundreds. When asked how many have had a fundamental impact on the business – how many have changed what they do or how they do it – the response is often a blank face.

Many executives do not know what they are supposed to be doing: they do not know what their job is. Collectively the leadership team has no idea where the company is going.

The confusion that exists in some companies is indicated when I ask executives what they think their company employs them to achieve. Often their answer is 'to earn a profit'. I then explore what they actually do to earn a profit, using examples of things they have done in the last week or so. Salespeople and production people find this easier, although even for them there are many aspects to their job that have only a tenuous link to profits.

What users of strategic business planning understand is that the firm has a purpose, a reason for being in existence. That purpose will sometimes be clearly stated, at other times only vaguely implied. Whatever that purpose is, everyone on the payroll needs to understand how he or she contributes to achieving it.

Of course profit is part of the purpose but, by itself, profit is only the result, the scorecard of doing other things well. The key word I am looking for is 'customer'. Without customers, there is no business. Everyone, from the finance director to the floor sweeper, is there to help the company provide the best possible service and products to its customers. That is the ultimate reason that they are employed. If they cannot answer how they serve that purpose, then they are at best of dubious value to the organization.

THE BENEFITS OF SBP

The benefits of strategic business planning are threefold:

- an understanding by all senior management of the business, its unique attributes, why customers buy from it, and the opportunities and threats it faces;
- a clear concept of where the business is going and the actions everyone will take to move it there;
- a commitment by the leadership team to make the strategic plan work and to ensure that the company moves in the direction they have decided is the best for its future.

The physical and immediate benefit – the plan – is summarized in a simple framework supported by an action program and a fairly short report. Its main purpose is to be a record of the process and to ensure on a regular basis, usually monthly, that the action program is being followed and is on schedule. What it is not is a sterile document; it is regularly updated, reviewed and made to live.

2

Understanding the framework

The strategic business planning framework is the glue that holds the strategy and implementation together. It provides the focus and direction and allocates the actions and responsibilities. It can accommodate revolutionary or evolutionary strategies.

The process of developing the framework, communicating it to employees and using its motivating implementation approach will create a dynamic company. The framework will prove to be very powerful in helping the leadership team to think and manage the business strategically. It is shown in diagrammatic form in Figure 2.1.

This chapter gives an overview of the framework and considers its component parts. The rest of the book then explains the process of how to develop a unique strategic business plan and framework for your company.

COMPANY PURPOSE

A company's purpose is the reason that it exists, and why it will continue to exist, providing it maintains a competitive advantage. A business, or any other organization, serves a need in society. It will only continue as long as society in general, or sufficiently large segments of society, want it to remain in existence through purchasing its products or services.

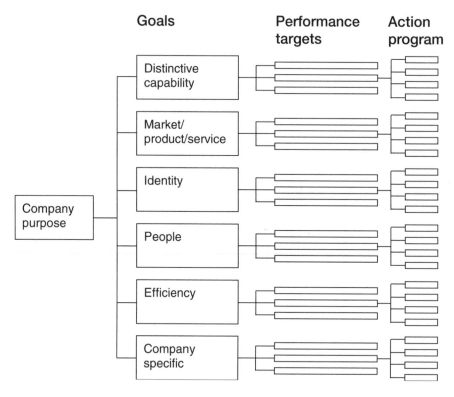

Figure 2.1 The strategic business planning framework

The armaments industry in the free world was created and continues because a democratic society elects governments who decide that national security requires armed forces. The armed forces in turn require modern arms, hence the need for an arms industry. Once the industry can produce sufficient armaments for its own country it can then, with its government's agreement, sell arms to others. In July 1989, when Gorbachov was changing Russia and peace with the West became the new policy, I wrote: 'But imagine for a moment that glasnost proceeds at a pace that at present seems impossible, that countries in Europe and the free world agree to stop equipping their armies with new weapons. Then society's need for an armaments industry is greatly diminished; its prime purpose no longer exists.'

That thought, intended to be over the top at the time, is already history. Since 1989 defense procurement has declined by more than 60 per cent in constant dollars. Estimates suggest that only 25 per cent of the 120,000 companies that once supplied the Department of Defense are now supplying them; the others have shut down altogether or left the defense industry. The loss of skilled employees over a period of time has been greater than that sustained by any other industry in recent times.

In the 1989 article I wrote: 'The armaments industry of the Western world is already repositioning itself to meet a new environment. And as the primary manufacturers, those companies that design, assemble and sell the final weapon, begin to develop a new purpose for their organization, so many of their subcontractors and suppliers will have to rethink their purpose. The situation is one that abounds with both opportunities and threats, because there will still need to be an armaments industry. The difference is that it will be smaller and have to meet different requirements. If they are to profit from the changes, companies need to rethink their purpose, their goals and their strategy.'

The successful corporations like Lockheed Martin have managed to do this through understanding the needs of the US Defense Department and adapting to meet those needs. Lockheed Martin set out to win a much bigger share of a shrinking market through consolidations with other companies. They also understood that today's military aircraft and fighting ships will have to last for decades. But the electronic and other technology-intensive parts may become obsolete in five years. Software components can require updating in two years.

Since in many ways military hardware needs to have relative rather than maximum superiority, the need is to continuously upgrade existing hardware at modest expenditure rather than scrap and replace. Companies that structured their business around this purpose have in a number of instances expanded their business and positioned it with greater security.

Purpose statements that can really affect a company's strategy can come from insights about the market requirements, as with military suppliers. These are often effective statements provided they are challenged every year. This does not mean they must change every year. Purpose statements need to last for a minimum of five years, even in this age of change.

It is already clear that increasingly company purpose will have to include not only the provision of products and services that meet the demands of the market in terms of performance and price, but also how their creation avoids harming the environment to an unacceptable degree.

Statements of purpose

The company purpose statement should be thought of as lasting for at least five and perhaps 10 or more years. However, every year it needs to be reviewed, challenged and justified.

The best purpose statements transcend product or market, level of service or performance criteria. They make sense of the corporation on a higher level. They explain what an organization means to accomplish in terms of the employees, shareholders and all other stakeholders. It defines why employees want to come to work in the morning, why people apply to join the firm, why banks, accountants and suppliers want to be associated with it in the long run. They explain why competitors admire the company and why non-customers would switch to it with only a slight change of circumstances.

Often a purpose encompasses an ideal, a value to strive after that lifts the spirit and gives the firm a place in the annals of business. One corporation that had that special quality for me personally was Philip Morris. I left the company in 1976, but I can still remember, almost tangibly feel, what it meant to be a manager there. The corporation was special, its people were made to feel special; products, advertising and employees 'traveled first-class'. Working for Philip Morris was a privilege. In all this I am ignoring the main product, cigarettes: it was the ethos of the corporation that was so exhilarating.

It has become fashionable to recognize that, generally, conglomerates are not any better at running a number of different companies than the managers of those companies are at running each on their own. The ownership and control of a number of separate and unrelated businesses have no purpose other than to achieve size and power. Conglomerating a number of businesses together is not adding value. The individual companies have a purpose, but the purpose of one company will often not relate to that of others in the conglomerate, unless there is a natural relationship between them.

GE is a conglomerate that earns most of its profits from finance, though it is most recognized for its manufactured and engineered products that cover a huge range from domestic white goods to aerospace. However, GE has clearly integrated its business through stating common goals, such as being number one or number two in every market, transferring business management ideas across the organization and having a common management approach inculcated in all levels of its staff. At its Crotonville management training facility Jack Welch personally discusses the business issues and strategy GE is following with company managers. Through these approaches it has become a business that adds value and creates purpose through its diverse business activities.

Purpose statements should help the strategists plan the strategy. This is the reason that those focused on stakeholders are almost worse than useless. They only restate the rules of the business game. They are little better than the old-fashioned objective of long-term profit maximization. At the basic level stakeholders consist of employees, shareholders, customers and suppliers. What company will not try to recruit and retain the most appropriate employees, ensure it has access to the cheapest and most secure capital, and will also try to stay in favor with the owners of the business, who can, if sufficiently provoked, sack the management? All companies try to retain loyal and profitable customers and want a partnership with suppliers that will create the greatest competitive advantage. And competitors, in the broadest sense, are constantly wooing all stakeholders; if their offer is better many stakeholders will change their allegiance. Hence a purpose that states 'to fairly reward all our stakeholders' is not only bland, it offers no strategic guidance and is of no real value.

In any company there is a set of factors critical to staying in business. Quality of product or service that meets the customer's expectation, cost of supply that will enable a profit to be earned on the price the market will accept, having a business delivery system that reaches customers and will not offend them are all critical. Meeting the set of factors does not create a purpose.

Which purpose statements, when fully lived and acted on, do motivate? Most people have triggers that motivate them. Technology, automobiles, the Internet and computer are all areas that motivate. They challenge technical ability and enable the creation of a new tomorrow. Caring, as in nursing, doctors and pharmaceutical companies, motivates. Meeting personal challenges and being trained and then trusted to do a job motivates.

If work is one way to contribute to society, as well as a means to earn a living, the purpose statement should create a motivation within the company to pursue and excel at activities that will delight customers and create pride in employees through meeting challenges and being able to develop their business skills.

Company purpose is thus the dominant theme, the glue that holds a company together, whether it is one unit or a number of businesses. It is the philosophy of the business. The statement of this purpose should make sense of the organization for its management, employees, financiers, customers and all other stakeholders.

Statements of purpose should not be so vague that they could apply to any business organization. To say 'our purpose is to be profitable' is effectively meaningless: no one could disagree; hence the statement does not help in understanding the company and provides no direction that employees can work towards.

There are two tests for a good company purpose statement. Think of a salesperson having to make a decision on his or her own, say about selling a product or service to a customer which will meet that customer's needs but not as well as some other product or service which could be purchased from the competition. The salesperson is unable to ask anyone else what to do. Will the company purpose statement help to make that decision? Then think of other people in the company, such as someone working the night shift in the warehouse, who have to authorize whether to send a spare part to a customer who urgently needs it to keep their night shift going. (This might be the case in the computer industry.) Does the employee in the warehouse pick the part and send it to the customer on his or her own initiative by the quickest means available; or wait until the morning, when the credit checks can be made and the proper procedures followed? Does the company purpose statement help to make such a decision?

Purpose revolves round two questions. One is Peter Drucker's classic question 'What business are we (should we be) in?'; the second is, 'What do we stand for?' (Drucker, 1974). This second question encompasses the fundamental philosophy that guides the business and the values inherent in that philosophy.

Effective Statements

Purpose statements are particular to a company. They may sound bland out of context to outsiders but have meaning to those associated with the company.

It is often easier to identify poor purpose statements. They can sometimes confuse and frighten rather than clarify and inspire. One accounting firm had as its company purpose statement: 'We want to be recognized as the accounting firm with an unsurpassed reputation for integrity, professional excellence, personal service and positive contribution to its clients.' In the three months after this was issued a large number of partners and managers were asked to articulate the firm's purpose statement. Only one partner could stumble his way through it. The message eventually went back to the senior partners that the purpose statement was as motivating as a bowl of cold rice.

The statement's problems lay in a number of areas. Firstly, it excluded a large part of the firm from its definition of the business, the management consultants. The use of the phrase 'accounting firm' was the writing on the wall for them. Possibly this was intentional, although the organization still has a large management consulting practice many years later. Secondly, it failed to define the market the firm wanted to be in. Thirdly, its standards could be applied to any large accountancy organization. Change the word 'accounting' and it could apply to almost any professional organization: legal, architectural, medical and so forth. It contains no meaningful definition, nothing that enabled the staff to say 'Ah yes! That's us'.

It is interesting that the firm added a second part to the statement, which said that they wanted 'quality people, quality service, quality clients'. This may sound even more bland, and yet it came much closer to hitting the button. This statement says, in effect:

- We want to grow at a rate that will enable us to recruit excellent people and train them well.
- We are not hell-bent on growth for the sake of boosting top line revenue.
- We want to give our clients a service that will make their business more competitive and financially stronger.
- We want to retain our clients.
- We want our clients to grow and achieve their business goals. In so doing our growth will be organic.
- We want relationships, even that hackneyed phrase, partnership, with our clients.
- Doing more for our existing clients is more important than winning too many new clients.

In short, the 'quality people, quality service, quality clients' summarized the purpose of the firm in a way that made sense to staff and could be explained to clients and other stakeholders. It answered the question 'What business should we be in?' with the answer 'Making our clients competitively and financially stronger.' The 'What do we stand for?' question was answered by 'Quality rather than quantity; quality defined by the positive impact we have on your business. It is achieved through our process of understanding your business and your goals, developing our partner and manager structure and by careful recruitment and training. Our obsession is that our clients are more successful because of our advice and input.'

This example brings out some of the golden rules of the company purpose statement. Managers need a fairly comprehensive statement to ensure that they are setting a clear and total direction for the company. But to motivate staff, to give them a purpose they can remember, the statement needs to be able to be summed up in one line. People need to be able to remember it ten minutes after they first heard it. That is why 'quality people, quality service, quality clients' was so powerful.

This type of slogan or statement that becomes a call to action really is an important element in communicating the company purpose to all employees. Properly developed, explained to employees and lived by top and middle managers in their actions and behavior, it can set a standard of performance to which employees throughout the company can relate and aspire.

One of the most famous is the Avis car rental slogan: 'We try harder'. This has stood the test of time. Originally a statement to distinguish Avis from Hertz and play the 'We're number two in size but number one in service', it now defines Avis against all other car rental companies. More importantly, employees still relate to it and know what they have to do to continually attract and retain customers.

Others that have been effective are 'The creative use of space' for a racking company; and 'Engineers in plastics' for a precision injection molding company. Each company made its purpose statement live. The racking company had a range of special, flexible products that used space efficiently. In addition it would customize those products for customers who had special needs. Finally it offered a computer-aided design service and trained its managers in the techniques of effective use of space. The plastics company made products with tolerances as tight as could be produced by machining steel. It was constantly developing new techniques to meet customer needs. The engineers in the company wanted to overcome the idea that plastics had a cheap image, which they did not want associated with their products.

In each case the important point is that the purpose statement distinguished that company from its competitors. It did this firstly in the managers' minds, because the statement meant much more to them than the words alone and, secondly, they could make it mean something for their staff, customers and suppliers.

Sometimes clients ask if there is a real point in having company purpose statements. Their accusation is that they are merely words to make the framework look attractive. The answer is that most companies are in business for the long run, not to make quick profit in the next two years and then disappear from the market. To build a long-term business you need a substantial number of long-term customers. It has been calculated that it is six times more expensive to acquire a new customer than to keep an existing one. Even more significant than this, service companies depend on their existing customers for between 85 and 95 per cent of their business; for manufacturing companies it is in excess of 65 per cent. Every customer represents an investment by your company. Every lost customer represents a loss; if you think of the annual sales made to that customer and multiply it by ten, this represents a fortune in lost business over the next ten years. This is why we need longer-term goals, so that we not only win in the short term, but also make the investment, in customers, staff, systems, equipment and infrastructure, for the long term. A company purpose is a commitment to the long term, which helps the company to win today, tomorrow and in the year 2020 and beyond. It is part of the answer to short-term management thinking.

That is one reason for having a purpose statement. The other is to do with the logic of the whole process. The goals have to contribute to achieving the purpose statement. This ensures the goals fit together and reinforce each other. Achieving performance targets attains the goals. The action program is what is done to achieve these performance targets. The whole process is therefore 'pulled along' by the company purpose. Where this process is not thought and worked through, whether in a multinational corporation or a small company, the result is a lot of action but no uniting strategic thrust.

There is one other reason for the purpose statement: for top management to think through why the company exists, and the purpose it serves creates insights into where the business should be going and what the future holds.

GOALS

Goals represent where the leadership team wants the business to go; they are the aspirations, realistic aspirations, for the future.

For most strategic business plans five types of goal are used in the framework: distinctive capability, market/product/service, identity, people and efficiency. Of these, three are position goals:

- Market/product/service defines the markets on which the business will focus and the products or services it will supply.

- Identity expresses how the business will be recognized and thought of by customers, employees and all the audiences it wants to influence.
- Efficiency determines how the business will perform operationally.

The other two are execution goals and are, generally, more difficult to articulate:

- Distinctive capability describes the unique attribute that leads to sustained competitive advantage.
- People encompasses the shared values, the desired culture and the type of organization the business has to be to succeed in achieving all the other goals and the company purpose.

These five goals enable the direction of the business to be comprehensively established. However, sometimes there is a need to include a sixth goal because of a particular requirement. This would normally cover areas such as safety, which is critical in a construction and heavy engineering operations, where this activity needs strong emphasis, or ethics, in medical, pharmaceutical, financial and legal businesses where there is a particular need to keep all staff focused on ethical issues.

When Jimmy Carter became US President, some of his advisers suggested that he should concentrate on only three or four goals for his domestic policy, because that is the most anyone could achieve in that type of job in a single term in office. So it is with SBP. The goals used in the SBP process will enable a clear direction to be set and comprehensive progress made to achieve them.

Some executives become very concerned with 'wordsmithing' the goals. It is of prime importance that there is clarity, that everyone can easily understand the goals, and that the language used enables people to relate emphathetically to them. However, they do not have to be erudite.

It is also important that the goals do not sound like long-term dreams that have no substance. Give them some immediacy. Performance targets and the action program will reinforce the feeling that the goals can be attained within the foreseeable future. The wording of the goals can reinforce this perception.

Distinctive capability

This goal answers the question: 'What business or organizational capability exists or can be created in the next three to six years that is superior to any competitor's, and will enable us to attain a significant competitive advantage in our chosen markets?'

The distinctive capability can be an inherent skill or competence that the company possesses. This might be that of acquiring new companies and integrating them profitably into the parent organization, or developing staff with certain skills that are in short supply. It could be a political skill, nurturing close relationships with the leaders of developing countries, or being able to work with investment banks or international aid agencies. This area of potential distinctive capability is so broad that it is generated not from a grid or checklist, but through an analysis of strengths and weaknesses, as described in Chapter 21.

From a customer's viewpoint a company's distinctive capability is similar to its USP (unique selling proposition). It is the attribute of the products or services created by that organization's distinctive capabilities/competencies that just cannot be bought elsewhere. It may be the factor that enables a company to charge premium prices. It could also be the factor that enables a company to have a low cost of delivery.

Distinctive capability is also the major area that must be monitored by the management control system to determine if it is still superior to the competition, and if it still represents a clear competitive advantage.

In business jargon, the distinctive capability is the business's critical success factor (CSF). If that goes wrong, the business will go wrong with it.

Sometimes this goal may be thought of as the distinctive competence goal. This is a key competence that is delivered to the market or used to develop the business. This overall key competence breaks down into a number of sub-competencies that need to be present in the functions and departments of the company. One approach to developing a distinctive capability is to identify and build a structure composed of the competencies within the organization, both those currently held and those needed in the future. Experience of this approach in large organizations has shown that it can be very powerful.

The distinctive capability goal is the most difficult goal to develop. It usually takes two or three times as long to determine as the other goals. Once it is developed the remaining goals seem very much easier to define.

Market/product/service

This goal defines the markets the company will operate in, and the products and services it will sell in those markets. It both describes this business domain and explains why it is attractive to the company.

One of the eight attributes of excellent companies is that they 'stick close to the knitting'(Peters and Waterman, 1982). Most profitable companies stay with what they know about. This does not mean they are not adventurous, but statistically the chances of succeeding with any new product are about one in seven, and that is in markets that are understood. There is obviously less chance of success with products, markets and businesses that are not well known.

When Philip Morris acquired 7 Up, the soft drinks company, it looked like a good strategic match. They had built the largest selling cigarette brand in the world with Marlboro, taken Miller from seventh position to second in the US brewing league, and so could really claim to understand consumer goods marketing. Philip Morris's skill lay in transplanting the brand marketing ability they had developed with their cigarettes and beers to the packaged food business. With the General Foods and Kraft acquisitions they studied the market and products until they understood how the brand would sell to the targeted customer group. Philip Morris was not an MBA type of management style, built on economic theory. It was built on knowledge of products and knowledge of markets developed over many years.

The difference with 7 Up, however, was that it operated through bottling franchises, and managing that relationship was a whole new ball game for the Philip Morris culture. When I spoke to one of the corporate marketing directors in Europe at the time and asked how 7 Up was doing, his instant reply (and this was still in the early days with the project) was: 'I'm not getting involved with that mess'. Philip Morris manages their brands with a strong hand. Having to work at managing the business with third parties was something at which they were unskilled, and eventually they sold 7 Up.

The market/product/service goal defines the markets that the company understands and wants to continue in, and the adjacent or new markets it wants to expand into. The products are those that are seen as being right for the company, defined either in terms of product or service type, production technology or business skill.

The market/product/service development chart (Figure 2.2) can be useful in developing the market/product goal at a particular stage in the process.

In this example, the company was already in racking systems for warehouses (option 1) and had extended into offering the same product to DIY retailers (option 2). Because it had met the needs of the retailers particularly well, it was being offered the opportunity to develop special products for these customers (option 3).

Products \ Markets	Existing	Extension of existing	Modification of existing	Completely new
Existing	(1) Storage racking for industrial and distribution warehouses	(2) Storage racking for home improvement warehouses		
Modification of existing	(6) Mezzanine floors for warehouses	(3) Special racking for home improvement retail warehouses	(4) Special racking systems for supermarkets	(5) Aircraft hangars for private planes
Completely new	(7) Computer control systems for industrial and distribution warehouses			

Figure 2.2 Market/product development chart

The products were essentially lighter and smaller versions of existing ones and could be manufactured using existing facilities and skills. This was moving the company in new directions, but they were opportunistically following up on leads, rather than deciding the market/product stance that was best for them. Their customers were driving them. The danger in this approach is that it is possible to end up in an overcrowded marketplace, with poor margins and little or no future.

In fact, for this particular company option 3 was an excellent choice and it went on to build significant sales volume in this market. What it had to decide next was if it was going to follow the route into developing the retailing market by, for instance, trying to sell to supermarkets (option 4), or whether it should concentrate on developing the markets it was already in. The managers also considered the possibility of developing their existing product to provide aircraft hangars for private aircraft (option 5). Manufacturing the frames would not be difficult, but the marketplace was totally unknown. They decided not to proceed with this option, even though they had a trial installation already erected at a nearby airfield.

They decided to stay with racking and storage systems for warehousing and retail, but only retail that used their existing technical and production base. This effectively meant heavy duty warehousing, such as DIY. They would also refocus on the needs of the warehousing market by introducing new forms of branded mezzanine floors (option 6). Finally, market forecasts were indicating that the growth in warehouse systems would come in the area of automated, computer-controlled warehouses. The managers decided that they would start seeking how to enter this market, either by acquiring a suitable company or through a strategic partnership (option 7).

This example shows how a company can begin to define its market/ product/service stance. The discussions evolved over a period of time and were combined with a number of other analyses. The value of the chart was in visualizing the discussion and in clarifying the options.

The timescale for achieving any changes is built into the performance targets, which are discussed later.

Identity

The identity goal is concerned with how the company is marketed. It is the image of the company that you want in the customer's mind. A good reputation and a clear image of what the company represents to customers is worth a fortune in future business.

In order to occupy a legitimate and rational niche for customers, a company has to be strategically positioned. Hence the marketing approach and the customer's initial or current perception have to coincide, even as the marketing seeks to influence that perception. An important element in this is recognizing where the company is positioned relative to its competitors: it does not make business sense for two companies to position themselves in exactly the same way.

The identity that a company or brand holds is easy to check with well-known names. Ford has been promoting the safety features of the Taurus, showing how a parent cares for the family through driving a safe vehicle. If the advertising is successful and supported by factual data eventually the image will stick with the public, much as the Volvo safety image has done.

A strong image makes it easy to build simple positioning statements into scenarios. For example, I am driving along an Interstate on a Sunday, behind a Taurus.

> Question: Who is driving, a man or a woman?
> Answer: A man.
> Question: How old is he?
> Answer: Mid 30s to late 40s.
> Question: Is he on his own?

Answer: No, his wife is sitting next to him and his two or three children are sitting in the back. There are also at least one, possibly two dogs in the back of the car.

You can see how safety, middle(ish) age, family and responsibility fit into an image. This game can be played further, guessing at the driver's job, the type of house he lives in, sports played, newspapers read. The fact that it will be incorrect for many Taurus drivers is not important. Many of my friends have Taurus cars and generally they had wives, children and dogs and many of the mothers used to drive their children to school in the family Taurus. The positioning of the product in relation to the customer is still very clear. It is a safe family car, and traditionally on Sundays father drives the entire family. That is the sort of family that buys Taurus cars.

This exercise is something that can be done with any product or service that has a fairly clear image: Honda mowers, Seiko watches, Yves St Laurent ties and Marlboro cigarettes. The picture or scenario will not necessarily be true, but it is the image of the product in customers' minds, what they aspire to or the statements they are making about themselves when they buy the product, that is the important aspect of identity. It is that aspect that gives brands a value, and every part of the marketing mix must reinforce it. The marketing mix includes every aspect of the company's operation, but especially the activities visible to the customer: pricing, packaging, distribution, advertising, promotion, sales and after sales service.

With large firms that are well known it is easy to see how products and companies are positioned. How does the identity concept apply to smaller companies? I was once talking to an estate agent that wanted to open a new office in Bournemouth, a coastal resort in the South of England. There are, he told me, a large number of retirement homes in the area and he wanted to focus the new office on providing a service to retired people wanting to move there. We discussed the needs, aspirations and assurances demanded by this market and what he needed to do to position the office so that it appealed to them. This involved, among many other factors, locating the office near public transport, providing parking facilities for those who drove, the design of the office, the design of all printed material, the age and attitude of staff to be employed, how staff should dress, extra services such as transport to view properties, and advertising image. The list grew and grew. The point is that everything had to be congruent to create the right image in the minds of the target market.

Once the distinctive capability of the company has been identified and the market and product decided on, the issue becomes one of promotion – how to achieve the image we want in the customer's mind. For an electrical fixture supplier to the building trade, for example, the distinctive capability might be speed of service and/or delivery in New Jersey. The identity goal might then be 'to be recognized by builders in the housing market as the fastest and most reliable supplier of electrical fixtures in New Jersey.'

It is a reasonable assumption that if achievement of this goal gives the firm a competitive advantage, other electrical fixture suppliers will also start giving rapid and reliable service. The company will not only have to keep improving its service to stay in front, but will also have to ensure that the market perception continues to be that it is the best. This will give a clear focus to the company's promotional activities.

An important point with all companies, but especially small and medium-sized ones, is to ensure that customers realize they have received superior service in some way or other. For example, if an advertising design studio works all night to have some artwork ready for the next day, or meets an impossibly short delivery time, they should make sure the client knows they have gone the extra mile. Importantly this needs to be done before or at the same time as the invoice arrives. With many customers when the invoice arrives they have forgotten what had to be done and they only see the amount, so the extra effort and work can even have a negative impact. In this case the client is the person who places the order and also everyone who influences the placing of the order.

One suggestion is to make a list of all major customers and for each write on one side of a page all the special things done for that customer last month, and on the other side any subtle ways of informing them of this fact.

One senior advertising executive was often dreaming up ideas for his clients. He was really steeped in their business and would spot opportunities for them to obtain free or low-cost promotion, or ideas for major campaigns. He would handwrite these ideas on special letterheads and send them to the clients. It achieved three objectives; firstly it let the client know he was always thinking about improving their business even when it did not generate business for his agency, secondly it kept his name in front of the client and thirdly, by hand-writing a note it made it personal rather than just a business relationship.

The concept of identity, the niche you plan to occupy in your customers' minds, is a simple one. Achieving a consistent message to those customers, however, both through the media and through personal contact, requires clear thinking, a subtle approach and constant work – it has to become a way of life.

People

The other goals will only be achieved through the efforts of people. Experience shows that the way a strategy is executed can matter more than the strategy itself. Execution is through the organization and its people: they must know what is expected of them and how their behavior and the culture they help create is essential to the strategy implementation. The people goal might be called the software side of the distinctive capability goal. It represents the organization's shared values, the behaviors that will be required, and the organization structure that will deliver the strategy, the culture that makes it live.

One of the most crucial determinants of all companies' success over the next 20 years will be the organization's value system. Companies that have a strong management, who know where they are going and are imbued with ethical and moral values, will be the winners in the business world. They will win the trust of their customers, and have an advantage in recruitment and employee morale over their more bland competitors, and these both lead to competitive advantage in the marketplace.

There is clear evidence of the demand for a more ethical stance. Both in the US and Britain there has been an upsurge in public concern about the ethical behavior of companies and business people.

The Wall Street securities house Saloman Brothers is an interesting example of the impact unacceptable ethics can have, and how this can be changed in a relatively short time. In 1991 the company announced that it had broken the rules in three auctions involving US Treasury notes. It became swamped by the subsequent scandal. As a result the firm lost clients, including governments, at an alarming rate and was not certain to survive. It appointed Warren Buffett as chairman of the executive committee. He sacked those who had broken the rules, virtually stopped operations in certain types of business, and made it obvious to all parties that Saloman Brothers would henceforth be a decent and honorable securities house. The consequence was that Saloman's fortunes revived and it once again became a major player in the market.

There are two interesting points here. Firstly, Buffett's reputation as a man of integrity could be transferred to apply to the company.

Secondly, he took visible measures to correct the unethical behavior, even though it might be argued that this made the immediate financial position worse. His appointment and the actions he took restored Saloman's reputation as an ethical organization.

More examples become evident every day. Perhaps the most powerful one is in Italy where, in the past, it has been necessary to bribe the right government or party officials to obtain government contracts. This has been known about by anyone doing business in Italy since the end of World War Two. Suddenly, in 1993, the practice was being talked about openly, and the public mood demanded that it be unacceptable and that those who are guilty must be punished. 'The guilty' range from leaders of major corporations, both private and state-owned, up to the most senior politicians. Many of them served prison sentences.

One of the winners from this situation is international conglomerate 3M. They have always taken a firmly ethical position and for that very reason have found that they are now preferred suppliers to the Italian Government.

Throughout the Western world, practices that were once overlooked are now being seen as unacceptable. Companies that become 'tainted' will not only risk public and customer condemnation but will be recognized on the university grapevine as companies that should be avoided. The best, most talented graduates will shun them. Their existing workforce will not feel proud of working for such companies and morale will not be high. It is very difficult to motivate a workforce when morale is low.

When British Airways admitted that its actions in trying to attract passengers away from Virgin Atlantic were improper, and the depths to which it had sunk in launching the covert operations became apparent, it is said that the BA managers became very depressed and despondent. From speaking to some of these managers at the time I do not believe that morale was poor. What the scandal did was to raise questions in managers' minds about their leaders and about how they will treat their own staff in difficult situations. In a business sense it also left BA very exposed.

The advantage of having business values that are recognized as being strong is that customers are increasingly buying a reputation rather than a product.

In virtually all products the service content is increasing, either at the point of sale or afterwards, and customers will look for a company they trust to give good service.

As technology becomes more complex and buyers only partially understand the capability of the product at the time of purchase, they will need to trust the supplier that the product will do what is promised. This applies in both commercial and consumer sales. Customers have to have confidence in the company they buy from. As more products are purchased over the Internet so customers require a solid reputation and reliable performance from the 'remote' supplier. As suppliers and customers link their systems together through the web so greater trust is needed that information and freedom to organize supplies will not be abused.

Product life cycles are becoming shorter, so buyers will need to upgrade or change the product more quickly. They need to know that the supplier will continue to maintain the original product and will design upgrades so that their cost is minimized rather than maximized.

There is more awareness that the way manufacturers treat the environment affects everyone: it is in all our interests to buy products from companies who minimize damage to the environment.

For all these reasons many customers will insist on dealing with companies who espouse and practise recognizably strong values and high standards. Business values and company culture are explored further in Chapter 7.

The people goal, therefore, deals with the organization structure of a company, its values, as expressed in its standards and behaviors and its relationships with people, both employees and others. Usually the two are so intertwined that they cannot be separated; but if the company's values do not encompass how it relates to its people then it has a major problem.

Efficiency

In the 1970s and early 1980s companies started competing on price through vastly higher efficiency. This was no longer a lowest cost or differentiated model equation. Companies like Dell, Home Depot, Southwest Airlines and Wal-Mart supplied high quality products or services at discounted prices. They developed new business models where efficiency was so great that they could significantly undercut the prices of their competitors. Spurred on by the re-engineering drive of the early 1990s, when processes were revamped and huge savings realized, efficiency became a key survival factor for most businesses, and a success factor for many companies.

The Internet will now spur an even greater drive for efficiency. Customers can now browse the Internet to find the lowest price for a product or component. A Pittsburgh company, FreeMarkets Online, holds online auctions for a wide range of buyers, such as The Royal

Bank of Scotland, the High Voltage Engineering Corporation, a manufacturer of high quality applications-engineered products, and The Allstate Corporation, the largest publicly-held US personal lines insurer. FreeMarkets claim to have helped companies around the world source US$30 billion of goods and identify savings of US$6.4 billion.

The Internet will drive down the cost of doing business. Re-engineering of processes will be replaced by total redesign of the business model with the primary aim of attracting more customers with lower prices.

Once inefficient companies could exist. Now even the most innovative companies have to be efficient, in how they innovate as well as operate. There will have to be continuous efficiency improvement systems, such as Toyota has, in all companies. They must drive out inefficiency, force intelligent business process re-engineering and provide quality products or services that give customers what they want at a comparison price they are willing to pay.

The purpose of this goal is to ensure that efficiency is high on the agenda of all companies.

The optional sixth goal

For some companies there is a need to highlight a particular issue with an additional goal. Such issues may include safety and the environment.

For many companies, especially in construction and heavy engineering, safety is an absolutely key issue. Achieving accident-free operations makes both human and business good sense. Therefore many companies involved in dangerous activities develop a safety goal.

Organizations that need to monitor their effect on the environment, in the mining industry for example, may have an environmental goal.

Using a sixth goal acknowledges that this aspect of the strategy is so important to the whole organization that it has to be stressed by its own goal statement. However, this approach should only be adopted when there is a compelling argument in its favor, since it produces a framework that is considerably more complex and makes it more difficult to communicate the strategy.

PERFORMANCE TARGETS

Performance targets are measures of achievement. They can be long-term, for results up to three years in the future, but usually they are targeted at a six month to two year time horizon. They are the backbone to the operating plan and should be reviewed regularly. The annual strategic business planning process should provide the framework for the following year's budget.

Performance targets are precise. They state exactly what will be achieved and when. If a people goal stated 'to retain and recruit quality people' there are a number of implied questions. What do quality people look like? How do we identify quality people at interviews? Do we need the same quality of people for all jobs? Often managers will agree that certain employees are quality people, but find it more difficult to say what makes them a quality person.

Performance targets will establish an approach that will identify 'quality people' for the organization and lead to an action plan for recruiting and retaining them.

Some years ago I was working with a major airline in reviewing its overall strategy. It had a list of six main goals, the last of which was to be a good neighbor. Then there was a list of perhaps 130 actions. Most of these actions were to reduce cost and improve quality in various areas of the corporation. It was like an unstructured brainstorm. And not one of those actions related to being a good neighbor. I worked with the managers in establishing performance targets related to the goals (in fact I had to work with them to establish meaningful goals, but that is not the point being made here), and then develop actions that would lead to the attainment of the performance targets. For the first time in years that company started to perform according to a thought-through strategy, and employees could see how their actions were directed towards achieving worthwhile goals.

Goals set the direction and are the key to strategic thinking and establishing competitive advantage. They state what the leadership team wants the company to become. The next step is to quantify measurable targets that will move the company in that direction within a stated timescale. Performance targets are vital to creating and monitoring an action program that will move an organization in the required direction within an agreed time frame.

The objective of performance targets is to establish the achievements and behaviors that will constitute steps on the road to reaching each goal. For instance, the distinctive capability goal of a contract cleaning company was 'to manage on a national scale, unskilled labor working in customer premises to produce excellent levels of service and customer satisfaction.' The company next wanted to identify exactly what would constitute 'excellent levels of service and customer satisfaction'. A group of senior field managers brainstormed the elements that they thought customers expected from the company. The elements were all defined simply by a noun or short phrase. For each element we ensured that everyone had a common understanding of what was meant. Each individual in the group was asked to score the elements in terms of how well they believed the company was performing. The scores were then compared and the group reached a remarkable consensus on performance.

Looking at the chart (Figure 2.3) it will not come as a surprise that this particular company had a number of field operating problems. They could not ask customers what they thought of the service because the managers did not believe they had the ability to correct the problem at that stage, although four months later they did start telephoning every customer on a quarterly basis to ask how the service could be improved.

	Poor				Excellent
	1	2	3	4	5
Hassle-free service			●		
Flexibility				●	
Cleaning performance			●		
Reliability		●			
Stability		●			
Confidence			●		
Security		●			
Package			●		
Communication			●		

Figure 2.3 Field managers' scoring of service to customers

The company management now had a subjective, but quantified, measurement of how good the service was at that time. They carried out the same exercise on a monthly basis, with each manager giving their reasons for any change in the score. One of the performance targets for that year was to move hassle-free service, cleaning performance and communication to between four and five by the year end, with every measure scoring at least three plus. Another performance target was to start telephoning customers by the year end to ask them if they were satisfied with the service, and to achieve 90 per cent of replies that were positive.

The performance target was written as 'continuously attain better than 90 per cent customer satisfaction in the quarterly telephone surveys.' That was fine as a key line performance target statement. When the action program team initiated the project and began to state how follow-up would be performed, they expanded this statement to clarify its meaning and ensure that it met its purpose.

For example, each survey would have a different theme, so that they did not become routine and lose impact. After asking customers if they found the overall service to be good and obtaining an affirmative reply, the researcher would ask: 'If you were to award us between one and five for reliability, with one being poor and five being excellent, what would you give us?' If the answer was less than five, the customer would be gently probed to reveal the problem areas. On another survey the customer might be asked how they would rate the company on communicating with them: poor, reasonable or good.

A list was compiled of all interesting customer comments and circulated to every employee. Prizes were given to anyone receiving particularly favorable comments. This ensured that employees did not see the exercise as some back door check, but as positive support for their efforts. Hence the performance target produced by the field managers did not only cover the customer satisfaction measure, but also broke it down into its different components and communicated the results to employees.

The final performance target read:

- Continuously attain better than 90 per cent customer satisfaction ratings in quarterly surveys.
- Action on problems to be initiated within 24 hours.
- Any problem that cannot be resolved in 48 hours to be notified to the Operations Director.
- Replies to particular questions on elements of the service to attain the top rating of five or excellent in 50 per cent of customer calls.
- All replies to be categorized by division and circulated. . .

This continued for nearly a page. Eventually field managers' performance reviews, and hence their pay, were partially based on the results of these surveys.

There was a particularly interesting side effect of this survey. Some customers gave low marks to try to beat the supplier down on price. The leadership team saw this as a clear indication that trust and communication with the customer was poor. In every case where this was suspected, a main board director, usually the chief executive, went to meet the customer's chief executive and discussed their relationship, including pricing policies, service levels and future expectations. In nearly every case this openness resulted in a stronger relationship being forged between the two companies.

Another type of performance target might be to do with the development of a new product. If this came under the market/product goal it might read 'to complete product development of XYZ circuit board production equipment by June 2002.' Again, this might be acceptable for the one-page SBP document, but it is too vague as a performance target to manage this project. A more specific and expanded performance target statement could be:

- To complete the product development of XYZ by June 2002.
- The product specification to be the completion of a prototype machine at a cost of no more than US$200,000.
- Production machines to be capable of being manufactured for a direct cost of US$30,000, able to produce 150 circuit boards per hour at a cost of less than US$1.00 per circuit board.
- The machine must be capable of being operated by semi-skilled labor after two days' training.

The greatest problems in setting performance targets occur with abstract goals. Take the statement 'our people provide solutions not problems.' What does this really mean? How do we know if our people are providing solutions?

The first approach with this type of goal, having written it down, is to list the words and phrases, the behaviors and performance that people will need to display if they are to achieve this goal. Some of these words and phrases will be as vague as the original goal. Unless they explain what you mean better than the original phrase, delete them. At this stage only behaviors and performance that contribute to the goal should remain on the list.

Write a complete statement about each behavior or performance, describing to what extent it is required. These statements can be tested by asking if an employee behaved or performed in the way described in these statements, would he or she have achieved the goal. If you can answer affirmatively you now have some behavior and performance measures that can be included in the performance target statements.

'Our people provide solutions not problems' was a people goal for a financial institution. After jotting down lots of ideas on what it meant, the following list was produced of customer contact staff behaviors and performance that the managers believed could be measured:

- trained and tested in product knowledge;
- trained and tested in their knowledge of the customer's business;
- able to ask questions about the customer's requirements;
- able to match the customer's requirements to the company's products;
- able to explain how the product meets the customer's requirements;
- able to convert 50 per cent of genuine enquiries into orders;
- able to resolve 85 per cent of queries instantly.

Another ten attributes were listed. The attributes were then turned into quantified behavior statements. The first one read: 'All staff can demonstrate a comprehensive knowledge of the company products. When asked they can explain any product, its features and benefits, relate these to the customer's market and ask intelligent questions to establish the customer's exact need.'

The performance target became: 'By March 1998 every member of the company having contact with customers will have a comprehensive knowledge of the company's products, the specified market sector and be able to relate them together to influence the customer. The success measure will be to convert 50 per cent of genuine enquiries into orders.'

Although it is difficult and time consuming, it is important that the performance target statements clarify vague, abstract goals. Performance target statements will be brief in the SBP plan but can be expanded in the supporting documentation, providing that none exceeds one side of paper. The reason for this limitation is that if the concept of the performance target cannot be defined in a single page, then it is too complex for strategic business planning purposes. Brevity makes for clear thinking and precision and stops the document becoming too big.

Performance targets, as we have seen, are the measures of success or failure. They chart progress towards attaining goals. As such they form the link between where a company wants to go and how it is going to get there.

Responsibility for achieving a performance target must be assigned to one individual. The action program will ensure that that person has the necessary resources to achieve the performance target.

If there is a warning about performance targets, it is not to define too many. It is better to have fewer and reach them, so that they become real achievements, rather than having too many that remain just words on paper.

ACTION PROGRAMS

Action programs outline how the strategy will be implemented. They are related series of actions that will be undertaken to enable the organization to achieve the performance targets. It is the management of the action programs that makes the entire strategic business planning process live. It is the action programs that ensure that management jobs have high impact: that the leadership team and managers stay in the 20 per cent high pay-off zone of the Pareto principle. Action programs help managers to delegate and help staff to see a purpose in their job. They are part of the key to restructuring the organization.

As with performance targets, it is better to have fewer, well-managed action programs than too many. This is especially important in the early days of using SBP. The action programs are related to the performance targets and are stated as in the following examples:

- Design and implement an annual survey of client opinion and perceptions.
- Identify means of effectively selecting and targeting the top 50 suppliers in new market sectors.
- Implement faster credit clearance procedures.
- Introduce flexible working hours/days.
- Develop a pricing model to reflect the economics of transaction costs.

Responsibilities

A named individual is responsible for achieving each performance target and a similar system is used for the action program. The performance target team leader and those named as responsible for the action program are the team for achieving the performance target.

The action programs are tied into the performance targets and the goals. However, the actual work will be performed by functional or product groups, departments, individuals or multi-functional teams under the leadership of the individual nominated to be responsible for achieving the performance target. Responsibilities are assigned by putting names against each action program together with a date.

SUMMARY

This chapter has explored the basic strategic business planning framework, including its main elements of company purpose and the five or six types of goal – distinctive capability, market/product/service, identity, people, efficiency and, if necessary, a sixth goal. Performance targets bridge the transition from goals to action and help to monitor how well the company is performing. The action program lists the tasks that have to be carried out to achieve the performance targets. The responsibility section allocates the work to individuals, functional groups or departments, or to performance target teams.

Most methodologies and frameworks are adaptable to the needs of the organization where they are being used. They are not sacrosanct but tools to help your business. However, my only caveat is that when the SBP process approach has been closely followed there has never been a failure. Where shortcuts and structural changes have been made in the process and framework, there has sometimes been a need to revisit some of the earlier work.

Therefore, for companies using this approach, at least for the first time, it is strongly recommended that you follow both the framework and the process closely.

3

Company purpose

THE OVERARCHING PURPOSE

For 99 per cent of commercial businesses there is an overarching purpose. It is to maximize shareholder value. That value will consist of dividends over time and the price for which stock or the business itself can be sold at a point in time. For owner-managed businesses dividends equate to the total remuneration received from the business.

For years I have wrestled with many other reasons for a business of reasonable size to exist, and this is the only one that both matches reality and can be intellectually justified. However, if the prime role of a leadership team is to manage shareholder value with the intention that it should be maximized, developing and implementing a strategy that pursues this objective is rare.

Determinants of shareholder value

The interests and behavior of direct stakeholders will strongly influence how shareholder value is managed. Figure 3.1 indicates how these stakeholders interact with the company and the potential influence they have on company performance.

Figure 3.2 outlines the pressures that influence each of these stakeholder groups.

There are three key points about these stakeholder groups:

- Shareholder value declines if direct stakeholders desert the company.

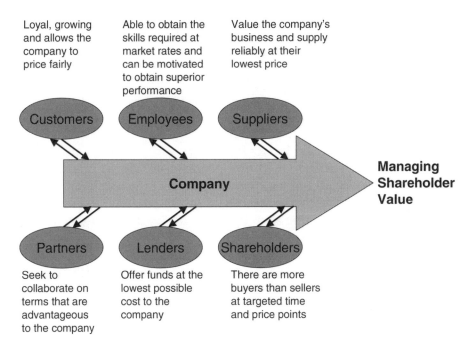

Loyal, growing and allows the company to price fairly

Able to obtain the skills required at market rates and can be motivated to obtain superior performance

Value the company's business and supply reliably at their lowest price

Seek to collaborate on terms that are advantageous to the company

Offer funds at the lowest possible cost to the company

There are more buyers than sellers at targeted time and price points

Figure 3.1 Influence of direct stakeholders

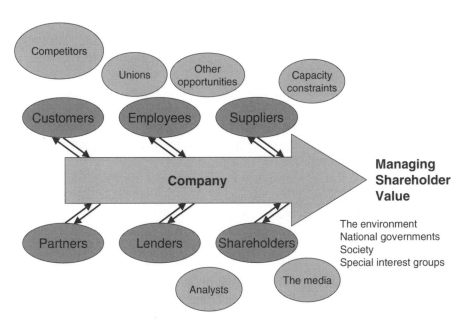

Figure 3.2 Influences on direct stakeholders

- Stakeholders remain committed if they obtain greater value than they could from alternative options.
- The relationship between the company and its direct stakeholders, including the feedback loop that exists between them, is a key indicator of the effective management of shareholder value.

Most business strategies do not seek to maximize shareholder value. Executives managing the business can appear to have many other priorities, often those that fit their own personal ambitions. This includes growth targets that do not maximize value, making acquisitions that appeal more to vanity than business logic, not undertaking activities that are critical to managing shareholder value because those activities do not appeal to the executives involved, and offering the wrong top management and employee incentive programs.

As an example consider two biotech companies that both launched their first product in early 2000. Company A has the less attractive product. It started by managing market commercial expectations. Its strategy focused on accentuating its product pipeline, which while not particularly great they knew would produce reasonable cash flows in future years. They also had a very clear therapeutic focus that they promoted to analysts at every possible opportunity. The chairman traveled thousands of miles to speak at industry conferences, giving a consistent, but interesting and updated, message. Press releases on the pipeline products were regular and encouraging. The company was also financially careful and tried to maintain reserves equal to one and a half to two years' cash burn.

Company B has a potentially exciting product, which it hyped to the market. On its failing to reach the initial revenue targets the market became disillusioned. Company B also has at least one other attractive product in its pipeline and a number of interesting in-licensing opportunities. What it has not done is communicate regularly to the market. Nor has it focused on maximizing those activities that would increase shareholder value.

The results can be seen in Figure 3.3.

Both companies were in the US$30–35 range in September 2000. By early November both peaked in the US$35–40 range. At this point both companies went into decline, but Company A slowed its rate of decline by an active program of communication and positive news based in reality. It bottomed out at US$12.5 in March 2001 and climbed back to reach another period high of just over US$30 in August 2001, before falling back during the difficult conditions of early September 2001 to US$20.

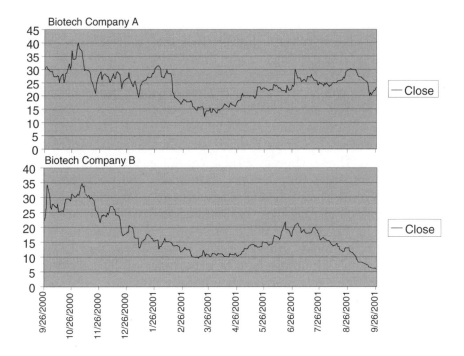

Figure 3.3 Stock performance of two biotech companies

Company B had a much steeper decline from its high in November 2000 to US$9.5 in March 2001. It too had a recovery to US$20.5 in July 2001. From this point its stock slid all the way down to just over US$6. Company B did not have an active investor relations/public relations strategy or process. Without news to bolster its stock price, short sellers were able to move against the stock. There are also a number of actions that could have been taken to increase company performance that were not taken.

One year is really too short a period of time to judge a business performance. However, over the period of one year when these two companies have been compared Company A averaged a 40 per cent higher stock price than Company B. This gave it freedom to explore other options that would ultimately increase shareholder value and also created higher exit values for any investor who needed to sell during this period.

Key in all this is understanding the value drivers that enable a leadership team to manage shareholder value. Research indicates that when leadership teams explicitly manage a business to maximize shareholder value it will increase total shareholder returns by over 61 per cent over a period of three years.

How do groups who manage for shareholder value differ from those who do not? One important point is that they do not worry unduly about the quarterly earnings. If they have an exciting new product or service opportunity they will accelerate development even though it will depress earnings over the next few quarters. Those who do not pursue shareholder value would not.

Another example is whether to expense or capitalize start-up costs on a new venture. Those who manage shareholder value will generally expense them. Those who do not will capitalize them. The message is clear. The companies that manage shareholder value are focused on creating economic wealth. The others worry about reported profits and will even destroy shareholder wealth to achieve it.

Throughout this chapter I will explore other approaches to establishing company purpose. However, the proposition here is that the overarching goal, which needs to be stated and explicit in everything the company does, is to manage shareholder value.

THE BUSINESS MODEL

For every successful business there is a clear business model. This describes how the company operates and competes in the market now. It identifies the distinctive, perhaps unique, strengths that enable it to win profitable business. It will answer the questions: 'How robust is this current model? What assumptions is it based on? What does the organization consider are excellent results, both financial and other meaningful performance measures?'

The hypothesis (see Chapter 13) will suggest possible changes in the marketplace, industry structure, society and economy. Part of the process of developing the new strategy is to bridge the change between the current business model and one that will meet the assumptions of the leadership team on the situation that will exist in three or more years' time. These assumptions will be based on the analysis of the hypothesis and other information that is gathered during the process.

The discussion on the existing business model, what it is now for a particular company and the future model for the company, will drive much of the thinking on developing the strategy. Central to this discussion will be an agreement on the changes that will most probably occur in the market and industry. Once a leadership team believes it has developed a probable hypothesis on how the industry and market will evolve or transform, they then develop a business model on how it will structure itself and the strategy it will follow to position the company and benefit from those changes.

The Amazon.com hypothetical example

Let us develop a hypothetical business model for Amazon.com, a company with which I have no personal contact so this is pure speculation.

The Amazon.com business model assumes that the expanding number of Internet users will create a new mass market who value low prices and convenience and will shop for a large number of their needs using the computer. By removing the overheads of a traditional bricks-and-mortar store Amazon.com is able to reduce the cost of supplying a product to a customer and so charge lower prices. This in turn leads to higher volumes and better purchasing which creates higher margins or enables the price to be lowered still further. Amazon.com will become the leading company with the most comprehensive range of merchandise for meeting consumers' needs. The key competences will be to design and market the most attractive Internet portal, to create the most recognized Internet name among consumers and develop the most efficient logistical distribution system so that all customers are delighted with the service.

In the original Amazon.com business model there was no focus on profitability. It was assumed that capital would be readily available and that the key performance measure would be the number of eyeballs viewing the Amazon.com web site. With the dot.com meltdown this had to change, but it only modified the business model, not totally changed it.

The three elements of the business model

There are three parts to a business model. The first is the environment in which the organization operates. This includes the market, customers, technology, social change factors, political and economic. It will usually include how short-term changes in these areas will impact on the operations and performance.

The second explains how the organization will benefit from the changing environment to build its business. This is the purpose of the organization, the reason for which it exists. For Amazon.com this might be 'to be the world's Internet retail portal'.

Thirdly is to understand the core competencies that will be required to achieve the purpose and how these will be developed.

This is a simplistic business model for Amazon.com, but it develops the concept of how a business model might be structured. A clear explicit business model is a powerful motivator. The purpose statement is effectively a statement of how an organization will exploit its business model.

Developing such a theory sounds simple. Amazon.com grew from a garage to an organization with a US$12 billion market cap in a few years. The speed of business means that the business model has to be developed, tested, refined, implemented, modified and then tested again in a never-ending sequence while the business is expanding and operations still developing. Even until the mid-1990s company managements had time, usually years, to develop and refine their business theory.

Now the whole process is faster and decisions have to be made with less knowledge, more ambiguity and a lot more 'gut feel' based on intensive research in a short period of elapsed time. Organizations have to be developed 'on the run' and not planned in detail in advance and then implemented. One reason for the problems of Japanese companies at the end of the 20th century is that planning is their great strength. Methodical, detailed planning means missing markets. The 21st century needs flexibility of approach, improvisation at introduction and rapid capability building during implementation.

Tesco and e-grocer

Tesco is the biggest supermarket chain in the UK. It has risen from a 'pile it high sell it cheap' mentality to take over the top slot from arch rivals Sainsbury's in the UK market. Its supermarkets equal any in the world for layout, décor, range and quality of merchandize and helpfulness of staff. With nearly 300,000 registered online customers and sales of more than US$450 million a year, Tesco is also the world's largest e-grocer.

Tesco launched the service in 1996. Harassed urban professionals found that ordering online and having deliveries made to their home for an US$8 charge represented real value.

Tesco did not create a whole new e-grocer facility. Instead it used its local stores to supply the merchandize. Pickers went up and down the supermarket aisles, just like an ordinary shopper, with their customer lists and large shopping carts. (Every item was scanned in so a wrong product could not be accidentally selected.) This approach enabled Tesco to offer 25,000 items compared to their main rivals' 5,000 through their warehouse-based system. Tesco has more than 300 stores online covering 90 per cent of the population.

The system worked and enabled Tesco to steal a march on those rivals building highly automated new warehouses dedicated to meeting the needs of the e-grocer business.

The approach was really that of a low cost market test and entry. But it had real deficiencies. At weekends, when most online shoppers place their order, the pickers had to jostle down already crowded aisles, adding to the crush of shopping carts in the supermarket. The system originally ran on Microsoft BackOffice software and inexpensive Dell servers. Neither of these could cope with many thousands of concurrent users.

Tesco satisfied the first criteria for new business: it developed a flexible system that met the needs of a small but growing market, improvised the introduction achieving both speed and low investment, proved the concept and then needed to rapidly consolidate its lead position with capability building through having a dedicated logistics approach and scaleable computer systems.

This is increasingly becoming the new strategic method. Rapid development of a concept and developing a flexible strategic plan, but one that clearly sets the direction, low cost trials to test reality and gain a lead in the market if it is successful, and full scale implementation once there are clear signs of it being successful.

Tesco proved the business model as an e-grocer. After that it had to develop a purpose for the new e-grocer division it had formed. Perhaps this could be along the lines 'to be the most efficient, customer-friendly, e-grocer portal and quality food supplier in our chosen markets'. However, it is more likely that Tesco would see its e-grocer business as part of its total customer service offering, as another channel in supplying the best quality and lowest priced grocery and other product requirements of their customers. The Tesco business model is similar to Wal-Mart, to continually increase the size of its operations, realize greater economies of scale and reflect them back into lower prices and/ or higher quality to generate greater sales and more economies of scale. It is a powerful engine and justifies continued growth.

Tesco has a great quality for business success: it understands its customers and markets. It adds costs where they add value. Hence Tesco's headquarters is an undistinguished concrete building in Hertfordshire, outside of London, in what is most charitably described as an unfashionable, slightly run down, location. Inside it is a utility building that is not particularly well furnished. Terry Leahy, the chief executive, is a down to earth character who understands the business well. His grasp of detail, customer surveys and sales data has enabled him to take major strategic initiatives that have been scoffed at by the industry analysts only to prove popular and business winners with consumers. It is this understanding of the market that enabled Tesco to develop a totally different e-grocer model to other competitors.

Now Tesco is co-operating with Safeway, California's biggest food retailer, to bring its successful Internet shopping approach to the United States.

The Tesco business model is founded on understanding its customers' needs and developing approaches to satisfy them. Its thinking is original, not just following industry trends, and it makes decisions based on the analysis of data and creative thinking.

All of this is summarized in their core purpose: 'Growing the business, to create value for our customers, to earn their lifetime loyalty.' They add to this in their values that drive the whole way they do business. 'No one tries harder than we do for customers' reflects the obsession with value and service. 'We treat people the way we like to be treated' expresses the consideration they give people within and outside the business.

The dangers of not understanding the business model

An industrial products company in the United States acquired a similar company about half its size. With combined revenues of US$600 million the new company was the largest in its industry. The companies were in the same products, in fact many were identical, but they were selling to different end users.

The acquired company ran a large, basically single plant operation, selling to customers such as the big construction equipment manufacturers. It was run on a 'mean and lean' basis and the president's response to any request for investment was ' What will it earn us?' He specifically meant 'in the short-term', though this was not stated. This approach had made it reasonably profitable, but its plant was old and it had no ideas on how to expand or develop the business. Being acquired was its main ambition. The president of the acquired company became chief operating officer of the combined operation and was given considerable freedom to integrate the two companies and cut out duplication.

The acquiring company had over 10 plants and had invested substantially in new plant and equipment. Its main customers were in the auto industry. To win profitable business they had to have the capability to work with design teams and developers in the Tier-1 and auto companies to create new products, innovatively meeting design criteria and specifications. This work can take three years to pay off, waiting for the next model range to enter production.

The new COO never understood this industry or the complexity of multi-plant operations. He started eliminating design and development functions and people who knew the auto industry and how to win profitable business. Initially he reduced costs and no immediate losses were evident. It was only nine months after he left that the realization set in that he had mortgaged the future for immediate cost reductions.

The COO was not a fool. The problem was that he did not understand the business model for the plants supplying the auto industry. He did not understand how to make money, how to allow for the annual five per cent cost reduction that will be imposed, how even sometimes it will be necessary to incur losses on a product, usually at the end of its life cycle, to help win the order for the new model from the customer.

His business model to supply large construction equipment companies and run a single plant operation was totally at odds with what is required to service the auto industry from a multi-plant enterprise. He also failed to understand that he could not obtain the volumes the combined business required from the niche markets the single company operated in before the acquisition. As the largest supplier in the United States the company needed the volume only the auto industry can provide. The merged company is still paying the price for his lack of understanding.

Such confusion becomes obvious, though not always agreed, when writing out the business model. Managers wedded to a theory that has proved successful in other situations and businesses are loath to abandon it in new circumstances. Their business model is not based on analysis but their own personal past history.

Understanding the business model as it applies to the company today and how it might change tomorrow is critical to developing a sound strategy.

Criteria for a business model

There are four criteria for a business model:

- The assumptions about the environment in which the organization operates and will operate in future, its role and purpose and the core competencies it has to possess, must be based in reality.
- The assumptions in all three areas have to match together.

- As with the Amazon.com example, the assumptions about the environment, the role and purpose of the company and the competencies it would need have to form a cogent and logical reasoning.
- The business model has to be known and understood throughout the organization and believed by all employees, customers, suppliers and investors.

The last point was the problem that John Peterman had (see Chapter 16). He never articulated the market, because he knew it intuitively. There was never a clear purpose; the philosophy 'people want to live life the way they wish they were' could have been a guide if it had been accompanied by the assumptions about the market and the needs of customers, the social and lifestyle changes driving these needs. The process would also have led to the discussion on the capabilities the company needed to succeed. Without these he could never communicate in a meaningful way the purpose of the organization or its business model to its growing numbers of staff.

There is one other element to these criteria. If employees cannot recognize the company they know in the statement, and believe it to be false, it will have a negative impact on morale.

The business model is grounded in the present and near future, unlike the hypothesis, which might look five, ten or more years ahead

In a rapidly changing world it could become obsolete more quickly, perhaps within three to five years. For this reason it needs challenging and modifying or completely reinventing on a regular basis

The company purpose statement, the cornerstone of the strategic framework, is often developed during the discussion of business models.

The role of assumptions

The business model is based on assumptions, about the industry the company is in, its trends and drivers, the margins that are possible, where revenues currently come from and where they will come from in future, who the industry leaders are and who the main competitors are, which technologies will dominate in future and which will not.

Internally the beliefs concern the risk level the company will stand, the growth rate it expects, its attitude to teams and to mavericks, its ranking of the importance of management, employees, shareholders and customers. These assumptions often predict decisions the leadership team will make. They close off minds to opportunities.

The approach I adopt is to document the key assumptions, and discuss these with the leadership team. Once they agree that these are the assumptions, then those that are unanimous and can be assumed to form the core base of assumptions are challenged to understand if they will still apply in a new business environment.

Testing the purpose statement

The purpose statement should answer two questions, either explicitly or implicitly:

- What business are we going to be in?
- What distinguishes us?

In the hypothetical Amazon.com example the answer to the first question is plain from the statement 'to be the world's Internet retail portal'. It clearly states they are in the business of being a retail portal. Nobody who knows Amazon.com could be unclear as to the business it is in and where it plans to position itself in that business.

The answer to the second question is also plain. Again this one simple seven word sentence implicitly says 'the biggest', giving a clear aspiration, indicating that everyone in every country is a potential customer and that many of them will use the service. It will be the global favorite consumer purchasing Web site. This is very distinctive.

In developing the business model other questions may be asked, such as 'Who is our customer? What is value to our customer?'

Amazon.com is a sexy company. Developing a purpose statement for them is relatively easy. One of my clients in the United Kingdom is a steel service center business. If ever there is a commodity product, it must be steel. I visited the top eight customers who accounted for over 50 per cent of sales. I was surprised at the loyalty and high praise evident in what these customers said about my client: 'the closest relationship we have with any supplier'; 'their quality and consistency is unbeatable'; 'their people understand steel and they are a good company to deal with'. Nearly all these customers used other steel suppliers as a second source, so there was constant competitive pressure. Yet my client had been their prime supplier for years. Even companies that were not customers spoke of them with respect; two suggested that they would be interested to hear from my client's salespeople. (This might lead you to think that their selling system is flawed because they have not picked up potential customers, but in fact they balance their sales against their capacity. Their target list of prospects has to match their slitting and storage capacity and working capital.)

One of the many interesting facts about this company is that its equipment is old, its range of services very basic and its level of computerization was negligible at the time of this assignment, though it now has an excellent IT operation. Its strategy does not envisage much change. Depreciation and interest charges are low, and in a low (at times nil) margin business there is no real need to change. It usually purchases used equipment to increase capacity and maintains a credit balance at the bank. Sales have increased steadily (15 per cent plus) over the years. In what must be almost the ultimate commodity business, this company differentiates its product with service and a friendly, knowledgeable, attitude.

The business model is that if costs, including depreciation, are kept to a minimum, existing customers, most of whom are medium-sized metal bashers, are retained and the company can grow with its customers' growth and, winning two or three new customers each year, it will steadily grow and prosper.

This is not exciting but it is realistic and grounded in years of experience by its executives. Also, if this sounds a dull company to work in, think again. The offices have a buzz, all employees understand customer service, training and transferring knowledge to new employees is managed through an effective mentoring program. The staff will never earn a fortune, but they are not unduly frazzled, they have great satisfaction through doing a job well and they do have a balanced lifestyle, something many of us might envy. Its company purpose is 'to be a reliable steel supplier and adviser to our selected customers and retain their loyalty to us.' This company and its staff lived the purpose.

Commodity companies can only sell on price. Margins are low and profits hard to make. However, the moment a company begins to offer guaranteed and quick delivery, a dependable quality standard, advice or consultancy on the best products or the best way of using them, special terms of business, salespeople who understand customers' business, invoices that are error-free, an organization in which the phone is answered on the third ring or sooner, and phone calls are returned as promised, then it is no longer a commodity company, it is a service company.

The unfounded purpose statement

Many companies have a purpose statement that is dreamed up by the chairman. It is often his fantasy statement, his view of what he would like to believe about the business. Sometimes these statements do ring true with employees and customers, but they lack logic and the whole framework is based on being logical and easy to understand.

In this category are some company purpose statements that their owners really love and have published widely. The problem with each of them is that they are not correct: for example 'to maintain the Fulton International ethic of response, commitment, endeavor and success.' This company was a dinosaur, slow to respond to customers, no commitment to improving the business or correcting its obvious problems, no drive or endeavor from anyone in the business. It was losing market share and needed a dose of realism and concerted action. Or take 'Hamble is a vehicle to provide our 'Group of People' with an enjoyable and stimulating working experience.' This company had high turnover rates and flogged its people hard.

PROFIT

Every business has to make a profit. For public companies this ideally has to be consistent every quarter, or the company has a credible explanation as to why it is not profitable. The profit driver focuses on the short-term and often obliterates the longer-term. However, just to say we have to make an increasing profit every quarter to maintain the stock price does not make it happen. There has to be a business purpose and goals that act as drivers of performance.

Profit is the parameter that establishes what the strategy has to achieve to meet its various needs, including those of the investors. It is a key element in the overarching purpose of managing shareholder value, but not as we have seen from the earlier discussion, the only or even the main element.

PROCESS

When developing the strategy, develop the five goals before the company purpose. The reason is that in developing the goals the business model is being developed and refined. Once this is done and the business theory can be briefly described, the purpose of the organization is easier to develop. All that really needs doing then is crafting the right phrasing to match with the culture and achieve the nuances required by the leadership team.

4

Distinctive capability

Where a company competed used to determine business success. As markets fragment and proliferate, as mass customization becomes more prevalent, so dominating a market segment is more difficult and less rewarding. Shortening product life cycles and totally new technical advances mean that rapid product innovation and commercialization are more important than just having leading products, since they will be ephemeral.

How a company competes is now the crucial strategic consideration. Distinctive capability is an execution goal. It is primarily about behaviors. The goal is to identify and develop hard-to-imitate organizational capabilities that lead to the delivery of products and services that distinguish a company from its competitors in the eyes of customers.

CHARACTERISTICS OF DISTINCTIVE CAPABILITY

Distinctive capability is the key to effective strategic planning. It represents a set of unique capabilities or competencies that have a special value to the customer base. In this sense, the strategy hinges on a capability that is ingrained and central to the organization and that enables it to deliver products or services that outperform competitors in meeting customer needs. This capability becomes the foundation of the organization's business success.

The distinctive capability goal must look forward for a number of years because, along with the cultural aspects of the people goal, it is the hardest to change and will take the longest to achieve.

Distinctive capability can be many things, but often it is the 'fit' of the entire strategy, organization structure and approach to business. Individual features are easy to copy; an entire business is very difficult even when competitors know what their capability is.

The key attributes of distinctive capability are that it is has a long-term financial impact and is difficult for competitors to replicate. It is depicted in Figure 4.1.

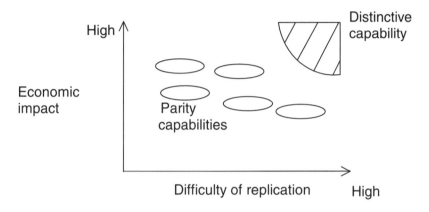

Figure 4.1 Distinctive capability

Distinctive capability is normally developed from the business model. However, this is an iterative process and some techniques can help in clarifying the leadership team's thinking on the company's distinctive capability.

The distinctive capability development model seeks to identify the greatest source of the company's strength. The distinctive capability goal answers the question 'What business or organizational capability does the company have which it will be able to develop further than any competitor in the next three to six years and will create a major, sustainable competitive advantage?'

The distinctive capability development model provides a starting point from which to develop the goal. It proposes that there are five approaches to creating a distinctive capability in serving customer needs. These approaches are not mutually exclusive, but in the initial review the focus should be on one or two areas. The complete model is shown in Figure 4.2.

Example	Distinctive capability approach	Factors
Sony e-Bay Millennium Pharmaceuticals Virgin Atlantic Tesco	Innovation	Ideas Development Commercialization
Wal-Mart Nucor Exxon Dell Computer Corporation Charles Schwartz Nissan	Operations	Tight controls Efficient scheduling Flexibility High quality Unique processes Purchasing
Coca-Cola IBM BMW Philip Morris Schering Plough Nike	Sales and marketing	Advertising Brand management Sales force – ability Sales force – management Technical literature Promotion
Wal-Mart Dell Computer Corporation Exxon Benetton McKesson	Distribution	Controlled channels Bulk transport Logistics systems High utilization Cluster markets Tight controls Piggy-backing
Nordstrom Lexus Talbots American Express Marriott Hotels	Service	Focused service on customer needs Individualized service Skilled operators Fast response Spares availability Excellent administration Replace faulty products or services

Figure 4.2 The distinctive capability development model

Innovation

The innovation approach concentrates on excelling at introducing new and successful products and services to the market as a recognized part of the company's strategy.

Sony is a good example of such an approach. It has a string of innovative new products, from the transistor radio to the Sony Walkman. Its record of introducing new products successfully to the market is first rate. Generally speaking it does not seek to compete on price, but on new and differentiated products. Its key capability is in miniaturization that allows it to make everything from the Sony Walkman through video cameras to notebook computers.

Innovation is not just about the big breakthrough, the new penicillin, but also about a process of continuous improvement, market segmentation and development. For instance, tea bags were a major innovation: no mess, no tea strainer. They became the dominant form of selling domestic tea. It was a major change, a big innovation. Now the market is being further segmented by the introduction of one-cup tea bags, special tea bags for those who make their tea in a cup rather than a pot. The product has special perforations in the bag to help the fusion process and has a specially formulated blend. The production process is only minimally different from that which produces ordinary tea bags, but this is nevertheless innovation. It is a new idea for a product, based on observation of the market, researched, developed, marketed and profitable.

Hence a process of continuous, successful, but perhaps incremental innovation can represent a distinctive capability. Equally, the capability can be in the generation of ideas, either for totally new products or services or for extending existing products to create new niche markets.

One of the base data forms in Chapter 19 is the innovation form. This gives a rough measure of the rate of innovation in the company. Innovative companies will have a high percentage of their new products or services as top-selling lines in their range.

The innovating company is recognized by both its high rate of introducing new products and services and the short timescale within which they are developed and successfully launched. It can also be a company that can continuously modify, change and improve its existing products to meet new opportunities in the market.

Operations

Operations and purchasing can provide distinctive capability through enabling the company to:

- be the lowest cost producer (Texas Instruments in calculators);
- be the highest quality producer (Wedgwood, Mercedes);
- be the most flexible producer (BMW, Honda being able to produce a number of different automobile models down the same production track);

- exploit unique (patented) processes (Pilkington float glass);
- use efficient controls (Ford, GE);
- have access to cheap supplies or scarce resources (RTZ).

This is an important area for companies whose products are considered commodities, or for those service organizations that sell labor, such as office cleaning or car valeting. It is also important for banks, supermarkets, oil distribution companies and so on. Generally, where the gross margin percentage is low, operations and purchasing are important, and will often be a key part of the distinctive capability goal.

Sales and marketing

Think of big international companies who are excellent at marketing and sales – Coca-Cola, Philip Morris (Marlboro), Nike and IBM – and generally you will find a profitable organization. Effective marketing and selling organizations often have a high gross margin percentage.

Many medium-sized companies lack professional marketing people at board level and believe they cannot afford to spend heavily on promotions and sales training. For those companies that can afford to invest in marketing, and develop the marketing function as they grow, there can be excellent returns.

Distribution

Some companies base their distinctive capability on distribution. Fashion retailers Benetton, for example, have built their market share through controlling their own retail outlets. This cuts down the number of locations from which their products can be bought, but guarantees that recognized outlets for their merchandise exist.

Controlling their own distribution gives them other advantages. One of the critical success factors in the fashion business is to be able to spot winning designs quickly and rush supplies to the market, at the same time stopping production of slower moving items. Each Benetton store has a point-of-sale system that tells the factory those items that are selling and those that are not. By combining this information with flexible manufacturing, Benetton is able to deliver a garment three weeks after the store places an order even if it is not in stock in the warehouse.

Besides controlled distribution channels, economies such as bulk distribution, clustering outlets close together to reduce transport, or piggy-backing on other products so that most of the costs are carried by another supplier, are all means of obtaining low-cost distribution or high distribution frequency.

Service

Service is becoming the key to many companies' success. The concept of customer care or customer service, giving customers more attention than they expect or would receive from the competition, is becoming one way of differentiating the company.

As society becomes more reliant on technology, so it requires greater reliability and faster repairs when something does break down.

Computer giant IBM built its business on marketing and service. Customers, and the service the company gives them, are at the heart of its business philosophy. Together with other companies who put service at the heart of their organization, IBM can obtain premium pricing for its products.

Efficient administration, issuing of correct invoices and well-presented letters are all indications of high service levels. Companies who can not only provide high service in their core activities but also in their support functions will be perceived as excellent by their customers.

DISTINCTIVE CAPABILITY COMES FROM BUSINESS PROCESSES

Start with the area that gives the greatest competitive advantage. Explore how linking with other processes can expand that area into a distinctive capability. Link these processes together so that they form a unique strategic capability that delivers superior value to the customer. This becomes the focus of the strategy.

The total fit of all the elements is defined in the business model. The distinctive capability is created by making investments in support infrastructure that creates a capability that is greater than the sum of its parts.

Distinctive capability begins and ends with the customer. It begins by identifying their needs and ends by satisfying them.

DEVELOPING A NEW DISTINCTIVE CAPABILITY

The crucial lesson is that it is difficult and takes time to change from one area of distinctive capability to another, or to add a second major capability. This means that the position occupied presently by the company not only determines how it competes now, but how it will be able to compete for some time into the future, and also how it will be able to react to strategic initiatives by its competitors.

All companies nevertheless have to achieve an acceptable degree of performance across the five distinctive capability areas; otherwise their customers will desert them. Virtually all companies need some ability to innovate. All companies need to offer some support services. In constantly striving for excellence, companies will be upgrading their abilities across all areas. The approach in which the company has a distinctive capability is the one where no other company in the same industry can match its particular standard of performance in the same way.

Distribution example

Esso, the United Kingdom Exxon Company, has a huge pipeline running down the middle of England. This pipeline gives Esso the cheapest distribution of oil products in all the areas it serves. This distribution advantage exists whether crude oil is at US$30 a barrel or US$10, whether the pound sterling is at parity with the US$ or there are two US dollars to the pound. The competitive reaction of one major oil company was to cluster its outlets, its service stations, only in regions where it could be strong, often a long distance from the Esso pipeline. In these areas it could still achieve the lowest cost distribution, because its outlets were so close together. It closed all outlets in those areas where it had only a few service stations.

This example demonstrates how a market leader can obtain an overall distribution advantage, but also how a smaller competitor can build competitive advantage using the same distribution approach, but adapting it to its own situation.

Innovation and operations example

As an illustration of how two companies can use their distinctive capability to compete, consider Yamaha and Honda.

In 1982 Honda was the leader in both global and domestic motorcycle markets. Yamaha was the number two in both markets. Yamaha believed that the Honda management was focusing on its newly emerging car business and that this gave them an opportunity to become the leader in motorcycles. They built a new, large and modern factory, and the president of Yamaha promised that they would be the world's number one motorcycle company within two years.

Particularly in the Japanese culture, this was a direct challenge that may even have been considered rude. Honda was driven to respond, whatever the cost. During the next 18 months it introduced over 100 new models, which meant that the range of motorcycles was replaced twice in that period. This rate of innovation was also twice the historical average and many of the new models were significant innovations, not merely facelifts or minor modifications.

The Japanese consumer is highly fashion-conscious, and Yamaha's products became obsolete as they were compared to the new Honda models. Before the Yamaha president made his statement, Yamaha held 37 per cent of the domestic market in motorcycles. A year later this had fallen to 23 per cent, while Honda's share had increased from 38 per cent to 43 per cent. Yamaha also went from a profit to a loss.

Yamaha chose to compete on price, long runs, and high volume. Its approach was for distinctive strength in operations. Honda chose to compete on innovation: rapid, consistent and visible innovation. Its understanding of the Japanese market, where both companies chose to fight the first round, its own strengths, beliefs and philosophy, enabled Honda not only to withstand the threat Yamaha posed, but also to benefit from it. And all this occurred while Honda's top management focus was undoubtedly on the emerging car business.

Had the president of Yamaha not bragged Honda might not have reacted so quickly. This would have enabled Yamaha to reap the benefits of low cost production and high margins, at least for a time.

Honda's reaction required the company to be organized in a way that was focused on strength in innovation. All functions had to be co-ordinated and be willing and keen to work together. The normal boundaries that divide design, research and development, engineering, production, marketing, sales and service cannot exist. Creating this type of organization is expensive and takes years, even decades.

The normal transition process is for a company to decide that it has achieved everything possible in developing a competitive advantage from its current distinctive capability approach. For instance, say it had focused on the operations approach and was the lowest cost producer for many of its products. However, it notices that the structure of the industry is changing. Afraid that it might be attacked through means other than price, and that such an attack might be successful, it starts to concentrate on developing a better distribution system. It needs to start by asking what 'better' means. Having analyzed the customers' needs, and how the company can satisfy those needs, managers then start developing the approach and structuring the organization so that it can provide the new capability. At the same time as developing the new capability, they must be careful not to lose their existing distinctive capability.

Honda's ability to develop and market new models rapidly is a classic case of distinctive capability. It is easy to observe what the company does, it is easy to define its distinctive capability, but it is very difficult to create an organization that can replicate this distinctive capability.

The ability of Honda to rapidly develop and introduce new motorcycle models has to extend right through its dealer networks. The logistics, support, promotions and training necessary to introduce a new model, or a succession of new models if that is what is required in the market, can only be accomplished with a dealer network capable of handling that type of workload. This does not mean that Honda is constantly introducing new models to the market, but that it has the capacity to do so if changes in the market or technology demand it.

The key is to create a distinctive capability that is hard to imitate and which distinguishes your company from its competitors in the eyes of your customers by delivering a highly valued benefit.

OVERALL COMPETENCE

Sometimes what is distinctive about an organization is not within the areas of the distinctive capability model, although this may trigger the thought process, but more to do with an overall competence.

For instance, in an airline engineering division the competence might be to keep an airline fleet flying on time anywhere in the world at minimum cost. This overall competence has many facets to it. When an aircraft is on the ramp at an airport with 300 passengers sitting aboard and there is a technical fault, that competence is shown by being able to work under pressure, to develop an immediate and safe solution that can be sold to the pilot. For the same company, the competence required of its regular maintenance operation, which overhauls aircraft, is a much more methodical and logical approach. For the logistics operation a third type of competence is required. When combined, all these competences contribute to attaining the overall competence, but the management style, recruitment and training necessary to develop each contributing competence is very different.

In his book *Thriving On Chaos* (1988) Tom Peters writes 'Tomorrow's successful corporation will be a collection of skills and capabilities ever ready to pounce on brief market anomalies. Any useful strategic plan or planning process must focus upon the development and honing of these skills (which translate into readiness to seek and exploit opportunities), rather than emphasize static approaches to market development.'

One key to the distinctive capability goal is defining these competences and skills, and nurturing and developing them. Philip Morris's competence of understanding markets and brands in relation to packaged goods is one competence; Honda's rapid innovation is another. At Tesco it is the ability to understand the needs of its customers from detailed analysis, develop creative solutions and then implement these even when they are counter to the accepted wisdom of the industry.

Distinctive capability is thus the 'core' of the business and it must be retained, maintained, developed, nurtured and monitored. Monitoring is necessary to ensure that the capability is still appropriate for the business and the markets in which the company operates. The heart of a company is not really its plant and equipment, its computer system or offices. It is the distinctive capability of the people at its heart. If that distinctive capability cannot be defined and articulated, then the company is doomed to disappear.

TRADITIONAL THINKING

In developing the future business model the capabilities have to be developed and decided. But, even with the introduction of the Internet and a whole new range of capability requirements, those that a company already has, its key strengths, will still be important and often will form the bedrock of future distinctive capabilities. In general, the approach is to build on what exists, rather than try to create totally from scratch. Tesco is an excellent example of this approach.

A few examples of traditional capability thinking are now given which help explain how it develops.

BMW and distinctive capability

BMW was the major aircraft engine manufacturer in Germany at the end of World War Two. With their factory in the Soviet sector and the ruination of Germany all around them their future seemed anything but secure.

While German industry recovered and manufacturers such as Mercedes-Benz started to re-establish their ranges and distribution network, BMW floundered. It produced bubble cars, which lasted briefly as a fad in Europe, and unattractive saloon cars.

In 1959 BMW was on the verge of bankruptcy and it seemed likely that it would be acquired by Mercedes-Benz. At this stage the Quandt family took control and arranged for an injection of funds to carry the company forward.

In 1962 BMW launched the 1500 and established a new segment in the car market, the quality production saloon. The 1500 was a small to medium-sized car with a sporty appeal. To the young European executive class it signaled the new age of business success and recognition. It was not Mercedes or VW, Rolls-Royce or Fiat, but its own expression of success and lifestyle.

The car was technically excellent, with good performance and handling. It was built on a production line but by a workforce with technical skills, the same skills that had built the aircraft engines for the Luftwaffe. The distinctive capability of combining technical design and production skills with high volume quality car manufacture aimed at a new market segment gave BMW its competitive advantage.

The reputation for engineering excellence and reliability, combined with sporty performance and distinctive styling, soon earned BMW a strong following.

BMW built on this foundation to become one of the great success stories of the second half of the 20th century. From its established engineering and technical base it moved back into aero engines, which built on its technical knowledge and skills. It built a new factory in South Carolina to help with the development of the US market, especially with the new SUV, the X5.

At this stage BMW decided that instead of remaining 'the ultimate driving machine', its advertising byline and a superb description of its distinctive capability, it announced it was a supplier of mobility. Makers of invalid chairs are suppliers of mobility, together with Ford, Chrysler and Toyota. BMW decided to acquire Rover, a British car manufacturer that had been in decline for 30 years, from being the largest UK manufacturer to having a small market share, surviving only because of support from the British Government.

'Size thinking' drove this acquisition. This is the 'if we are bigger we are better' syndrome. For some companies this works, and there are genuine synergies and benefits from growing through acquisition. BMW did not have expertise in acquiring a company like Rover, in either size or market position. The plan was to move Rover up market, closer to BMW's own positioning, probably as a competitor to Audi. To do this it would have to sort out the huge problems at Rover.

BMW's distinctive capabilities lay in its engineering and technical excellence, which derive from its German engineering heritage, and in its brand. How would these be deployed in turning round a company that had been in 30 years of decline and had tried to reinvent itself at least three times and failed? The answer is they were not. BMW management, inheritors of one of the century's great success stories, decided to follow a management fad on having to be the right size, a big size, and forgot the distinctive capabilities that had made them strong and delivered competitive advantage. The result has been the loss of several billion Deutschmarks and a huge sapping of energy and confidence.

Wal-Mart

In 1979 Wal-Mart was a small discount retailer with 229 stores located in the Southern United States. The discount industry was dominated by Kmart with 1,891 stores. Its huge size gave Kmart the economies of scale in purchasing, distribution and marketing that are considered the key elements in being successful in a mature industry.

Today Wal-Mart is the largest retailer in the world with sales in 2001 of US$200 billion versus Kmart at US$37 billion. Wal-Mart also has some 4,500 stores worldwide with average revenues per store of close to US$45 million, versus Kmart with 2,100 stores with average revenues per store of under US$18 million.

The major factors in turning Wal-Mart from minnow to mighty are that they identified their goals and developed a strategy and implementation plan to achieve them. Their goals were:

- to provide customers access to quality goods;
- to make these goods available when and where customers want them;
- to develop a cost structure that allows competitive pricing;
- to build and maintain a reputation for absolute trustworthiness.

The key to achieving these goals was to make the distribution system, from placing orders on suppliers to stocking what customers were buying on the shelves, the focus of the strategy.

The Wal-Mart process starts with ordering full container loads from suppliers. These full loads are delivered to the warehouse where they are selected and cross-loaded onto containers going to the stores. Most goods never enter a warehouse inventory system. This process saves costs through ordering full containers of product and eliminating inventory and handling costs. It also means goods move from manufacturer to store quicker, improving the cash conversion cycle. The approach results in Wal-Mart's costs of sales being two to three per cent below the industry average.

Cross-docking, as the system is called, is very difficult to manage. It needs continuous communication between suppliers, distribution centers and all points of sale in every store to ensure orders can be placed, consolidated and delivered to the correct store within a matter of hours.

Wal-Mart ensures this system works effectively by owning its fleet of vehicles that deliver goods from its distribution centers to the store, replenishing stock twice a week on average.

The approach is effective because of the tremendous amount of communication throughout the organization and a drive to make the system work. Its distinctive capability is in a strong system operated by a staff that knows how to turn it into a major competitive advantage. Systems that require understanding and a co-operative culture to wring the advantages from them are both difficult to replicate and deliver strong economic results.

STRATEGIC ASSETS

The distinctive capability will most often be an organizational ability. Occasionally it will be in the form of an asset the company owns, such as British Airways' landing and take-off slots at London Heathrow Airport or being the industry standard, such as Microsoft's Windows operating system.

IBM

Recognizing the distinctive capability is important even as new business areas are entered, to ensure it is retained in the new strategic plan. It could be argued that IBM's distinctive capability until the advent of the PC was a strategic asset. At the peak of its power IBM had many distinctive capabilities. However, with hindsight, its greatest capability was probably the ability to determine the technical and operational standards of the mainframe computer industry. Software written to run on IBM computers could not be used on competitors' machines, so customers became locked into IBM. However, when IBM entered the personal computer market it purchased the two most important parts of the machine, the microprocessor and the operating software, from outside suppliers, Intel and Microsoft. Because it did not negotiate an exclusive arrangement with these suppliers they were able to supply their products to other manufacturers, and so an entire industry was started producing IBM PC clones. That change has led to the total redefinition of the computer industry and the demise of IBM before its reincarnation as a service led company.

The lesson from IBM must be that understanding the business model and the distinctive capability embedded within it is vital not only to building the future, but also to defending it.

British Airways

British Airways has sought many ways to become the global airline. Firstly it sought to take a major stake in US Air. The political lobbying of US airlines blocked this. In June 1996 BA and American Airlines signed their deal making them the most powerful airline alliance in the world, with control of 70 per cent of the flights across the North Atlantic. Again it failed as it faced opposition from industry regulators, other American airlines and Virgin Atlantic in the UK.

However, the major stumbling block was the condition laid down by the European competition authorities that BA would have to surrender more than 250 flight slots at Heathrow to other airlines. The dominance of Heathrow is the major strategic asset of BA. Even when surrendering some of this dominance could enable it to achieve its other strategic objectives it refuses to lose that which it already possesses.

It can be argued that losing the Heathrow strength would lead to the creation of a new and stronger distinctive capability of which Heathrow would be an integral part. However, BA has held tightly to its current distinctive capability asset and not in any way sought to make its global ambitions easier by diluting its Heathrow dominance. This clearly indicates how well the company understands the value of its asset, even when it makes the implementation of the broader strategy more difficult. It will not give away today's strength for tomorrow's opportunity.

In general strategic assets owe much to the history of the company. BA's domination of Heathrow was not consciously planned. IBM's ownership of operating systems grew out of its market domination and then became a marketing weapon. IBM realized its value intuitively but failed to build it into its strategy for the PC. For anti-trust reasons this may have been difficult, but by not doing so the company lost sight of this key factor when it developed PCs.

Most companies do not possess this form of strategic asset. Strengths will carry through from their history, but will not be a distinctive capability as they currently stand. The distinctive capability will come from the organizational capabilities produced by the strengths.

THE NEW DISTINCTIVE CAPABILITIES

In periods of rapid change, which we are going through now with e-commerce and the Internet, the development of new distinctive capabilities will become important. With transitional and change the business model strategies it will become important to develop new distinctive capabilities that still meet the definition of having high economic impact and are difficult for competitors to replicate.

Using two of the examples from Chapter 13, pharmaceuticals and automobiles, we can imagine the possible distinctive capabilities companies will have to develop. Their strategy might be to start taking positioning strategies to allow them the greatest flexibility when the picture becomes clearer.

Pharmaceuticals

The first step for a pharmaceutical company wanting to develop positioning capabilities for the period from 2005 onwards is to determine what they need to know about genomics in general in order to be able to compete in the new world. Having defined the overall genomic knowledge capability the next decision is to focus on which therapeutic areas it will have the greatest possibility of success and those areas where there will be the greatest potential for financial reward. These may not necessarily be the same. Once these decisions are made then it has to start recruiting and developing leading edge knowledge in those areas. This is the first step, to decide the market it wants to dominate and the knowledge it will need to achieve this and then develop that knowledge.

Step two is to decide the potential structure of the company. Assume they will still have a number of blockbuster drugs that have wide applicability and use. Then the assumption must be that these will be marketed as now. The new drugs, though, are likely to be far more in number and have much smaller revenues. The business model needs to be reconfigured so that it can manage a larger number of drugs with smaller revenues. There is a school of thought that says the major pharmaceutical companies do not want to market drugs with a potential of less than US$100 million, some say US$300 million, per annum. This culture will have to change.

The whole process of clinical trials will have to be simplified. Because it will be possible to identify if a molecule will interact unfavorably with specific genomic fingerprints, the trials will not need to be on thousands of patients, but on the smaller number for whom the drug is genetically suitable and where it is known the drug will treat the problem.

Managing a large number of clinical trials, possibly hundreds, and minimizing the cost will require a whole new approach to clinical trials project management.

Speed of development will also become more important. The marketing approach will be in 'owning' a gene, knowing all its variations and impacts so that any disease associated with it can be treated with the products of the one company.

Along with this will be the ability to develop disease management regimes, again rapidly, obtain recognition from whatever authority lists the treatment on the database and ensure it is placed on all the formularies. This is a whole new capability.

Just as with Wal-Mart where the distinctive capability was composed of many attributes that together created a whole new capability, so with pharmaceutical companies many factors will create a new capability. Even if they build from the existing expertise in certain therapeutic areas, the development of a new distinctive capability will be essential to their ongoing success.

Automobiles

GM has already announced its intention to totally reinvent itself. It plans to allow customers to specify their car online, exactly as described in Chapter 18, and deliver to their doors in four days. Such is the pace of development that ideas generated only two years ago, that were said to be over the top, are now being planned by the world's largest car maker.

As at February 2000 GM had yet to consider, at least in public, the implications for the dealer network. They were exploring the design, build and ship issues. The implication for dealers is huge. Once GM and Ford, who are said to be neck and neck in the race to build a custom-made car, can build to order, the power base of the dealer, huge stock lots and the ability to manipulate data disappear.

If GM, Ford and Toyota can achieve build-to-order configurations and manage the issues of what will happen in a sales downturn (can they economically shut down excess production?) they will have a totally new capability and one that could enable them to challenge even the imports such as BMW, Nissan and Honda.

This is a totally new configuration of the business model. The impact on suppliers, who may until now have thought that the key to success in being a parts supplier to the big auto companies was in meeting price, quality and delivery schedules, may now find it is in also in adding flexibility to these three. One of the keys to building custom-made cars is to precisely schedule the delivery of 3,000 or more parts, sometimes from hundreds of miles away. For some of those assemblies, those that are affected by customization, then the Tier 1 suppliers who provide those parts will have to have the same customizable ability as the auto manufacturers. If the order-to-manufacture time is three days, the customer order-to-parts supplier lead time will be two or less. Production scheduling for a supplier providing a range of parts will be difficult: he will not know on Tuesday his production schedule for Wednesday. This requires a whole new set of capabilities.

Even though customized cars will affect only a relatively small proportion of the parts in a finished vehicle, once suppliers are used to supplying these in a two to three day time frame, the practice will spread because of the increased efficiency it will create along with the flexibility to change models down a flexible production line.

The result is that the business model changes, the distinctive capability of the automakers changes, the distinctive capability of the parts suppliers and dealers has to change and whole new opportunities are created.

This is the challenge on the distinctive capability front that now faces many businesses. The key is to understand what the new business model will be for each company.

COMPETITIVE ADVANTAGE

This leads to one of the key concepts of distinctive capability. It is only of value in markets where its application will lead to a competitive advantage. Therefore, being the highest quality producer of a given product only becomes a competitive advantage in a market that demands, or can be encouraged to demand, that higher quality. If the market needs are satisfied with the current level of quality, and there is no reason to believe this will change, then the capability to produce higher quality products does not lead to a competitive advantage.

Determining distinctive capability stems from an understanding of the company's strengths and culture and the needs of its customers. Hence its development is closely related to the market/product goal. The analysis of distinctive capability and customer needs must show the existence of explicit benefit. The company then has a potentially profitable competitive advantage. It is this hard and difficult analysis and synthesis that stops the strategy process from becoming a 'wish list' and ensures that it delivers a real improvement in company performance.

DEVELOPING NEW DISTINCTIVE CAPABILITIES FROM THE OLD

Reynolds and Reynolds is a Dayton, Ohio company that was incorporated in 1889. It helps new car dealerships provide service to their customers. Its dealer management services include ordering parts for repair jobs and to remind owners when it is time for their car to be serviced. It has built a strong reputation and customer base with a presence in over 90 per cent of the automobile retailers in North America. Some 1,900 of DaimlerChrysler's 4,400 dealers use Reynolds. All of Toyota and Lexus dealerships in the United States and Canada will soon be using Reynolds' dealer-management systems. This customer base is a real strategic asset. Its distinctive capability is in the knowledge it has about the industry in general and the individual dealerships in particular.

Throughout its long history Reynolds and Reynolds has grown both organically and through making acquisitions. It recognized the importance of computers in streamlining auto dealers and was an early entrant into the new business.

Now it is putting its services online. It has recruited Lloyd 'Buzz' Waterhouse as president and COO. (Waterhouse was formerly general manager of the IBM e-business services division.) It will compete against some powerful competitors, including Waterhouse's former company, IBM, who want a slice of the online automotive market.

In order to strengthen its position Reynolds is entering into some strategic partnerships with the dealer services and claims solutions groups of Automatic Data Processing Inc and with CCC Information Services Inc, an electronic parts network to link buyers and sellers in a cost-effective, user-friendly solution for the multi-billion dollar automotive parts market.

Leveraging off its current distinctive capability Reynolds and Reynolds is developing new competencies in e-commerce that will reinforce its competitive advantage and stop any threats from new entrants to take its business away.

DISTINCTIVE CAPABILITY AND THE STRATEGIC PLAN

Effective strategy is founded on distinctive capability. Providing it is developed from a solid analytical base, this will be the factor that determines which products and services a company will provide and the markets in which it will compete.

New rules have been formulated for the development of a strategic business plan: the current distinctive capability will either be an organizational attribute or a strategic asset; sometimes it will be a combination of both. Where companies do not have a clear distinctive capability they have to review the competitive strength of their business and its survivability potential.

The future distinctive capability will ideally be built from the current position, but with the transformation of whole industries driven by technical development and e-commerce it might also need to be a completely new capability. This new distinctive capability will still have to meet the key criteria of high economic impact and being difficult for competitors to replicate

The key to developing the distinctive capability is to understand and develop a clear business model. Once this is complete it becomes clear what capability is required to create sustainable competitive advantage, and this, together with an understanding of the current major strategic strengths, will indicate the area where the company has to create the distinctive capability.

OUTSOURCING AND DISTINCTIVE CAPABILITY

Outsourcing is becoming more common in all areas of business. The point at which a company starts to outsource its distinctive capability is the point at which it can conceivably start its demise.

To return to our earlier example, BMW. The match between its distinctive capability in engineering and the market opportunities that it identified – translated into a major competitive advantage.

Now the BMW brand says the product stands for engineering excellence, prestige, an upmarket, sporting image. This distinctive capability is the fit of the whole strategy encompassing design, quality control, marketing, sales, service and maintaining a high trade-in price for used cars. Its original distinctive capability, engineering production, is now transportable. BMW has opened a new manufacturing facility in South Carolina to produce the X5 SUV, and there is no perceivable damage to the brand image.

BMW is now considering outsourcing the development and entire assembly of its latest SUV, the X3, to Magna International. It could lead to Magna's Steyr subsidiary in Austria assembling up to 60,000 vehicles a year.

This project involves using Steyr's research and development capability as well as their production capacity. BMW also says it will consider further collaboration with other carmakers as it expands. BMW is now no longer dependent on its production engineering for its distinctive capability.

With its strong branding BMW is able to outsource what have been considered key core competences of all automakers, R&D and manufacturing, without undue risk providing it maintains control of the quality of the vehicle. This has to include the driving characteristics, performance and quality of manufacture. Its strength now is in understanding the market niches where its brand gives it a strong competitive advantage, and being able to style and specify a concept that will appeal to that market. The vehicle development and production can be handed to another company, albeit under the close supervision of BMW's own staff.

Because BMW have minimized the risk of outsourcing this strategy makes sense, and gives the company tremendous strength to flex its production provided it has structured the right type of contract.

In contrast both Ericsson and Alcatel have outsourced the manufacture of their mobile telephone handsets. Whilst design and functionality is important in marketing handsets, price also has an important role. Control of costs is important, and by outsourcing this function both companies lose control of a key competitive weapon, one that might one day be a factor in the overall distinctive capability.

In contrast Nokia, the world's leader in mobile handsets with an estimated 35 per cent market share, outsources only 10 per cent of its production for this product and says its volume enables it to strike more competitive deals with suppliers and telecommunication providers, which in turn affords it wider profit margins. Interestingly, Nokia outsources 60 per cent of its networks infrastructure business, recently announcing a deal to transfer two more factories and 1,250 employees to SCI Systems.

Cisco Systems, Apple Computers, Motorola, Lucent Technologies and Ericsson amongst many others outsource to Flextronics, Solectron, Celestica and SCI Systems. These global companies, and others, manufacture some of the biggest brands in the world. In many cases it must make sense. However, there is also a herd instinct in business, another fad, and outsourcing amongst electronics manufacturers is flavor of the month. Not though, to our knowledge, with Dell, which uses its manufacturing strategically to create competitive advantage.

There is perhaps a lesson here. With high margin/high volume items, where price is not the main issue, be it BMW or networking equipment, outsourcing can make a lot of sense. With low margin/high volume items it appears to make the most sense, in the short term, but in the medium term a potential competitive advantage is being given away, a certain type of knowledge is inevitably lost, and the strategic options for the companies will be narrower in the future.

5

Market/product/service

The objective of the market/product/service goal

The approach to the market/product/service goal developed here is primarily strategic. The goal, together with the performance targets, is the leadership team's focus on how the markets/customer/products/service strategy fits together. It is their decision on the breadth of offering, in terms of customer segmentation, product and/or service range, that the company will take to market. It is the framework for marketing people to work within, whether they are handling industrial or consumer products or services.

My experience over the years is that those companies that have a strong and focused market/product/service stance are more profitable than those who have broad offerings, but with the new economics of e-commerce this may not necessarily be true in future.

Segmentation

Market segmentation is a process to analyze the market and creatively identify customer groupings to which the company can currently and potentially offer superior value. The market/product/service goal and the identity goal aim to target the mix of customers, products and services and then establish a communication program aimed at those customers. The distinctive capability goal is focused on developing unique internal capabilities to satisfy those customers and the organization goal establishes an operating structure, culture and set of values that will enable the organization to relate to and serve this market. The segmentation and the identification of potential new customers is a key element of the strategic business planning process.

Segmenting the current customer list is the best approach to understanding the current market. From this grouping of existing customers, potential customers are identified through brainstorming and market research projects. From this combined set of groupings a future market goal can be developed.

Start by reviewing the customer list in revenue order, using the ABC analysis discussed in Chapter 19. Segment this list as shown in Figure 19.6.

Using the chart in Figure 5.1 (Segmentation), start with the Group A customers by looking for SICC (the US four-digit standard industrial classification code) or use the new NAICS (North American Industrial Classification Standard).

Continue this through the Group B and C customers. Compare the top 20 per cent of customers to the bottom 20 per cent of customers. Generally the top group will generate two to five times the revenues of the bottom group. In searching for new customers, the top SICC customers will be the ones to focus resources on.

Repeat the analysis with geographical regions. Again the top 20 per cent of regions will be a number of times better revenue producers than the bottom 20 per cent.

Cross-referencing the top SICC code customers with the top geographical customers will show a correlation: those SICC customers will be located in the top regions. In what other regions of the country are there also strong groupings of these SICC groups? Also, what other SICC groups outside of the top 20 per cent are strong performers in the best regions?

Next repeat this analysis with products and services. Review which products or services are sold by SICC. What is the mix of product in regions? To this analysis factor in the salesman or channel that is producing the revenues.

From this analysis a mix of customers, marketing approaches and products/services emerges which can lead to maximizing revenues – and margins.

Predictable revenue streams from current customers

The key element in forecasting a customer's probable future trend is to be found in the transaction history. This is at the heart of the customer relationship management (CRM) software.

Rank	Customer	SICC	Region	Products or services	Last year's rank	Last year's revenue	This year's revenue*	Revenue by quarter**				Marketing approaches	Channel used	Revenue per channel
								Qtr 1	Qtr 2	Qtr 3	Qtr 4			
1	Name Department												Sales person order internet	

* If possible keep this as the revenue over the last 12 months versus the previous calendar year

** Each quarter should be the most recent: eg, in July 2001 the quarters might read:
Qtr 2, 2001, Qtr 1, 2001, Qtr 4, 2000, Qtr 3, 2000

Figure 5.1 Segmentation

As an example, Merrill Lynch focuses much of its marketing effort on what it calls 'prime customers'. In one study they analyzed the probability of a customer being in the 'prime' group this year:

Probability of Being Prime This Year

Prime each of the past two years	0.63
Prime last year, but not before	0.46
Not prime last year, but prime the year before	0.14
Not prime either of the past two years	0.06

This analysis explains why the quarter figures always record the last four quarters. Recency and frequency are the most reliable indicators of future business. Customers at risk of departure can often be dissuaded at reasonable cost.

From the segmentation analysis it becomes possible to identify relationships between the SICC, geographical location of customers and products and services supplied. This can be correlated to revenue changes and frequency to gain an insight into potential losses or increased opportunities in a defined set of customers. This ensures that however the market/product/service goal is defined it is always being monitored for actual performance.

From this tracking it becomes possible to identify new products or services that will be required for particular groups. This moves towards the mass customization approached discussed in Chapter 13. If the marketing goal is focused on supplying specific groups then this type of analysis is crucial to tracking performance in these groups. Creatively used, together with the business model approach, it helps to identify those groups that will enable the company to best achieve its goals as established by the leadership team.

Segmentation and the business model are usually the main analyses used in developing the market part of the goal. However, other forms of analysis can create additional insights and a selection of approaches is included in the following pages.

Competitive scope

One of the key decisions for the market/product/service goal is the breadth of the competitive scope. This establishes whether to compete across the market/product/service range, or to choose a limited number of market/product/service sectors and meet the specific needs of a carefully targeted group of customers. The analysis begins where the company is now, and moves on to determine what the company wants to aim for. Start by analyzing the competitive market scope, followed by the product scope and then combine the two.

Market scope

There has to be a strong correlation between the major services or products and the major markets. However, at this stage identify the markets in which the company is strongest. In addition to the segmentation suggested above it could be by market sectors as in Figure 5.2, by lifestyle characteristics, by socio-economic criteria, or demographic features. The only requirement is that the approach and output makes sense to the leadership team.

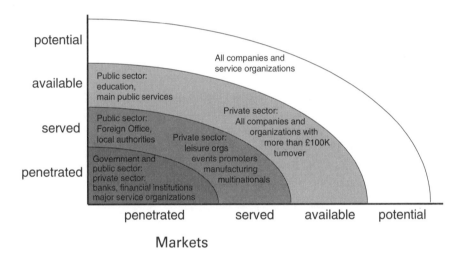

Figure 5.2 Competitive market scope for a management consultancy

The broad definitions used in Figure 5.2 are:

- penetrated – the customers who actually buy your product.(Using the customer analysis conducted in the data collection and presentation stage, these will be the category A and perhaps some of the category B clients or customers.)
- served –the part of the qualified available market that you decide to pursue. (It will contain the C clients or customers and some of the B. It is a potential market for growth but if this is followed it will broaden the focus and may dilute the company's continued development of the penetrated market. It might also have an impact on the image of

the company in that it will no longer be seen as such a specialist operation.)
- available – the customers in the market who are likely to be interested in your product offer and are able to finance the purchase. (Equally important is that customers in this market can access the product or the sales team. It is self-deception to estimate the market potential for an entire area when your sales effort is only effective in one part of the market.)
- potential – every customer who might be in the market to purchase a generic product or service of your type. (This may be segmented into market size.)

Using this type of analysis, with market sectors categorized by definitions and potential market size, encourages debate about where the company should position itself.

Product scope

Figure 5.3 breaks down the competitive product scope for a management consultancy into five areas. Only three or four could be used, depending on the products and the markets.

From the work that has been done during data collection, a similar chart should be easy to produce for your company. If it is difficult, then part of the earlier process has not been completed to a satisfactory level. The easiest way to draw up a chart is to write all your products or services on Post-It notes, draw the basic framework on a flipchart, and then agree among the leadership team where to place the Post-it notes on the flipchart.

The broad definitions used in Figure 5.3 are:

- primary – if you went to most of your clients (or customers) and asked them what they would purchase from you without hesitation, it would be this list of items. (This is the area where the company has undoubted expertise or products acknowledged as market leaders or superb, and this is recognized by your customers and potential customers. It is also the area where you see yourselves as offering your best products and services, primarily the A products from your product ranking list.)
- accepted – the area where the company is acknowledged as having the expertise or good products, but not perceived as the market leader or the natural choice. (The purchaser has to be convinced by selling that the order should be placed with the company.)

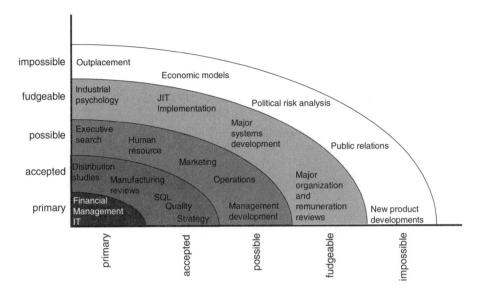

Figure 5.3 Competitive product scope for a management consultancy

- possible – the area where the company is able to do a job or supply a product, but normally it is either starting to develop in this area, or it forms part of a bigger job where there is a need to show competence across a range of abilities or products. (It is an area of business not to drift into without making a clear strategic decision to do so.)
- fudgeable – jobs where a business needs the work to maintain cash flow, or takes it on as a challenge where management is sure that their abilities (not capabilities) will enable it to be seen through. (It is a 'suck it and see' type of approach; usually the customer does not know this. It is also a classic area for losing money.)
- impossible – the job is outside the business expertise and no attempt should be made to win it.

The most important areas are those designated as primary and accepted. If they are very large in relation to the total area, then you have a broad product offering with a potential lack of definition. The large management consultants such as PricewaterhouseCoopers, Cap Gemini Ernst & Young or KPMG would probably claim to offer expertise across most of the disciplines in Figure 5.3. Other, even quite large, consultancy firms would have a more focused product range. For instance, Accenture concentrates more on information technology, systems work and e-commerce. It is not a question of which is the right approach, but which is the correct strategy for your firm.

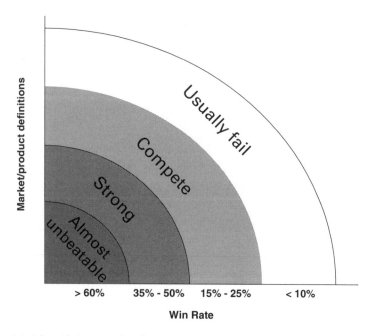

Figure 5.4 Identifying market/product segments

Another approach to deciding where to focus the business winning effort and to understanding the market is shown in Figure 5.4. This is particularly useful for companies in contracting businesses supplying a wide range of industries. A software house would be a good example of the type of business.

The win rate is the ratio of contracts won to proposals submitted. Here the gaps between the various sections are only to show starkly where the business has unassailable strengths and where it is relatively weak. It is interesting that some companies spend almost as much time and effort in trying to sell to market product segments where they have little success as those where they have huge success. If this was accompanied by the introduction of new products or services or even targeted selling campaigns to those sectors it would make some sense. However, often there is no such initiative and the company seems determined to waste its resources and depress its sales staff by letting them bash their heads against brick walls.

Future product and service offerings

Having analyzed your existing product range, the next step is to decide what your future product offering should be. It may remain as it is now.

If it does, you may need to develop better marketing to ensure that it becomes recognized as the primary product range for your organization.

On the other hand, it may be that future products or services might not just evolve from what you do now. Brainstorm products or services in the impossible sector and you might uncover significant new business areas that could create a whole new future for the company. For example, a management consultancy might set up a negotiation consultancy to help clients negotiate deals with other companies. This might include arranging agreements with third-party suppliers or conducting sales negotiations for major contracts. This is different from anything we are aware exists now: many people offer to train your staff to negotiate more effectively, but this consultancy would negotiate for you or as part of your negotiating team. When considering products and markets keep an open mind for a really radical approach.

The end user market

Every company has to understand its end user market. For some this is their direct market. However, even with consumer goods it is not unusual to find manufacturers thinking in terms of the retail outlets and not the final consumers as their customers. Many companies sell derivative or part products, demand for which is primarily decided by sales of another product. If the company is producing batteries for notebook PCs, for example, then it has to understand what is happening in the notebook PC market. The simple chart in Figure 5.5 starts the process of establishing just how much managers know about the trends in their market.

There may be a number of trends, some of which can appear contradictory. They need to be articulated and the forces that are driving them need to be identified. This is a critical element in the business model.

The process starts by defining the main product/service groups and the main markets. The starting point is ensuring that you can agree how to segment the markets; this could be by geographical location, industry, size or whatever. Try to keep the matrix as small as possible at this stage. Then complete the chart for each segment of the matrix.

If the chart cannot be completed relatively easily then it is a fair conclusion that there is a lack of market understanding. This is, quite simply, a recipe for failure. In many companies there is very muddled thinking about trends and drivers and the leadership team needs to understand those forces that impact on their industry before deciding the marketing goal.

Product Groups Markets	Product Group A	Product Group B	Product Group C
Europe	Trends: Drivers:	Trends: Drivers:	Trends: Drivers:
USA & Asia	Trends: Drivers:	Trends: Drivers:	Trends: Drivers:
Rest of world	Trends: Drivers:	Trends: Drivers:	Trends: Drivers:

Figure 5.5 Market analysis – end-user trends and drivers

Once this chart is complete, summarize exactly which products and markets appear most attractive. Obtain agreement from members of the leadership team and the marketing and sales staff about the trends and drivers. Then establish a small working group with the objective of developing a thorough understanding of the market as described below, relating this to the company's strengths, and making a proposal about the size of the market and product scope. Be prepared to vary the approach to meet your own needs and only use analytical tools that you consider will really help you.

The output from the analysis so far might include:

- analysis of current customers;
- other customer segments in the market, their value and strategic importance;
- loyalty of customers to current suppliers and what generates that loyalty;
- the top three reasons that induce a customer to select a certain supplier;
- other customer requirements;
- customer communication channels;
- overall market prospects;
- pricing trends;
- market/product/service segment attractiveness.

Using the segments in Figure 5.5 as a basis for defining market/product/service groupings, and keeping in mind the company strengths and weaknesses analysis, complete Figure 5.6.

MARKET/PRODUCT ATTRACTIVENESS	COMPANY STRENGTHS		
	Low	Medium	High
High	Opportunity Test growth potential	Selective potential Focus where strength can be maintained	Concentration and investment Maintain strength and profit structure by investment
Medium	Limited potential Test for expansion without high risk	Focused potential Low-risk/high profit segments only	Build competitive advantage Selectively invest to raise productivity and added value
Low	Loss limitation Lower fixed costs Explore best exit	Overall harvesting Switch from fixed to variable costs Brainstorm profitability options	Limited harvesting Protect profitability Risk losing market share

Figure 5.6 Market/product/service segment attractiveness

In each section of this matrix there is a strategy indicator. For those sections that appear interesting, see if the leadership team agrees with the statement in the context of your business. If you do, discuss the implications for your business to strengthen further your position in this market/product/service segment. From this point write ten to twenty lines about the strategic implications of continuing or further developing your presence in this market/product/service sector. One reason for carefully completing the strengths and weaknesses analysis can now be clearly seen.

Deciding on future scope

The key decisions concern whether to follow a broad competitive scope, in terms of products/services and markets, or a narrow competitive scope, focusing on specialist markets or specialist applications or both. For instance, a strategic consultancy could be said to have a narrow product focus. A strategic consultancy focused only on the pharmaceutical industry would have a narrow product/service and a narrow market focus.

Often this decision about concentration is the most significant one a company has to make. It can lead to enormous success if it is founded on good information and planned and executed well.

One client spent the first nine years of its existence growing to US$1.5 million revenue. It then expanded in consecutive years to US$3m, US$6m, US$10m, US$18m, US$26m, US$34m and now plans to grow at 25 per cent compound over the next four years. Its key decision, made when its turnover was US$1.5m, was to focus on supplying one product range to one defined market sector. Having made this decision the leadership team became really creative in their approach to this market, the structure of the sales operation and the reward model, after sales service and product design. In many sales situations they were virtually unbeatable and often were the only company invited to tender. Tight market/product/service focus gave them the ability to out-think their competitors and implement new business models.

Having decided on the market/product/service stance to adopt, locate it on Figure 5.7.

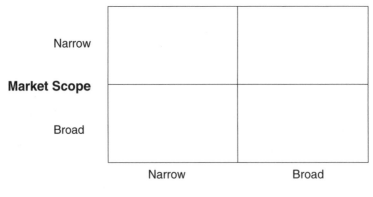

Figure 5.7 Market/product/service scope and range

The four options are thus: narrow product/narrow market, narrow product/broad market, broad product/narrow market or broad product/broad market. Then identify the market/product stance of your three major competitors (identified in the competitor analysis) on the same matrix. If you and your major competitors are in different quadrants of the matrix, then it is possible for all of you to have strategically sound businesses. If, however, all of you are competing in the same or adjacent segments, then competition will be fierce and profits much lower.

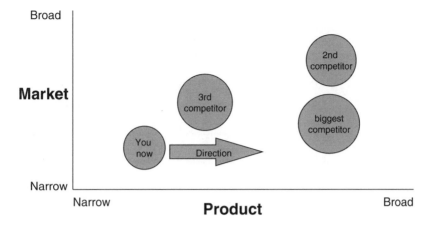

Figure 5.8 Competitor market/product stance

Figure 5.8 indicates a business that at present occupies a reasonable position, perhaps a large niche. Its strategy as indicated by the direction arrow shows that it is headed for problems by moving into more direct competition with its major competitors.

The next step is to identify (yet again) the advantages that you can offer your customers from this position. Does the offering that you will be making to your customers have greater benefits or a better price-benefit ratio than your competitors can offer from their strategic position? Also, thinking of the identity goal, what will your customers recognize about you from your marketing approach, what will strike them as different, positive and remain in their mind?

Market/product segment (MPS)

As markets become smaller and more focused, as we move towards mass customization, a concept that is useful is to consider the number of market/product segments (MPSs) offered by a company.

This involves drawing up a chart of products and markets and examining how they are distributed. For a company with a narrow product/service offering and a narrow market focus, this is fairly simple. With a broad market scope, it can become more complex; in this case group products into ranges that fit together logically. An example is shown in Figure 5.9.

Having broken the market down into small segments, each with its own distinct needs and buying habits, mark on the chart the product or services that each segment purchases.

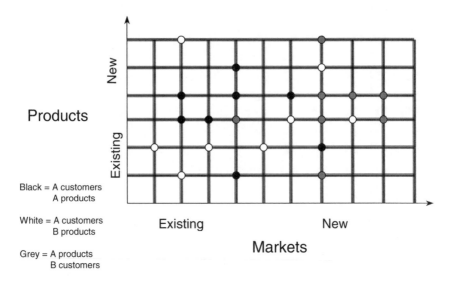

Products

Black = A customers
A products

White = A customers
B products

Grey = A products
B customers

Figure 5.9 Product/market segment chart

In looking at this chart of market/product segments, try to arrange them in an order that makes most sense to both your own staff and to customers. Use the product-ranking chart in Chapter 19 and the coding shown on Figure 5.9 to identify distinct market segment. This will often result in clusters of MPSs that represent the core business of your company. From this determine where you want to go and what types of products or services you want to sell in which markets.

One interesting fact that would come out of Figure 5.9 is that new products are primarily sold to B customers, and very few to A customers. Another way to define the MPS is by products sold to customers in different SICC codes.

One of the main benefits of the MPS concept is that the segments are small enough to enable the marketing, sales and operations departments to 'smell' the customer: no longer an abstract market concept, but a living, breathing, visualizable person or company.

Product/service range perception

If the products or services form into a related range, it is important that the customer can clearly see how the range fits together. There are many examples of new product introductions causing customers to be confused about how they relate to the existing range, sometimes with the result that total sales across the range are reduced. One approach is

Figure 5.10 Product/service range perception

to develop a chart similar to Figure 5.10 for your range of products and services.

In developing this chart think what, if anything, defines the characteristic of the range for the vertical axis. For instance with the Ralph Lauren Polo range of products there is a wide range of formal and casual clothes for men, women and children. Within the range are also underwear, sleepwear, lingerie, accessories, fragrances and home products such as sheets and towels. This range does not 'fit together' in terms of price per se, even though all the products are upmarket. Its 'fit' is in terms of a lifestyle image.

Some companies' product brands are unrelated: Marlboro is not related in the consumer's mind to Virginia Slims though both are manufactured and marketed by Philip Morris. However, Marlboro Lights are a brand extension and strongly related to normal Marlboro cigarettes, and the way the consumer perceives this is vital consideration in the brand management program.

In a large company with a number of product divisions or subsidiaries, consider how the whole business fits together. For example, Philip Morris is in many different businesses, but they are tied together by being packaged consumer goods. Philip Morris explains its expertise in terms of market understanding and branding. This level of fit in the range may not matter to consumers, who are usually buying the individual brand, but it does matter to an investing institution, so ranges have to make sense at the corporate level as well.

The need is to plan how the market will perceive the total offer in terms of range size and logical fit. For instance, think of a Mercedes car: the image is immediately upmarket and luxury. But Mercedes also manufactures trucks and vans: how do these fit the luxury image? In fact, Mercedes uses its name in a generic sense to mean engineering quality and design. This applies to all it vehicles, trucks and vans as well as cars. Besides this generic branding there is a specific branding that applies to luxury cars as well as rugged commercial vehicles. Now consider whether a Jaguar truck would fit that company's image. It is this strategic positioning and the customers' perception of it that is so crucial to success.

Another good example is the Porsche Cayenne. This off-road SUV, yet to be seen, will be the third model range after the 911 and Boxster. As is the case with the legendary 'Carrera', the Spanish word for race, Porsche has not chosen an artificially concocted word, but rather a living term understood in almost every language and associated with spirited qualities.

Yet Porsche is a sports car brand. How will enthusiasts react to a SUV under their marque? The words above are taken from the Porsche Club News. The positioning includes Cayenne within the marque, as a member of the brand, and its sporting credentials are already being established. No one can know for sure but there is already a feeling of certainty that Cayenne will extend the brand but not dilute it.

The start, in what can be a very complicated process, is to decide the vertical axis and the types of measures that will be used to define it. Price is easy. Socio-economic status is reasonably straightforward. Life-style can be more difficult.

Hence, when planning your market/product/service position, think of how the company will appear to the market. Does the overall offering make sense in terms of the potential customers' perception?

Consider the BMW range: the three basic Series – 3, 5 and 7 – clearly move up a price chart and socio-economic status. The Series 3 can be thought of as for young aspiring executives who will be upwardly mobile. It might also be a second car in wealthier families. It can clearly be seen as an entry-level option for anyone wanting to be associated with the BMW brand and the statement it makes about the owner. The Series 5 is a middle management brand with options that can endow it with either a sporting image or present it as a more practical family vehicle through the Sport Wagon choice. The Series 7 is a senior executive option, which states 'I am a financial success in life'. The two SUV options enable those who really like this type of vehicle to combine a sports image but still be a BMW owner with the prestige that that conveys. Finally there is the real sporty image from the Z3, at between US$31,000 and US$38,000, which conveys a young, fun and successful image. This young – at least at heart or in self-perception – image is

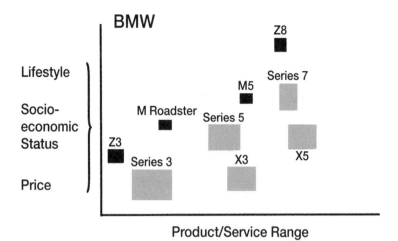

Figure 5.11 BMW

fostered further at increasing prices through the M Roadster, M5 – a powerful luxury sedan which sits between the sports and fun image and the Series 5 and Series 7 ranges. Finally, there is the Z8, the flagship high performance roadster, which conveys a sophisticated, sporting and highly successful image, but one not tied to the corporate ladder. At US$130,000 it is the most expensive BMW. From this example it is clear that this can be a complex exercise. The key at the start is to understand and define the vertical axis. It is also possible to make the horizontal axis increasing price and have the vertical axis as an image concept.

There is one very simple example where *not* considering how customers would perceive a range profile cost one company dearly. The company manufactured and supplied office furniture for the largest companies in Europe. There was one basic range that covered all needs, from the workstation, which generated the bulk of its revenues, through to the director's suite. There were variations in the range, but it had one defining feature. Its great virtue, beside being a well-designed and quality product, was that it could be easily reconfigured and additional modules purchased to meet companies' changing requirements.

At one major exhibition this company put a new range on a large raised dais in the center of its exhibit. Other than a range name, it had no pricing, no explanation of whether this would supersede the existing range, in which many customers had a huge investment, or how it would be sold. Customers were confused and business reduced significantly until the company clarified the situation.

Just thinking through how a product or service range will be per-ceived by customers, and how the supplier can influence that percep-tion, can be a valuable exercise.

Pricing decisions by MPS

Segmenting the market by MPS helps to develop a better understanding of what is sold to each market/product/service group and facilitates pricing decisions.

As an example, one manufacturing company made specialist machines that could be sold both to end-users and to OEM customers (manu-facturers who used the machines as part of their own equipment). They were also sold through distributors overseas. The machines were classified as: standard, which were similar in terms of price and performance to those offered by competitors; high performance, which could do work which competitors' machines could do either not at all or not as well or efficiently; and specials, where a system would be designed and manufactured to meet the specific requirements of a particular customer. A final group of customers was identified who did not want a machine at all. They wanted the service the machine provided and wanted to enter into a contract in which the supplier would guarantee a 98 per cent service level. They were not concerned whether this meant having spare machines to replace defective mach-ines, large numbers of spares, or a planned maintenance program or whatever. What they wanted to purchase was guaranteed performance, for which they were willing to pay.

All pricing in this case was effectively cost plus. OEMs and distrib-utors were given a 33 per cent discount on list prices. When the market was analyzed the company found that there was no reason to offer huge discounts to OEMs and distributors on either high performance equip-ment or specials. Having an across-the-board pricing policy was costing the company a good deal of money. The market/product segment chart helped the various segments to be identified and the pricing and marketing policy to be modified appropriately. Using this selective approach to pricing increased overall gross margins by 8 per cent and met no significant customer resistance, even in the tough market of the early 1990s.

Know the MPS customer

The rate of new product introductions has increased enormously over the last 10 years. With the move towards mass customization this will increase. As each market becomes more crowded, as products are aimed at ever smaller niches of specialized need, so understanding what a customer buys becomes critical. There must be sufficient information about each MPS to enable the company to 'know' the customer within the segment. You need to begin to think like the MPS customer.

Edward de Bono says in his book *Sur/Petition* (1992) that there are three stages in product or service development:

1. getting the product or service right;
2. making the offering competitive with similar products on the market;
3. 'integrating into the complex values of the buyer.'

Prudential Assurance in the United Kingdom used to run an advertising campaign which showed someone hang-gliding in the distance and the caption: 'You can spot a Prudential pensioner a long way off'. There was a series of advertisements including rock climbing and sailing. The company was harmonizing with the values of those who are retired but still have an active life in front of them. With the average retirement age in the United Kingdom being about 57, that is a vast number of potential customers with low expenditure, reasonable income and who perceive themselves as still having a lot of life to live and the energy to live it. In other words, they have a complex value system, probably including family and grandchildren, the need to care for one's spouse, but also to do the things there was never time for when at work. This can be researched and understood.

Creative use of the MPS

Understanding MPSs is critical for new products, or where potential market gaps are identified.

For instance, General Electric dominated the US commercial electric light market with over 50 per cent market share. The buying decision was usually made by the corporate purchasing department, who used two criteria for placing orders: how much does it cost and how long will it last? Electric lights were a commodity product where all manufacturers competed on price, brand name and established contacts. These were all areas where GE was strong and could utilize to continue market domination. The major problem with traditional light bulbs is not their up-front costs, which is what concerned the corporate purchasers, but the disposal cost. A new lamp generally costs around 80 cents to buy. A replacement lamp costs around US$1 per light. The higher replacement costs are because normal bulbs contain levels of toxic mercury that prevent them being disposed of in dumping sites because of the risk of pollution.

In 1995 Philips Lighting, the North American division of the giant Dutch electrical group, launched the first environmentally-friendly light bulb. It uses a low level of mercury and can be thrown straight into a rubbish bin. It was not attractive to purchasing departments; it was more expensive than current lighting. But Philips did not market to purchasing departments. They rethought who the customer was, a company keen to reduce overall costs, and focused on who saw the overall costs, including disposal. Purchasing agents saw only the initial price. The disposal costs were later seen by the CFO.

Philips used both the CFOs and environmental public relations to drive the sale of their environmentally-friendly lamp, with its lower overall lifetime cost to the purchaser. The result is that Philips now has over 25 per cent of the T-12 fluorescent lamps market in public buildings and offices.

Philips also has superior margins and a rapidly growing market share. The MPS here is not just a market segment. It is a function within large corporations and understanding who will perceive the benefits of a new product. Convention was not only stood on its head, Philips also risked alienating the traditional decision-maker, purchasing. The rewards of a carefully planned marketing program have clearly outweighed the risks.

Buyer value analysis

For each MPS it should be possible to complete a buyer value analysis. This really tests your understanding of the customer you visualize in the MPS.

This model suggests how to analyze the buyer's value criteria and approaches to securing the sale. It follows a simple sequence as shown in Figures 5.12 and 5.13.

Firstly, analyze the benefits sought by buyers. These may be either tangible or intangible, but time spent identifying them is never wasted.

Secondly, buyers often need to justify to themselves in logical terms why they should make this purchase from this supplier. You need to

Benefits sought	Benefit measures	Action motivators
Improved performance	Time	
Security Freedom of action	Quantity	Fear
Image		Greed
Enjoyment	Quality	
Knowledge		Excitement
Health	Money	
Hassle removal etc		

Figure 5.12 Buyer value analysis

Time:	Elapsed, speed of delivery User time saved
Quality:	Appearance, can be seen to be well made/presented Easy to use, no faults, comfortable Gives long service, durable Hassle-free Pride of ownership Quality of life Quality of relationships
Quantity:	Enables user to produce more Move faster
Money:	Reduce costs Increase profits Free up cash

Figure 5.13 Benefit measures

convince them of the additional benefits in terms of values. Benefit measures are how you help customers to justify the purchase logically. Besides logic, there is an emotional element in making a purchase; engaging this emotional element can clinch the sale. When IBM dominated the mainframe computer market it used to be said, purportedly by IBM salespersons, that nobody was ever fired for choosing IBM.

This was certainly a way of using fear to encourage IT and purchasing managers to place their order with IBM, who could be relied on to continue in business, provide a high level of service and generally look after the customer. This enabled it to charge premium prices.

Buyer values are at the heart of understanding customer needs. The difficulty is that the exercise takes time and can seem tedious and sheer hard work. However, it does pay off. Together with the answer to the question, 'What is value to our customer?' the buyer value analysis will help to begin logically thinking through what will encourage customers to purchase your company's product.

Price and cost comparisons by MPS

The chart in Figure 5.14 seeks to identify where there are price and cost mismatches versus your competitors. Even when product prices are under pressure, this will not necessarily be the case in all market sectors for that product.

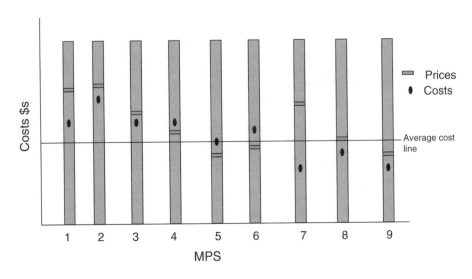

Figure 5.14 Product/service value analysis by MPS

Start by researching your competitors' costs (the financial analysis approach may help if they produce a limited product range). Having obtained a feel for their financial performance and structure conduct a base level value engineering exercise on their products or service offerings. Identify features that you offer that they may not and consider if these offer real value in the customer's perception. Check if their product or service has a simpler design that delivers the same benefit. If your company produced a product or offered a service exactly like the competitor you are analyzing, would your cost be higher or lower than it currently is? From this analysis it is usually possible to strike an average cost line for an MPS.

Only in MPSs 1 and 7 does the company in this example have a clear price/cost competitive advantage. In MPSs 2 and 3 it is vulnerable to losing its differentiated advantage because of its high cost structure; in MPSs 4, 5 and 6 it is at a clear competitive disadvantage, with higher than average costs and lower than average prices. It could be losing money in these areas. Only in MPS 7 does this company have an overwhelming competitive advantage.

The company analyzed in Figure 5.14 is in a strategic shambles. Because it does not have a clear competitive position, it cannot project one to the market. It is vulnerable across a wide range of MPSs and must think through where it is going to focus its effort. It will probably find that most of its sales are in the MPS areas where its prices are low. If these are mature markets then it must develop a marketing strategy to milk these products through to extinction, however long that might be.

In the 1980s Imperial Tobacco was the leading cigarette manufacturer in a highly profitable mature UK industry, which was in a steady state of slow but steady decline. Hanson, a UK conglomerate, in a fiercely contested takeover battle, acquired the company. Hanson stripped out every department and overhead that was not essential to the day-to-day running of the business. It ended up with a superb cash generator and profit contributor.

With the Internet making price comparisons easier, it is becoming ever more important to be a low cost producer, or at least a reasonable cost/high benefit supplier. This type of analysis guides leadership team thinking into developing a strategy that will move the company into MPSs where it can maintain a clear competitive advantage. It should also stop it from competing head to head with the competition, which is usually a route to reduced profits, even if you are the strongest company in the market. This exercise can also encourage a business to undertake benchmarking exercises and conduct studies of other businesses, their processes and business models, to establish where and how they manage aspects of a similar business better.

All companies must look at managing their MPSs to the benefit of the total organization and be clear on how each MPS contributes towards achieving their goals.

At the end of this process there should be a clear description of the broad market/product/service trends and drivers, the markets that are attractive and their fit with the company strengths, the detailed MPSs and the buyers' values, comparative pricing/costing to your competitors and its implications.

Discriminators

In their book *Positioning To Win* (1982), Beveridge and Velton explain how to produce business proposals that win, using a concept that is appropriate to understanding an MPS customer. One product is differentiated from another by discriminators. These are the facts or beliefs held by the customer about your product or service, and they can be influenced.

Customers buy differences, especially positive differences. Being like three similar competitors is not a reason for a potential customer to buy your product or service.

Discriminators are not necessarily matters of verifiable fact, but of buyer perception. If the MPS customers and their needs are really understood, it should be possible to develop discriminators for each.

A discriminator may be strength or a weakness. It may exist in you or in a competitor. The four types of discriminators can be described as:

- An 'Aha!' is a strength (yours) – the golden nugget that will unlock a sale to a customer or open the door to an MPS. (Generally there will only be two or three really effective discriminators in a sale or market situation.)
- An 'Oh-oh' is a weakness (yours also) which you need to neutralize.
- A 'Ho-hum' is a feature that is neutral and does not count. As they have no positive impact on the process they are excluded from the analysis. (We have over 300 offices. So does every company competing for the account.)
- A 'ghost story' is a way of making the customer worried about your competitors' weaknesses.

The need, therefore, is to identify all the relevant discriminators and decide how they will influence the customers' choice. This paves the way to highlight your strengths in relation to your customers' critical needs, neutralize your weaknesses, counter competitors' strengths with a view to discrediting them, and expose your competitors' weaknesses so that they worry the customer. Remember that they worry the customer; you are not trying to knock the competition. Blatant attacks can lose sales by making the seller look unprofessional.

For each MPS first identify the 'Aha!' – what it is about your offering to that market that will make the customer go 'Aha!' Then categorize the other discriminators that you identify, of which there may well be twenty or more. Produce a chart like the example shown in Figure 5.15. When you can complete this then you are really beginning to understand your MPSs and your competitors' positioning.

Discriminators	Aha! Your strength	Oh-oh! Neuter your weaknesses	Ghosts Features Competitors Weaknesses
Strong reputation in market	X		
Unrivalled experience in this type of work	X		
New system already proven in USA. Cost saving 35 per cent	X		
Previous new system did not work as well as quoted		X	
Company has large debts: financial viability in doubt		X	
Top management changes: might withdraw from market			X

Figure 5.15 Discriminators

Competitor analysis

Competitor analysis is towards the end, not because it is less important, but because there is no point in thinking about how their strategy should impact on your company until the leadership team has creatively thought through their own strategy. At that stage it is useful to see how it is different from those of competitors and how it will position the company to gain competitive advantage.

Use this competitor ranking and analysis form to establish the profile of your competitors. List your main competitor companies. They may be the biggest firms, those you compete against most frequently, or those

Competitor ranking	Key strengths (max 3)	Key weaknesses (max 3)	Main product range (over-lap with our product range)	Marketing proposition	Strategic thrust
Biggest competitor					
Next major competitor					
Third major competitor					

Figure 5.16 Competitor ranking and analysis

you fear or respect the most. It is frequently the case that members of the leadership team will identify different companies as their three main competitors; resolving this is an interesting exercise in its own right. If this happens, decide on the criteria to be used and then rank the companies suggested in terms of market share, recognized leadership position, or how often you compete against them.

Describe each company's major strengths (a maximum of three) and major weaknesses (again, up to three). List the overlap between their product range and yours as shown in the competitor product matrix (Figure 5.17).

Products	Your company	Biggest competitor	Next major competitor	Third major competitor
1	x	x	x	x
2	x	x	x	
3	x	x	x	x
4	x		x	
5	x	x	x	
6	x	x	x	x
7	x		x	
8	x	x		x
9	x		x	x
10				x
11				x

Figure 5.17 Competitor product matrix

This clearly shows where there is overlap and indicates any segments where there is less competition. For instance, in the example shown only one company is producing products 10 and 11. Perhaps this is because they are specialist products, the market is too small, or the margins too low. It might also be an opportunity.

Next, describe the competitor's main marketing proposition (eg quality, price, customization, service, delivery time, reliability, financing, image), and enter it on the form.

Finally, describe each major competitor's main strategic thrust. This may be expanding into new markets either at home or overseas, changing distinctive capability, merging or acquiring new companies, developing different types of product, expanding production facilities, or just trying to solve some significant problems which are plaguing them. It is interesting how often another company's strategy may be known, or guessed at, by managers, but never thought through. It can encourage managers to pursue their own strategic direction more aggressively. Ensure, however, that you avoid a 'looking over your shoulder' approach to SBP.

Having gathered this information, much of which is subjective, carry out a financial analysis of the competition, as outlined in Chapter 20. This will begin to provide a factual base against which to test some of the information that has already been gathered. Review all that has been stated about your competitors in the light of this financial information and complete Figure 5.18.

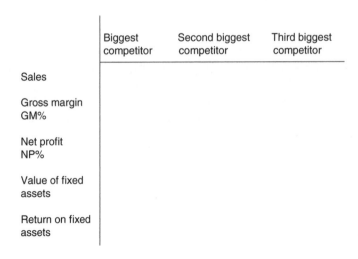

	Biggest competitor	Second biggest competitor	Third biggest competitor
Sales			
Gross margin GM%			
Net profit NP%			
Value of fixed assets			
Return on fixed assets			

Figure 5.18 Competitor financial analysis

There is the option to start with the financial analysis or with the competitor analysis. Experience indicates that starting with the competitor analysis leads to a more in-depth and insightful discussion that can be reviewed in the light of the financial figures. Comparing the competitor matrices again at the end of the discussion will often provide new insights into how the market operates.

SUMMARY

In developing the market/product/service goal the leadership team and/or the marketing/sales group will have undertaken a number of exercises. They will have:

- analyzed the market in terms of its end users, trends and drivers;
- analyzed the market attractiveness in relation to your company strengths;
- considered the breadth of your offering in terms of market and product;
- compared your strategic position to that of your competitors;
- analyzed your total range to ensure that it makes sense to your potential customers;
- broken down your market/product offering into its smallest practical segments;
- analyzed the customers for each segment in terms of their buying values and potential discriminators.

From this analysis, and others that might be particularly relevant to the company and its business, the leadership team will have developed a clear, and shared, view of the market and where the company should direct its resources. This needs to be framed into a goal; the performance targets will flow naturally from that goal and the analysis that has been conducted.

6

Identity

The identity goal is concerned with positioning the company's image as well as its products and services in the minds of all the target audiences.

THE VALUE PROPOSITION

We have moved from a world in which there was an excess of demand, with the ability to pay, to one where there is an excess of capacity in most products and services. In this scenario the value proposition becomes critical. This is true for most businesses now and even where a company has a position where demand is greater than supply, in the modern world capacity can usually be rapidly established, even when this requires expensive R&D.

The ultimate value proposition is a guarantee that a service or product will perform as agreed, or better, or there will be no charge. If this proposition is accepted, how close to giving a performance guarantee could a company move? Carefully structured, could this become a differentiating value proposition?

Consider Graniterock in California. The company sells crushed gravel, concrete, sand and asphalt. Two brothers head the leadership team. They decided that Graniterock would provide total customer satisfaction and achieve a reputation for service that equaled or exceeded that of Nordstrom.

They instituted a radical new policy called 'short pay'. On the bottom of every invoice they put 'If you are not satisfied for any reason, don't pay us for it. Simply scratch out the line item, write a brief note about the problem, and return a copy of this invoice along with your check for the balance.'

If customers scratch out a line item they do not have to return the item, it remains theirs free and gratis. They have the power to decide how much they will pay. The system provides a feedback mechanism about the quality of the service and products. It compels managers to track down the real causes of problems to prevent them being short paid again. Customers know that Graniterock is serious about its quality pledge, and so do employees.

Financially the company has prospered. It has 6 per cent price premium and profit ratios with a pre-tax return of approximately 10 per cent. In an outright commodity business dominated by giant corporations this is exceptional.

Aside from this rather radical approach, one of the keys to positioning is to define what a good company in your industry should be – for instance if yours is a software company then what a good software house should be.

Airlines do this when they keep changing the definition of what a good flight experience or good value is. Virgin is constantly refreshing and changing its positioning. Its total travel experience means being picked up by a limo from home, office or hotel and being driven to the final destination in another limo – provided both the pick-up and drop-off are within specified distances. In between it is possible to have massages, haircuts, manicures or pedicures. Flying now gives the opportunity to spend the hours traveling doing some of the things that take personal time, and arrive relaxed.

Before Virgin redefined it, the generic airline value proposition was a comfortable, on time, no-hassle flight from the club lounge to priority luggage. Before and after that you were on your own. In between it was food, drink and films with limited space to work. Now it is from start to destination with time-consuming services being available en route. BA is positioning itself as the business and first class airline, with smaller planes, less waiting and traveling without the coach class hordes.

From positioning the company, identity can be developed which will help with how we influence the perception of customers, prospective customers and other audiences will have of your business.

Suggested approach

Define the value proposition of a generic company in your industry.

Either name four recent projects and succinctly explain how they have delivered competitive advantage to your customer. Within these projects is there a common value proposition that could be used generally by your company? Develop this value proposition.

Alternatively, review four products or service lines and trace the customer interaction from pre-order to payment to servicing, a defined end-point of the transaction. Where is value added from a customer perception? Is there a common value proposition that could be used generally by the company? If there is, develop it.

From this value proposition, which should clarify the positioning statement, attempt to decide how it will be perceived by a number of different audiences.

From a selling viewpoint for many companies working in the business to business arena, there is only a need to create an identity, an understanding of the value proposition and a clear perception of the company, with a few thousand people – those who place or can influence the awarding of business to your company. Complete Figure 6.1 (audience value perception) for all customer sub-groups.

Divide others into different audiences, employees, investors, suppliers, partners etc. Develop a list of audiences and complete the exercise in Figure 6.1. (Suggestions for staff are shown as one example only.)

Identity and recognition of the position a company occupies within an industry has become a vital component of strategy, influencing the customers' perception of the company and encouraging them to purchase its products and services. It is also equally important in persuading shareholders, investment analysts, employees and governments of the strength and values of the organization.

WHAT IS IDENTITY?

A company's identity is how an audience will perceive it. The audience may be customers, shareholders, employees, investment analysts or governments. A positive perception is worth millions of dollars to shareholders in profits and share values. Corporations with a strong, positive identity will generally have higher price/earnings ratios than their counterparts in the industry.

Identity needs to start with the customer. It is not just advertising and marketing; it is the total relationship with the customer. It begins

Audience	Variation on perception	Key factors in creating perception	Possible actions
Clients: Client sub-groups CIO CEO COO CFO CCO Divisional heads Etc Potential clients and their sub-groups Investors			
Staff	A good CV with a good name on it	Identity in computer industry	
	Challenging assignments that will develop them technically and professionally	Managing careers to maximize value to the business, clients and staff	
	Training	Clear training and development program	
	An enjoyable company to work for	Culture management	
Potential staff Potential acquisitions Media			

Figure 6.1 Audience value perception

with a deep knowledge of your customers: their lifestyles, ages, preferences, location, hobbies, socio-economic situation; or, for business customers, their industry, sales value, sales profile, contacts, purchase trend by product/service type and value, purchase growth rate, new product introductions, competitors who are selling to them, and much more. You enter into a relationship with the customer whether you are manufacturing lipsticks or machine tools, whether you sell consultancy or airline seats.

In their book *MaxiMarketing* (1987), Stan Rapp and Tom Collins discuss share of the market and share of the mind. The difference is that share of the market measures the breadth of market penetration, while share of the mind measures the depth.

Clarks Shoes, a United Kingdom company, certainly had a depth of penetration in my mind when we were buying shoes for our young children. They provided shoes in different widths, which is as important in allowing children's feet to develop properly as the correct length. Fifteen years later the message is firmly imprinted on my mind, and providing they can maintain a reasonable fashion image that will appeal to any future daughter-in-law I might have, I would certainly buy my grandchildren Clarks shoes.

What creates a really positive customer perception? There are many books written on this, and it really does need some serious study, but what follows is a possible route for a first attempt at the identity goal, performance targets and action program.

Parameter setting

The first part of parameter setting is to establish the emotional feel for company identity among the leadership team. In many companies this is never done, and this simple exercise serves to align the mindsets of the members and eventually, the entire company.

It begins by deciding the words the leadership team want associated with the company, and, as important, what positive words they do not want associated with it. The leadership team are asked individually to complete two lists, one of three to five positive words they want associated with the company and one with three to five positive words they do not want associated with the company. Short sentences are also acceptable.

When they have individually done this the two lists are written up on a flipchart. The example below (Figure 6.2) is taken from an actual workshop. Sometimes the same or similar words will appear in both columns. This makes the point that if the leadership team is confused about the words they would like to describe the company, it is no wonder customers are confused.

This was a small but complex business and eventually the leadership team decided they would like to promote the identity of 'Excellence at all levels'. In a business where five departments had close interaction with the customer this was an excellent goal that they have now put into action, both operationally and as an identity. It is important that the identity fits with all goals, but especially with the distinctive capability, market/product/service and people goals.

This part of the exercise thus reaches agreement on what you want to be recognized for and, just to sharpen the image even more, what

Positive words associated with the company	Positive words not to be associated with the company
Quality	Tried and tested
Dynamic	Comfortable
Innovative	Largest
Expert	Superior
Enthusiastic	Dominant
Excellent	Good
Aware	Aggressive
Focused	Traditional
Aggressive	Proven
Leading edge	Competitive
Highly profitable	Friendly
Responsive	
Solutions provider	

Figure 6.2 Clarifying words

you do not want to be seen as. These represent the parameters for your identity goal.

CUSTOMERS' ACTUAL PERCEPTION

Strategy is the program of initiatives that will take a company from where it is to where it wants to be at some future date. In terms of the identity goal, the previous exercise, along with others, will establish where the leadership team want to be. Establish this before going into detail on where the company currently is.

If a market survey is conducted, as outlined in the data collection section, ensure that one question asks which words the interviewee would associate with the company and its competitors. Remember that normally the interviewee does not know which company is conducting the survey. The results are usually interesting, if also painful at times. The information on competitors can be fed into your competitor analysis and can be used when selling against them; ensure the sales force is briefed on the results.

Summarizing this data is sometimes difficult, especially if the interviewee is given total freedom to choose any word or phrase. Allowing a limited choice of words does not give the type of feedback being sought – the spontaneous, emotional response. The responses can be divided and summarized into groups; whichever allows the most sensible interpretation to be made. The difference between what the leadership team wants the company to be recognized for and what the customers and potential customers say is the gap that has to be closed.

As an example, I conducted a small exercise in the United Kingdom on name recognition/word association. A limited number of business-people were asked in one to one interviews what words came to mind for each of the companies in Figure 6.3. They were asked for one word for each company and then when the first list was complete had the opportunity to choose a second word.

Company name	First words associated	Second words associated
IBM	Computer services	E-commerce
Shell	Oil	(Many different answers)
BMW	Prestige	Engineering, quality
CostCo	Good value	No frills
Rolex	Expensive	Oil sheiks
BKT Strategy	Strategic business planning	Clive Reading

Figure 6.3 Word association

This survey is not meant to be at all significant, except for my own company, BKT Strategy. The other company names were used purely to accustom people to this way of thinking and to loosen their minds so that they gave a reasonably honest answer for BKT. I chose the companies almost at random. No competitors were included because I wanted an instinctive reply, not a relative answer. What struck me as interesting about the first five companies is that two were associated with a positive image, while the other three were associated with factual statements. BKT was also associated with factual words, a product and a name, rather than a value; I too have work to do. (The actual list contained a much wider range of words and has been simplified, perhaps over-simplified, for this illustration).

Making the goal real

Sometimes there is a need to make the identity goal more tangible. Members of the leadership team need to have examples of how the company and its identity will improve and change. They also need stories and examples they can use in explaining the strategy to their staff.

Having given the leadership team feedback on how customers perceive the company, which is usually not as great as expected, ask them to write a short half page account about how it will be viewed after achieving its identity goal. Each person should only address one or two aspects of the business interaction.

In order to ensure there is balance, paint different scenarios for them to use as a guide in their description. Examples of such scenarios could be:

- the customer's goods inwards inspection team unpacking the latest shipment from the company;
- a salesperson visiting an established customer (perhaps name the customer, maybe one whose feedback was not so great);
- a salesperson visiting a prospective customer;
- reading customer service reports;
- meeting a group of Wall Street analysts to discuss the company's performance;
- talking with your biggest competitor about changes in the industry.

Such exercises visualize what you are trying to achieve. Reading these short scenarios out to the leadership team can also be quite amusing. As the scenarios are read out capture the key words on a flipchart.

Having developed and visualized the identity goal, brainstorm the factors involved in achieving it. This should cover areas such as advertising, promotions, public relations and public speaking, developing relationships with customers, what is service to the customer and how can it be improved, improving customer support and response, what training will be necessary (a people goal issue, but identify it now), how can emotional bonding between the company and the customer be developed?

What does emotional bonding mean? One audit partner I knew talked about 'being there when the lightning strikes'. Such occasions might be when there is a tax inspection and something is wrong; when the bank manager wants to reduce the overdraft, dramatically; when the biggest customer goes into liquidation owing the company a fortune. Then the CEO might need a 'friend' to call on. Be there then – that is put the phone down, make any necessary excuses and leave to see the client. That is when loyalty is created and emotional bonding takes place. Reinforce it by not sending an invoice for a year if the company is in trouble. If you can stand it, you will have a relationship for life.

Identity is a tough goal to make happen. Partly it depends on all the other goals being achieved to create the right image. These goals are within the company's control. Identity is an influencer. It builds slowly and can be lost quickly, and lost by anything, from an unfavorable newspaper report to a bad employee. When it 'clicks' it is worth a fortune, far more than all the physical assets added together. The reason is, of course, that it is all the assets, especially the human assets, added together. Identity must be managed. The message we want to convey must be clear, and all performance targets must focus on reinforcing and repeating that message. There is so much confusion already in the customer's mind, so much noise, so many competitive offerings, that if the leadership team are not clear about how they want to be perceived, then they cannot be surprised if the customer perceives them in a way they do not want.

Developing the goal

As well as considering the generic words to be associated with the company, list all the audiences that need to be influenced. Some of this was done earlier in completing the chart. Just to check back, these may include:

- customers;
- employees and prospective employees;
- investors;
- government;
- partners and joint venture associates;
- current and future prospects;
- suppliers;
- the media.

Think about what attributes of performance will influence each audience. Emphasize those that are reasonably attainable in the short term as immediate performance targets and plan how to reach those other attributes that are desirable in the longer term. Ensure the plan for each audience hangs together. While each will be addressed by a particular message, they are not islands of influence but constituents of the whole. The perceived company identity for all of them must be consistent.

As part of this planning process there are a few other areas that need to be considered. Do you want to have an independent company identity, that is, independent of the brands marketed by your company, or do you want the brand to be synonymous with the company image? For instance, the Volvo Company identity is closely linked to the Volvo brand, whereas the General Motors image is separate from its various brands.

If there are a number of companies in your group, it is advisable to ensure that they all carry a corporate logo as well as their own brand name so that the strength of the group is apparent to its various audiences.

What do you want your logo to be? Some companies consider their logo to be their identity. In fact it only symbolizes that identity, but it is crucially important.

Finally, a true story about what can be achieved with a clearly targeted identity campaign in a short time. One of my engineering clients had a 1950s image and worked in a 1950s factory, which looked dowdy. He changed the company name, developed a new, modern logo and produced a smart new corporate brochure, decorated the factory and smartened up the appearance of the offices. He then ran a trade advertising campaign. The total cost was about US$160,000. Within six months he had sold the business at a 30 per cent premium. As the buyer said, the company was bigger than its sales: its identity was all-important.

7

People

Business organizations in the Western world are undergoing a fundamental change in the way they are structured. This is only the next stage in a pattern of employment and work that has been changing for over 200 years. In 1800 about 85 per cent of the population worked in agriculture. Today it is less than 3 per cent. In the mid-1950s some 55 per cent of the working population was in industry. That figure is now below 13 per cent.

Fewer people produce more food and there is more industrial production with a smaller workforce. The service sector, which it was hoped would provide work for those leaving industry, has probably already peaked in terms of its employment potential. Yet at the start of the third millennium US unemployment is at record lows and in Europe the high unemployment rolls of the last few years are at last beginning to fall.

When I was at business school in 1972 we were discussing the automated and leisure society. Computers and robots would do the work and we would enjoy the rewards; the only problem was how the rewards would be distributed.

Since then there have been periods of nearly full employment, interspersed with periods of unemployment, such as 1982–83 when unemployment in Britain touched 13 per cent and the 1991–93 recession which was the longest since World War Two.

These employment cycles have combined with major technological developments to change the nature of work. The result is that traditional jobs in traditional companies will be steadily disappearing over the next

20 years. It is reasonable to assume that in future a business organization will offer only transient employment to the majority of its employees. The task for managers is to make all employees as productive as possible during the time they are working for the company.

THE RESOURCE POOL

Companies have a pool of human resources available to them. This can be summarized in simple terms as:

- those employed in the company who will remain in their current positions for a number of years;
- those in the company whose jobs will change radically over the next few years or who will leave;
- those employed in other companies who might join and follow either of the above routes;
- the unemployed who might join and follow either of the above routes;
- those just entering the workforce;
- those on temporary contracts;
- those who work in the company full time, sometimes for long periods, but are employed by an outsource company who pays their wages, sets their conditions and with whom their future career lies.

At any one time the company's workforce is an amalgamation of the elements in that pool. The amalgamation is continually changing and the number of people employed in the company also frequently changes.

The percentage of people that will stay with a company for only a few years is probably increasing. The young, under 30, know that they need to develop new skills rapidly to be sought after in the job market, and this often means moving from company to company. This increasing rate of change in staff raises particular questions:

- How will new employees make an effective contribution to the company – quickly?
- How will this ephemeral organization be structured so that it can remain competitive?
- What will hold it together so that it remains a recognizable entity to customers, shareholders and the employees themselves?

One approach is for businesses to have strong operational systems and processes so that new people can be trained and made productive rapidly.

For many non-management jobs this means jobs having a tight specification with measurable outcomes over short periods of time – daily, weekly or, at the most, monthly. The jobs will initially tend to be narrow so that new employees can become reasonably productive quickly. Where possible jobs will be designed on a modular basis.

It also means intensive training on a hierarchy of modules so that new employees can rapidly learn job modules and start contributing to the company. Progressively new modules will be taught until the job is rounded and reasonably challenging

Thirdly it means strong systems so that training, starting the job and replacement of staff can become a smooth operation.

This sounds like Henry Ford's mass production. Except that jobs can be built up as fast as the employee can learn, it creates a continual challenge of job expansion and enables management to identify good performers quickly.

For instance, project management is a major element in the success of companies in many industries and service sectors. If project managers are allowed to manage projects using their own approach and methodology, senior management will find it harder to know exactly what stage the project is at, staff on the project will have to learn the project manager's approach and if the project manager leaves before the project is completed then there will usually be chaos.

If the business has rigorous project management systems and controls that everyone knows and follows, then senior management have a better understanding of progress against budget and schedule, project staff have a better understanding of project performance and problem areas and if the project manager leaves it is easier for another manager to pick up the project without a serious hiccup.

Throughout the business, strong processes and systems achieve the goals of making new staff productive quicker, enable the company to remain competitive by having efficient approaches to work and ensure the company remains recognizable to customers even when staff leave.

The process of teaching job skills through modularization also helps to create a flexible organization. As the business environment changes, companies that are competent at developing, teaching and implementing new job modules quickly have the ability to redirect the resources of the business to the new opportunities.

None of the above is meant to imply that staffs are automatons simply following the book; there is still a huge need for initiative and creative thinking, but it is implemented through processes that everyone can comprehend and follow.

BUSINESS VALUES AND COMPANY CULTURE

One of the difficulties leadership teams have is in fairly rapidly establishing their own value sets and identifying the culture they want the company to move towards. These two exercises help management think through their attitude to these issues and decide the key strategic initiatives they need to take to establish their shared business values.

In all organizations the inherent business values of the leadership team strongly affect the decision-making process. In many companies these values are not made explicit or thought through. The result is a muddled decision-making process or contradictory decisions being made in different parts of the company. There is, in short, confusion.

There are many different values in business. Loyalty, trust, integrity and honesty are some that are easy to recognize as being desirable. It is hard to be against them; they are key parts of the human character. The difficulty arises when you try to measure them.

Therefore the values explored here are more specifically related to business. They are easier to define and the process of defining them makes it easier to develop other values later.

Policy-setting values

The SBP process identifies the leadership team's attitudes to ten policy-setting values, as described below. They are basic to the way the business is managed, but are often not fully understood or agreed on even by the leadership team.

The values are defined as follows.

Risk

What level of risk is the company willing to accept?

The accelerating rate of change in the business world ensures that the option to avoid risk is not open to any company. Equally, every company can undertake projects in which the risk is too great, where the continuing existence of the business relies on a specific outcome of events.

It is in establishing the level of risk that the company will accept, in return for a minimum level of projected benefits, that decision criteria are required. Companies need some guidelines. These might consist of something like: 'we will not undertake any project whose complete failure would reduce forecast company profits by more than 50 per cent over the next three years' or 'any project that is pursued must produce a realistic forecast of at least x per cent return on investment in y years'.

This is a simple approach and can be challenged on a number of grounds. However, the reasoning behind it is also simple. Having discussed the policy, few managers are so dogmatic as to say no project will ever be allowed that is outside it. The future is too imponderable for most to say that. What it does mean is that any decision to move outside the policy will be carefully thought through and the impact of failure on the company carefully considered. Many of us have become excited about a project at some time in our lives and thought of going ahead without considering the risk of failure. The idea behind this approach is to ensure that no management ever bets its company on the success of one new project without thought of the consequences.

It is interesting how Richard Branson minimized the risk when he started the Virgin Atlantic airline. Instead of buying a new 747, which he could not afford, he bought one that was two years old. He also had an agreement with Boeing that they would buy the aircraft back after the first, second or third year if the project failed. Finally, he calculated that if the airline flopped, the group as a whole would not be bankrupted. At worst the Virgin Group would lose two months' profit. This is an example of moving into a new and high-risk venture without betting the entire company.

Growth

Does the leadership team want the company to grow and expand, or are they content to keep it at about the size it is now?

There is risk in both these approaches. What are the implications of growth on the independence of the company or in the owner's participation in the business? Fundamentally the questions to be answered about growth are: 'If we want to grow, why? What might be the consequences of not growing?'

Independence

If the company is medium-sized, or an autonomous division of a large company, the question can be phrased as follows: 'Do we want the company to stay independent, or want it to grow into a publicly quoted company, or sell it off to another organization?'

If it is a large corporation, independence becomes more an issue of how much autonomy should the operating groups and divisions have. Independence may then be phased. The leadership of the corporation is willing to give as much autonomy to operating divisions as they can accept commensurate with the corporate strategy and the required financial performance expected from the division.

People

The biggest challenge for many businesses, if they are to expand or even just survive, is to recruit and retain the right people.

There are two elements in this: who are the right people and what do you have to do to retain them? The important point at the values stage is to recognize the worth of the employee's contribution and its effect on the business.

Teamwork

Many managers do not believe in teamwork. Successful entrepreneurs are not often known as team players. The business success is often due to their individual flair, not the competence of the management group. They see the role of the management group as supporting and making possible their vision by efficiently executing their decisions.

Other companies see teamwork as the most vital component in their success. Team consensus and cohesion is more important than individual flair in these companies and will be preserved at all costs.

Communication

Does your company value secrecy or open disclosure of information to employees?

In one of my early client companies the executive directors were not informed about the ownership of the business. When it was pointed out they had a legal duty to understand how the business was financed so that they could determine if it was solvent, I was asked by the chairman to keep quiet on this issue. It was an interesting point for me to examine where my own values stood.

There is, however, another important aspect of communication. For the senior managers, company and departmental information is of great interest. However, to excite employee interest communication should be aimed far more at the work group and individual level. People are interested in what affects them. If communication is initially focused on what affects the individuals it is aimed at, then it will be more effective.

Quality

The recognition that quality is important, and that there is a correlation between quality and profitability, is the key in establishing values.

Often the difficulty with quality is understanding what quality means to the customer. Does it mean appearance, durability, lightness, speed, user pleasure, lack of hassle or uniqueness? Accountants, for example, often think quality is technical excellence, whereas for the client it often means reducing the tax bill to a legal minimum.

One definition of quality is ' meeting the agreed requirements of the customer now and in the future.' Be precise about what the requirements are. Measure how they are met. It is not always easy to determine customers' requirements, but without finding out their exact needs it is difficult to meet them.

Innovation

Without innovation organic growth is hard to sustain over the longer term. The company's attitude to innovation largely determines its growth strategy. A positive attitude to innovation is indicative of managers who are willing to invest for the future of the business, and will certainly affect its spending on research and development.

Investment

The attitude uncovered here is whether the leadership team believes in reinvesting money back into the business in acquiring the best assets to improve performance, or whether they believe in giving high dividends to shareholders.

Ethical stance

This may be last both in this list and as a priority for many companies; but meeting social, legal and moral obligations to society as a whole is becoming increasingly important.

Recently the big pharmaceutical companies were in dispute with the Government of South Africa over the cost of AIDS drugs. These drugs could be obtained from generic manufacturers at less than 10 per cent of the price charged by the big companies. African countries cannot afford the high prices being charged by these companies.

Having managed the situation incredibly badly, the pharmaceutical companies withdrew their legal action and offered to supply the drugs at cost price (though in many cases this was still more expensive than the generic company prices).

Now they have opened Pandora's box. Many people in the United States without prescription cover cannot afford the high prices charged for their medication. Suddenly the public understands the numbers. For instance GlaxoSmithKline sells Combivir, an AIDS drug, for US$7,000 per year in the United States. Cipla Ltd, a manufacturer in Bombay, India, says it is offering a finished generic version of Combivir for US$275.

No longer can the pharmaceutical companies talk endlessly about R&D. In a recent report to its investors GlaxoSmithKline said it spent 37.2 per cent of its revenue on marketing and administration costs, and only 13.9 per cent on research. Bristol-Myers-Squibb spent 30.4 per cent on marketing and administration and 10.6 per cent on research.

With pharmaceutical companies spending more than US$13 billion a year on medical reps pitching their products to doctors and another US$2.5 billion on consumer advertising, they are now more marketing organizations than scientific developers.

Ethically, can the whole edifice remain as it is today? Pharmaceutical companies might be better to ask themselves that question now than face another public relations disaster.

Establishing business values

To establish business values, members of the leadership team use the definitions in Figure 7.1 to (individually) complete the values chart, Figure 7.2. The definitions used are deliberately provocative.

The exercise is normally conducted as follows: members of the team independently develop their own individual business values charts.

Use the following definitions as criteria for marking:

Risk	The company is prepared to take risks to achieve high performance
Growth	The company wants to grow and expand as fast as its resources will permit
Independence	The company, and my operation within the company, should stay as independent as it is now (or become more independent)
People	We are prepared to invest in people to improve the skills of the company
Teamwork	The company believes in teamwork. It will sacrifice individual flair to build a strong management team
Communication	We will give the employees and other stakeholders any information that is of interest to them, except where disclosure could damage the company's competitive position
Quality	The company believes in high quality products, services and relationships, even where this might reduce short-term profits
Innovation	We believe that innovation is vital to the future of the business, and we will invest to create innovative products, services, operations and methods of business
Investment	The company believes in investing profits back into the business rather than paying dividends to shareholders
Ethical stance	We believe in meeting social, legal and moral obligations to all of society, even where this reduces profits in the future

Figure 7.1 Business value definitions

They do this for both the values they believe the company has now and for their own personal beliefs on what the future values should be. The two lines on the business values chart indicate those areas where the team believes there should be a change. On the example shown, which is for the leadership team of a US heavy manufacturing operation which had merged ten months before and was undergoing considerable business stress, the main areas the team believes should have priority focus are:

- growth – the company wants to grow as fast as its resources will permit;

	Strongly oppose	Oppose	Support	Strongly support	Priority value
1. Risk		LHD	R rh	JT l·djt	
2. Growth			T	D dj	LRJH lhrt
3. Independence			LRJTH lhrd	D	
		jt			
4. People			DT	LJ	HR hrdjt
5. Teamwork		J	LHR hj	D lrtd	
6. Communication		DT t	HRJ h	rdj	l
7. Quality			DJ	LT rd	HR lhjt
8. Innovation			LRJT j	HD lhrt	d
9. Investment		L l	HRT ht	D rj	J d
10. Ethical stance		LT lt	d	HDRJ h	rj

Code: ——— Current business values .... Personal business values
R = Roger   T = Tim   J = John
D = David   L = Len   H = Harvey
UPPER CASE = Current culture
Lower case = Future personal culture

Figure 7.2 Business values chart

- people – more needs to be invested in people to improve the skills of the company;
- quality – the team believes in high quality products, services and relationships, even where this might reduce short-term profits.

Also in the example, two areas where there needs to be significant change are teamwork (this will need developing as a result of the merger of two companies) and communication (this is starting to be addressed through a variety of initiatives).

In the example there are strong indications in the business values of the preferred type of strategy that the team would like to pursue. The business values exercise uncovers the subconscious business drive of the participants. Very few, if any, participants are thinking about the hard strategy the company should follow as they complete the form. Its value is in correlating the subconscious drive of the strategy team with the embryo strategy that emerges. In this company the main drive of all the leadership team is for growth, people and quality, which were marked as 'priority value' by the majority of the group. There is also a need to improve teamwork and communication. With the strategic thrust focusing on global growth and acquisitions, these values will be critical to success.

The business values, the Belbin output and the attitude of the team in the workshop often indicate to the observer/facilitator whether the team is able and has the drive and inclination to implement the strategy they develop.

Organizational values

This list of policy-setting values begins to establish the business values that will be accepted within your company. However, organizational values are equally important. These concern acceptable behaviors and therefore express your organization's desired culture.

Some years ago I was working with the board of directors of a software company. We were considering what customers bought and what the company sold, which often turns out to be an interesting exercise. The managing director had already told me about his career and why he had eventually started his own business. Much of this was to do with the fact that he was a man of great integrity, who wanted to earn a good living by honest means.

During the exercise one of the directors suggested an intangible product that the company sold. Everyone agreed, except the managing director. For two hours the issue was discussed, which was far longer than the analytical benefit warranted. But that was not what was being decided. What was actually being laid down was a key value of the company, its degree of honesty in what it sold and its own understanding of that honesty. A basic and core value of the company was being established.

In another company I was working in I used a video on management. The operations director of the company asked me if he could borrow it and I agreed, on the strict understanding that it was not copied. He returned the video and confirmed it had not been copied. At a later meeting in front of 20 senior managers the managing director of this company said he would like to see the video again and I offered to loan it to them. 'That won't be necessary, we copied your original,' he said. The operations director went bright red and the 20 managers, who either knew or suspected the truth, smirked. I did not need any more convincing that the top managers of that company were less than honest. Later it emerged that nearly everyone in that company was involved in some sort of dishonesty; the managing director, for example, was purchasing goods from companies in which he had an equity share. It came as no surprise when the company went into liquidation. The biggest loser was the venture capital company, who lost millions of pounds. To this day they do not really know why the company failed.

Of course, it is not easy when you are starting a new company to be full of virtue. It is essential to stay within the law and be fair to those you deal with. However, once this condition is satisfied survival and growth of the business are natural priorities. Entrepreneurs need to practise 'creative frugality', and perhaps more of us need to be entrepreneurs in that sense.

One of the key foundation stones of the company, what it stands for, the driving value that keeps it going, is decided during the company purpose exercise (see Chapter 3). This belief, and the other key values that keep the organization going, are of critical strategic importance. In many of my client companies the values of the organization have overridden all other considerations in making key strategic decisions; and these were not just for show, or to look nice on a strategic framework.

One of my clients was relocating his office and warehouse. He had the choice of moving it 20 miles away into a development area, where government assistance meant that he could have super new premises, rent-free for four years. It would significantly improve the profits of the company. The office in the development area was also nearer his home and was a shorter journey for at least half his senior executives. There were no real business reasons why he should not take this option, and many reasons why he should. The one problem was that many of the clerical and less skilled staff would not be able to continue to work for the company if it moved to the development area. It would not have been a significant problem: new staff could have been trained fairly quickly and the development agency was prepared to pay for their training, so that they could learn what they had to do before the move. The managing director, a self-made multi-millionaire, did not think staffing or training would be a problem. However, there was high unemployment in the area where the business was currently located and many of the existing staff would not find it easy to obtain another job. Some had been with him for a number of years, seven or eight in many cases, and had worked for him while he was becoming successful. He would not 'betray' (his word) their loyalty for a few hundred thousand pounds. The business reasons and the strategic advantages counted for nothing. The owner's values were all that counted.

However, values come in many guises, and it is difficult to pin them down in a written description. It is best when defining values to start with the down-to-earth business values and then build up to more elusive ones.

Culture

Values and culture are closely linked. Culture is the set of behaviors the company would like to see exhibited by its managers and staff. All companies have a culture, although not all companies overtly recognize what theirs is.

There are as many cultures as there are organizations, and therefore each needs its own description. However, on the public SBP courses I have categorized organizational culture as:

- power culture – authoritarian and hierarchical; dominated by a strong leader; people strive for status and influence; political skill important; motivation by fear and insecurity;
- achievement culture – opportunities for intrinsic satisfaction; personal commitment to goals; integration of values and company purpose; integrative skills important; internal motivation;
- support culture – bonding through warm relationships; trusting and caring style; responsive leaders foster responsive staff.

On the SBP courses participants equally favor the power and the achievement culture. Many say that there are elements from two of the three in their own company cultures, though I have never met a company that claims to have a strong support culture. Perhaps all my clients are relatively hard-nosed businesses.

Changing the culture

In the belief that even those organizations with a strong culture will need to change their organizational capability in the next decade, the next part of the SBP process is to form a description of the culture now, and then a description of how the leadership team wants it to develop.

In your own company one word or a short phrase will summarize a huge volume of meaning that everyone on the inside will understand, if not always agree with. A managing director of a government-sponsored research organization summarized it as 'From institution to wanting to own equity in the business'.

Other 'from to' examples might include: from 'dependence' to 'empowerment'; from 'follower' to 'leader'; from 'fear' to 'satisfaction'. The bigger the difference between the two words, the greater the cultural change that is desired. Usually this change is worded in a short phrase rather than a single word.

The next step is to think of the issues that will be critical to making that change and list them down the left-hand side of a chart, as shown in Figure 7.3.

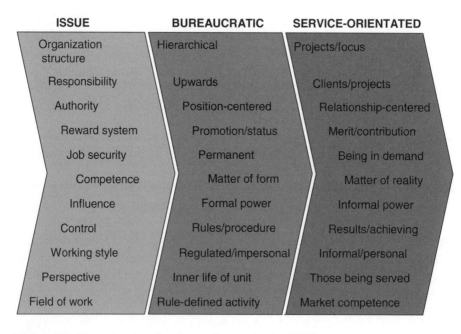

ISSUE	BUREAUCRATIC	SERVICE-ORIENTATED
Organization structure	Hierarchical	Projects/focus
Responsibility	Upwards	Clients/projects
Authority	Position-centered	Relationship-centered
Reward system	Promotion/status	Merit/contribution
Job security	Permanent	Being in demand
Competence	Matter of form	Matter of reality
Influence	Formal power	Informal power
Control	Rules/procedure	Results/achieving
Working style	Regulated/impersonal	Informal/personal
Perspective	Inner life of unit	Those being served
Field of work	Rule-defined activity	Market competence

Figure 7.3 Organizational culture change in the NHS

This example is taken from the British National Health Service (NHS) at the time when it was going through huge change. Here the cultural change desired is 'from bureaucratic to service-orientated'. For many companies a simpler chart is better with a more action-focused framework. The idea is to make the words more relevant to the leadership team.

One of the best examples is a company that described its current state as 'happily chaotic' and its desired state as 'happily one team'. The mangers used equally descriptive words throughout the culture change chart. Another example is a company whose performance had been lackluster for a number of years and was now faced with the prospect of a hostile takeover. It was one of those companies that if you walked in as the end of shift pips went you were likely to be trampled by the horde of helmeted and dungareed workers rushing to leave the premises. Their clocking out was a master of coordination, picking their card from a large number on the rack, putting it in the clock and inserting it in the exit rack in one smooth and well-practised movement. This was the highlight of their working day.

Management described its current state as 'static', and used 'dynamic', 'expanding' or 'growing' to describe the desired state it rapidly wished to achieve. The outcome is shown in Figure 7.4. Indeed the management did make huge efforts and some progress in changing the culture – before the acquiring company relieved most of them of their jobs.

This exercise really helps managers to decide on the type of culture they want and the changes required to obtain it. At the end of the

ISSUE	STATIC	EXPANDING
Attitude	9-5 with tea breaks	The best we can do
Management style	Orders	Enthuse and excite
Relationship	Distant	Close
Work	Chore	Fun
Purpose	Vague	Clear
View of employees	Expendable	Expandable
Mentality	Difficult/can't do	Can do

Figure 7.4 Organizational culture change in a static company

exercise they can review their business values to see if these still hold good. After that the next step is to start (and I emphasize start) planning what will be changed and how it will be changed.

The key to effective culture change is to identify two or three, or even one, high leverage issues that will impact many areas of the business. Concentrate on these leverage issues; ensure there is a clear performance target for how their attainment can be measured at the end of the year, publicize them and ensure they are achieved. Once the ball is rolling cultural change momentum can be maintained each year.

Changing culture is a journey, not a move from here to there. Twenty years ago most management writers thought the IBM culture was a corporate asset. When IBM recorded the biggest corporate loss ever it became viewed as a liability.

The plan for bringing about the culture change is often easy to produce. Symbols can be used which make the change clear to all employees.

However, it is much harder to make it happen. Employees observe behavior and actions, rather than just listen to statements. To live, and be seen to live, the new culture is harder and takes longer than most managers expect.

One idea that came out of this type of exercise concerns how to show loyalty to employees. The client involved wanted to offer security of employment to all employees, but we had discussed the changes that were taking place in the market and industry and decided that this was just not a realistic possibility. However, if they could not offer security of employment, they could try to ensure that all their employees had skills that made them employable elsewhere. As part of the process of creating a skilled workforce, it was decided that employees would not complete a standard appraisal each year, but would write their curriculum vitae. This would detail how they had developed during the period and what they could now offer to an employer. If they wanted to leave the company, they had a CV already written to help them.

The other side of this idea, though not the reason for introducing it, was that it also identified to the company those employees who were most valuable and had marketable skills. And it indicated employees who did not have great skills: it was difficult to read some employee's CV and not wonder 'If he or she was not already employed here, would we offer him or her a job?'

The two culture maps are good examples of how to produce a first draft change, but not good examples of a total program. They are too all-encompassing and need to be reduced in scope to the high leverage items.

Summary

An agreed set of business values and a clear concept of the current company culture (and how it has to be changed) are vitally important in developing the strategic business plan.

Business values are relatively easy to agree; the culture map is much harder. Generally any organization should only attempt a maximum of three issues at once. Even three become very hard to plan and make happen. The company might have many issues that are important to developing the culture that it wants to achieve, but the key to success is to prioritize the issues, identifying those that need to be achieved first, in, say, the next one or two years, and then those that need to be achieved in the longer term. Using this approach, managing the company culture becomes a rolling exercise involving a constant state of managed change.

This rolling approach also avoids the risk of the culture becoming a block to change in the organization. The strong culture in corporations such as IBM has been blamed as one of the causes of their lack of flexibility. The concept of a rolling culture change maintains the benefits of a positive culture, but also emphasizes to everyone that the culture is also continually changing to meet new requirements. In fact change becomes implicit in the culture itself.

The people goal and company philosophy

As we have seen in previous chapters, strong companies have recognizable philosophies. This philosophy will show through in the business model discussed in Chapter 3. Underlying many of these philosophies is an acknowledgement that a competitive and responsive organization cannot be built on a paper-driven, computer-driven, administration-orientated system.

A successful organization will only exist in an environment where employees will commit a huge amount of personal effort to achieve goals that they identify with in an organization that they are proud to belong to. The philosophy will not be effective if it is foisted on managers and staff; they must have input to it and the right to modify it. They must feel ownership of it before it is implemented. If the principles and philosophy are clearly understood and agreed, then managers will welcome soundly developed processes and systems and make them work. This applies particularly to the organization's philosophy towards its people.

People are employed by organizations to produce results. They are not employed for their own self-development, unless that self-development brings tangible results to their employer. Developing people to their fullest extent is good business sense, but that development must correlate to the needs of the company.

Therefore the people goal must be consistent with the overall company philosophy and business model and must relate to the company's key business issues.

Management and organization structure

In many medium-sized companies and the divisions of large corporations the members of the leadership team are effectively functional managers for 85 per cent or more of their time. One of the results of this is that the senior managers have less headroom than they would like or need if they are to make the greatest possible contribution.

One of the benefits of the SBP approach is that it can start to create a situation where leadership team members spend more time acting as sponsors, reviewers and mentors, and managers are given greater freedom to run their projects.

Figure 7.5 shows an organization structure that exists in many companies. Leadership team members each control a functional department. The pyramid is broken between the leadership team and the

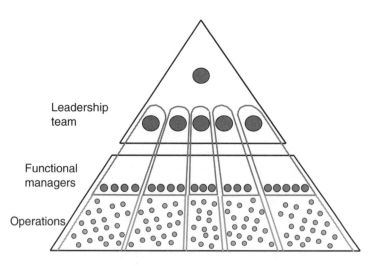

Figure 7.5 Traditional management structure

functional managers, which is notionally intended to indicate that we want to break the close bond between them. Why?

When the leadership team are heavily involved in managing departments there is less opportunity to 'de-layer' the organization than if they can be removed from too much contact with the day to day operations. A functional role absorbs leadership team time and energy, and tends to make the organization rigid and inflexible. Many organizations are finding that it is better to devolve more authority to the senior managers, which frees the leadership team to deal with more complex and ambiguous issues. However, leadership team members are usually more comfortable running their function, where they are the leader, than being in the leadership team, where they are with their peers. One result is that in the leadership team they tend to be the champion of their function rather than an executive deciding what is best for the entire business.

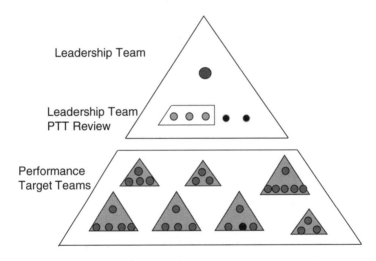

Figure 7.6 Management of performance target teams

Figure 7.6 illustrates a management structure for achieving performance targets. Here there are three roles for the leadership team in managing and controlling the process. A number of leadership team members form a performance target review group. The membership of this group can change from meeting to meeting, although at least one member needs to be present on a regular basis to provide continuity. They approve the initial performance target project plan and then monitor the performance target team (PTT) to ensure that the plan's milestones are being met. This role removes the leadership team from day to day involvement in the project, but ensures that they never lose ultimate control of its progress.

For some projects the leadership team will lead the project team. Experience indicates that this route should only be followed if the member of the leadership team is the sole candidate for the role. More often, although still in a minority of project teams, a member of the leadership team will participate in the team as an ordinary team member.

This form of performance target management leads directly to a more flexible, empowered and performance-focused organization. The role of the leadership team subtly changes over time so that they become less involved in functional duties and have more time to undertake the critical work of developing the company strategy, ensuring that performance achieves the strategy, being the living symbol of the culture and values, and making the critical connections with financial institutions, government and joint venture partners that have to be conducted at the top level of the company.

One of the reasons for this change is that project teamwork gradually becomes part of the way the company is managed. The creation of project capability throughout the organization will thus create a different type of management structure, almost without having to design it overtly.

Another advantage of this approach is that the number of members of the leadership team can be reduced, perhaps to four, five or six. This will result in a more coherent group, quicker at making decisions, with a better grasp of what is happening throughout the organization and more likely to be a team. One of the big problems I believe with leadership teams is their size; often I work with groups of 10, 12 or more. This is too big: too much waste of executive time, too slow in making decisions, too easy for members to avoid real commitment to a decision. It is also easier for one man to dominate, which removes the advantage of team decision process.

The project teams are directly related to the performance targets. For companies embarking on strategic planning for the first time, the initial performance targets tend to be those needed to establish a sufficiently good operating position to begin to implement the overall strategy. Those companies experienced in strategic planning will establish more challenging performance targets that will have a major impact on the company.

Project leadership

Chapter 10 explains the development and structure of performance targets. These in themselves become part of the organizational and people development process. However, there is one area that needs to be considered now: the learning experience and personal development of the performance target team leader. This might also apply to other members of the team. Therefore, if the project involves knowledge of marketing or selling, the leader may decide to go on a course to gain some understanding of those skills. The aim is not to become the marketing or sales expert for the team, since there will usually be someone from the marketing or sales department as part of the performance team, but to be able to understand and contribute to those aspects of the project. Other skills, which might need to be developed further, are building and leading high performance teams.

A study of many of the current leaders of industry indicates that many of them attribute their professional success to leading a successful project at an early stage in their managerial life. Managing the project gave them the confidence to know that they could obtain results through leading a team.

Achieving the performance target organization structure

There are two approaches to achieving the performance target organization structure. First, make challenging performance target teams the norm for tackling all new projects within the organization. Performance target teams become a mechanism for change, particularly in a high-performance organization with a transient workforce. If part of the team ethic is to accept new members, while acknowledging the contribution of departing members, new members of staff become productive quickly.

The second approach is to operate departments as projects. Think back to the market product segments (MPSs) defined in Chapter 5. Either select a new MPS, which is generally best, or use an existing one, and set up an ongoing project team to manage it. If the MPS is a product you will need to decide how to link up to manufacturing. There may be one manufacturing cell producing only this product, and in this case the link is comparatively easy. If manufacturing is more complex you may need to establish some compromise solution. If the MPS is a service, then it depends on your operating structure how far you establish the project team as an autonomous unit.

Follow the outline for developing performance targets given in Chapter 18. Let the new unit run under monitored conditions for a trial period. If it is successful then gradually extend it to cover other MPSs.

Over time the structure of your company will completely change. It will become more responsive to changes in the market, productivity will increase, customer service will become unbeatable, and staff will become motivated, creative and committed to the achievement of the specific performance targets.

Another advantage is that because projects are subject to ongoing review by the leadership team, who are monitoring progress rather than managing it, successful MPS teams are more easily developed and allocated additional resources; and those that fail are more easily cancelled. Removing the leadership team from personal involvement makes this process much easier. Staff only have to relate to a small unit rather than a whole function and become productive more quickly. The result is that the organization structure becomes more flexible and responsive to the opportunities in the market.

Building performance target teams

High performance teams need demanding and precise performance targets that every member of the team can believe in and work towards achieving. They must feel a common sense of purpose in the performance target and be committed to its attainment. The process of defining performance targets is covered in Chapter 10.

Leadership teams and boards of directors frequently talk about themselves as a team. However, when managers and the leadership team get together to discuss the future of the organization, it is not unusual for senior managers to question whether there is in fact a team at the top.

In my experience it is very rare for the leadership team to be a true team. They may believe in teamwork as a practice, but usually they will only be a working group with no real joint effort to achieve a single, clear purpose or performance target. The leadership team are involved in pursuing, or helping others to pursue their targets. Their type of work and breadth of activities mean that they rarely become a true team. One big advantage of the structure outlined in Fig 7.5 is that the leadership team can become a true team, with smaller numbers, tightly knit, and mutually accountable.

True teams make joint decisions for which everyone is accountable. Joining a performance target team is a risk; the performance target is challenging and it might fail. Nobody likes being associated with a failure, even if the company says there is no stigma and a certain level of failure is to be expected. However, once people are committed, it is the very risk of failure, the mutual accountability, the thrill and satisfaction of overcoming obstacles that make teams high-performance units.

There is a general acceptance that a company that can develop a distinctive capability or distinctive competence in its core activities will have a sustainable advantage over its competitors. The product or service itself is not so important – MPSs will be created, meet a market need, and then disappear as the market moves on. It is the ability to be flexible that is becoming more and more crucial. The best and perhaps the only organization structure to enable this change is the performance target team. That is why it may be no exaggeration to say that it is the key to remaining competitive for many organizations.

Here are some important points to bear in mind that will help create successful teams. Firstly, there is a difference between a team where its members will be involved full-time in achieving its target and a team where its members will only participate for part of the time. A full-time team generates far more commitment and better results, and has the potential to become a really strong team. This is much more difficult to achieve for a part-time team. However, there are ways of making a part-time team effective, such as ensuring that they have their own recognizable project room, where they can meet as a group and under-take their project work. This becomes the home of the performance target team; home is a good place to build commitment.

Secondly, ensure that the team members' functional managers do not see the performance target team as a rival for their resources. Ensure that they will assist the team by encouraging members and giving them the time to make the project work. For all initial performance target teams, ensure that the team leader has the ability and, ideally, the personal charisma, to resolve any organizational problems that may arise.

Finally, if this system of organization is to succeed and become the norm in your company, the first few performance target teams must succeed. The performance target must be significant to the future of the company and challenging, so that there is a real risk of it not succeeding. Resolving this dilemma of needing to succeed but risking failure is important to the long-term creation of a new organizational structure. Part of the solution is to select people who are known to perform well as part of a team. The brilliant individual player can be a disaster. The performance target must also be carefully defined. If all this advice is followed, there will be enough success among the initial performance target teams to convince everyone that it is the route forward.

Training

When you are changing your culture or organizational structure, there may be a need for some training. Since I am convinced that a large amount of management training and development is wasted, if not outright negative, in its impact on companies, I believe in a very hard-nosed, pragmatic approach.

Knowledge and skill training are essential to a company. So training staff to operate computers, manage a new budgeting system or interview applicants for jobs is worthwhile. It is so-called management development that is often wasted. Some large corporations spend millions of dollars each year to develop managers who go back to their offices and within a few weeks are more de-motivated than when they left them. When jobs are plentiful this training leads directly to an increase in staff turnover.

Based on your distinctive capability goal, decide what knowledge and skills you need to develop in your company. From the culture map identify which attitudes need also to be changed to achieve this goal.

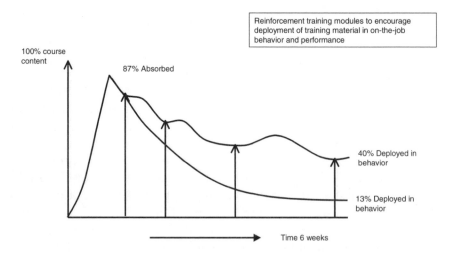

Figure 7.7 Reinforcing training to increase behavior deployment

Decide whether you will be able to fulfill these training and develop-ment needs without sending managers on a course. This requires creativity. If you decide it is not possible, consider how a course might achieve, or help to achieve, the objective. However, remember that if someone attends a course and then nothing is done afterwards to reinforce the learning that took place, after a period of six to seven weeks only 13 per cent of the content taught on that course will be deployed. Therefore before sending anyone on a course, ensure that there is a system of 'pit props' (as shown in Figure 7.7) to maintain the knowledge. Being part of a team can be a significant developmental exercise in its own right and can also help to consolidate learning or new skills.

8

Efficiency

E-business, technology and increased computing power will drive a change in business that is unprecedented. Whether in automobiles, pharmaceutical, sports shoes or any other business, the customer will move from being a purchaser to being at the center of business. Mass customization will become a reality in many industries.

To achieve mass customization in a world where it will be accompanied by price transparency will require efficiency of a new order. Traditionally we think that uniqueness implies a higher price. To accompany individual customization with reducing prices is almost counter-intuitive, yet it is what will happen. This will require high-level corporate action as well as nimbleness – I use the term 'nimbility' – to seize local opportunities that match the corporate profile. This really is both effectiveness, doing the right things, and efficiency, doing things right.

Perhaps it can be said e-business will drive e-fficiency, and e-ffectiveness.

Energy expenditure in an organization

In any organization there is only so much resource. The key resource of the business will be its brainpower, primarily the management and the knowledge workers. Many companies squander this resource as if it is infinite. One example is the countless meetings attended by too many people who neither really contribute to nor need to know about the subject under discussion. However, this is only one example of the waste of brainpower.

Much of this waste can be found under S G & A (sales, general and administration) in the accounts. Dell, who does not waste these resources, is at the 10 per cent mark. Other companies are in the 20 to 30 per cent range. And S G & A only hints at the total non-productive use of brainpower.

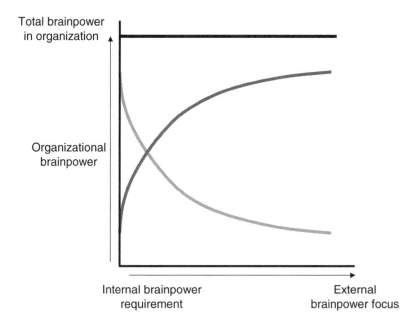

Figure 8.1 Brainpower expenditure in an organization

Figure 8.1 conceptually shows the issue. Efficiency means focusing more brainpower on the external parts of the business, primarily customers, investors, suppliers, media, analysts and government. Correspondingly less brainpower will be focused on the internal requirements of the company.

Efficiency is not about the lowest cost per se. It is about utilizing the entire resources of a business to deliver the greatest result. This is not cost minimization at every level, though the entire operation will use the least resources to deliver a given performance. Oracle, for example, consolidated its databases and changed its pricing model so that there is only one contract and one price for a specified product across all customers. In total these initiatives saved Oracle US$1 billion in the first year after full implementation. The effect of e-initiatives on Oracle is shown in Figure 8.3.

This is typical of the impact the Web will have on commerce. In business to business transactions where suppliers offer their products over the Net they will offer various configurations at fixed prices. Volume discounts will be open for all to see and it will possible for a customer to construct a spreadsheet which they can use to calculate the best product configuration and volume order to satisfy their requirements.

The argument is that increased volumes will offset lower prices and that other efficiencies, taking and processing orders, will reduce administration costs. But reverting to the argument that in most businesses there is an excess of capacity over demand, increased volume for some will mean decreased volume for others. With transparent pricing, the need to reduce costs, or add greater value for the same resource input, thereby become more efficient, is going to be critical.

As John Chambers said to a group of business leaders, 'Your franchises are under attack. Prices will fall. Margins will decline. You must get on the Net and find new ways to add value.' Perhaps Jack Welch summed it up even better: 'Everyone has access to Net technologies; the crucial question is who's got the vision to take full advantage.'

The impact of the Web will be to change the business models of most companies. This is a huge opportunity for many companies, especially those who manage to combine e-business with their traditional business. However, in this goal we want to look at how these changes will affect our own business model.

Suggested approach to improving efficiency

Take the following actions to increase efficiency:

- Review the efficiency survey (Figure 8.2) and decide if and where the business needs to change.
- Develop a flowchart of the current business model.
- Decide on the areas that are critical – the fulcrum points that give real leverage – and review where improvements or total re-engineering might be appropriate.
- Review the areas, processes and functions where the greatest cost is incurred and explore all the cost reduction possibilities.
- Explore the potential internal impact of e-business on the company (not market).
- Develop a new business model or models if/as appropriate.

	COMPANY POSITION				
	Very Weak	Weak	?	Strong	Very Strong
Conversion process					
Achievement focus					
Strong external focus					
Growing without consuming more internal energy					
Local adaptation					
Greater than the sum of the parts					
Time management					
Cost reduction					

Figure 8.2 Efficiency survey

Pre-e	e-initiative	Post-e	Benefits and results
• Over 100 customer databases • 140 product and pricing databases • 70 HR databases • 97 e-mail databases • Each country had own data center, IT staff and procurement department • Systems integration nightmare • Disparate customer service	On consolidating databases into one information unit	• 1 customer database – centralized CRM • 1 product and pricing database – centralized pricing • 1 HR database • 1 e-mail database saving \$30m pa • Centralized procurement department • Increased co-operation with distribution partners	The consolidation of IT led to economies of scale both in labor costs and purchasing of hardware and services Marketing costs decreased as duplication of effort was eliminated All product demos went online improving the productivity of the sales staff \$1 billion savings first year

Figure 8.3 The effect of e-initiatives on Oracle

Definitions for Figure 8.2

One would expect an efficient business to have the following characteristics:

1. The conversion process – from idea or decision to implementation and monitoring – is well managed.
2. Employees focus their time and effort on doing and delivering what they are expected to achieve. Other issues, and management, do not intercede and reduce individual and team effectiveness.
3. There is a strong external focus to the business. The employees and management do not spend more time than is absolutely necessary on internal management.
4. As it grows the company manages to keep the same resources, or even a higher percentage of resources, focused on clients, the market and changes in the industry. The Internet and other customer communication channels improve relations with the customer and the company manages and leverages the additional information flowing from these new channels.
5. The company is like a large number of organisms, adapting individually and collectively to change.
6. Management teams must act locally with nimbility and corporately with strength, to greater effect than people working individually.
7. Time is managed well at all levels; awareness of time management is high.
8. Low cost is being driven by e-business. Cost reduction features regularly in management and project discussions. (This is cost reduction in the business model, not on projects to meet client expectations.)

Having the leadership team rate the business on these questions is a first cut at establishing an effectiveness and efficiency assessment. From this output it is possible to establish the key blocks and how these can be removed.

Current business model review

Developing a new or modified business model is a key part of creating the SBP. One element that is often not given sufficient attention is the efficiency of the model. As well as exploiting changes in the market and the business environment it must be efficient, particularly for the longer term when competitors will be adopting similar models if yours proves a winner. Asking the following questions helps to ensure that efficiency is considered as part of the development of the business model:

- Where is the model strong in delivering results efficiently? (The fulcrum points.)
- How will e-business and other technical changes impact on the current business model, particularly in how the company will operate internally rather than in the opportunities that will be realized?
- Is there an opportunity to spinout a new business, adapt e-business to the current model or are competitors so far in front you are in danger of disappearing? (Unlikely given recent experiences but consider it.)

Develop concept models of a spinout e-business and an adaptive e-business, where the new technology is applied to the current model.

Outsourcing

Outsourcing can be a major source of cost reduction. BP Amoco plans to transfer most of its US accounting and back office operations to PricewaterhouseCoopers in a US$1.1 billion ten-year deal. Generally outsourcing the accounting functions will reduce costs by between 10 and 20 per cent.

Most of the major oil companies, with BP Amoco in the vanguard, feature cost-cutting as a regular business activity, not just something to be practised when profits decline. Sir John Brown, who is a demanding CEO, expects BP to deliver the planned savings of US$2 billion from its takeover of Amoco one year ahead of schedule.

Reducing the use of high cost resources

Another effective and efficiency driver is Randal Scott, Chairman of Incyte Genomics Inc., a company pursuing the decoding of genes with an absolute focus on their commercial value. He is not interested in mapping the human genome, just the genes that are medically relevant.

Randal Scott had seen other businesses he worked with encounter problems. He applied factory production techniques to the scientific discovery of genes. He used computers instead of PhDs to do repetitive lab testing and sifting of results. His engineers stripped down the machines that did the DNA decoding and made them more productive.

He ran the machines in three shifts over 24 hours. He speeded up the steps before loading the machine to make it more efficient. At the end of the line were patent writers who roughed out applications as placeholders on fragments of the gene until the scientists could decode the full length.

This approach has made Incyte the largest holder of gene patents in the United States, with 350 granted, 6,500 pending and applications at the rate of 100 per week.

Incyte's marketing approach was unique to the pharmaceutical industry. Instead of exclusivity all companies could have access to the data by becoming subscribers. They signed agreements not to sue one another over data they contributed. Randal also listened to what the customers wanted and focused on providing it.

When a subscriber to the gene database finds a gene it wants to study in more detail it orders a physical copy from the factory in St Louis. It is shipped overnight and the order triggers a license. If the research into the gene draws a blank Incyte receives no payment. But if that gene can be turned into a product then Incyte receives between 1 and 5 per cent of sales revenue.

Randal Scott built a company on strong scientific knowledge, but also on being effective in focusing on where the best commercial opportunities existed, and efficient in utilizing all the resources, both human and equipment, to reduce the cost of building a gene database. He also used the approach to patent the biggest number of genes of any commercial company.

Incyte has some tough competitors. Mainly these are high cost and take a 'Rolls-Royce' approach to gene hunting with expensive facilities and staff. They may yet win over Incyte. But in my book Randal Scott is a model of creative frugality, how to achieve stunning results with minimal spending.

External Relationships

In an article in the *Harvard Business Review* in September 2001 Michael Hammer suggested that after all the internal re-engineering and other efficiency initiatives businesses had taken, the new efficiency gains would be in creating more efficient links with external suppliers. Some of this has been in progress for years, for instance, allowing suppliers to restock supplies in a customer on their own initiative within agreed parameters, invoicing automatically triggered after receipt of goods.

He takes it further than this and looks at integrating the entire supply chain through transparency of data throughout the chain, by exploring the possibility of common delivery services to large customers and by sharing the information to make the product development process more efficient, quicker to market and increasing the possibility of success.

SUMMARY

Strategy is a marathon, not a 100 meter dash, yet running at over 12 mph for 26 miles takes disciplined training, a tough mental attitude and a superb physique. The longest economic boom in US history led many companies to forget the fundamentals. Without that they may not have grown to their current size, yet neither would they have had the huge write-offs and pain. The efficiency goal forces management to consider the real business over many years and not just the froth business that lasts a few years.

9

Synthesizing the strategy

EFFECTIVE STRATEGY

An effective strategy has to contain position goals, where the company wants to be, and execution goals, the resources the company wants to develop and have available to implement the strategy and operate the company.

Of the five goals in the SBP framework, three are position goals – market/product/service, identity and efficiency – and two are execution goals – distinctive capability and people. Therefore a balance between position and execution is built into the framework.

The strategic plans of some organizations do not seem to reflect any coherence between the various things the company does, or between position and capability. Executives often have the same problem in deciding what they are trying to achieve with their company's actions. That is why their plans are such a mess: full of good ideas, but no structure. The managers cannot differentiate the 'what' and the 'how'. The result is that they put in lots of 'hows', unsure of what they are meant to achieve.

Large organizations need to ask themselves two questions about their strategic process: 'What is the "group strategic plan" trying to achieve?' and 'What is the process being used to achieve it?' The process defines the achievement. If the planning process is bottom-up, from operating companies to the group, then the definition of the business will always remain with the operating companies. The group's power to influence them is limited, both managerially and psychologically.

If the planning process is top-down, with the group defining the high-level goals for the operating companies to interpret, then influence remains at the group level. It is the mechanism which keeps the 'herd of companies' moving in the same direction. It is the way large groups should proceed if there is to be business coherence between the different companies in the group.

There are two high-level questions that top managers in large groups need to answer. One is the classic 'What business are we (should we be) in?' With the advent of e-commerce and companies reinventing themselves this becomes a crucial question to answer on a regular basis. The other is 'What do we stand for?' This is concerned with the values that define the business purpose.

When both are answered they become the glue holding the businesses together.

In answering them management needs to be mindful of its use of words. It is easy to use words such as 'world class', 'first in leadership, quality and performance', but what do they mean? Exactly how is a company first in leadership?

When you have decided on your business purpose and the key goals, make sure that every board director, VP, manager and employee can look any customer, any competitor or any other stakeholder in the eye and say why they can claim them as legitimate aims for the group to achieve.

Strategic options

By this stage in the process the members of the SBP team will have discussed and made an initial decision on the direction they want the business to take. The company purpose and many of the goals will be agreed, at least in outline. The team will be working together as a unit and will be keen to develop a clear strategy. Verify and agree where your direction is taking you. Make sure that you have defined a position for the company that you have the capability to execute and which has special value in your market or to your customers. At this stage it should be possible to outline the first draft business model if this has not been done already.

However, even if the strategy is emerging fairly clearly, ensure that you are considering the full range of strategic options that you could pursue.

Start by reviewing where the process has reached. Next prepare a brief synopsis of all the input documents, as shown in Figure 9.1.

Figure 9.1 Synthesis of strategic options

Some of the comments made in this synopsis will be controversial, but don't worry about this. Discovering what people disagree with often makes for more rapid progress than lukewarm agreement. Head the synopsis 'Synthesis of Strategic Options' and cover at least the areas detailed below.

New business opportunities

During all your discussions it is likely that a number of new business opportunities will have been identified. These will concern new product/service opportunities, possible new markets, and new approaches to business or possible acquisitions. These should all be described and prioritized.

Market trends

Outline the main trends in the market. Where some of these trends appear contradictory, such as one trend towards higher service levels and another towards lowest cost, then outline both, including the volumes and types of customers that are following each trend and what is driving the trend. Sometimes there will be a number of trends, with interrelationships between them. Ensure that these are fully understood and explained. Try to forecast what you expect to happen to each trend over the next ten years.

This analysis is at the heart of generating the strategic options and helping to decide which one the company will eventually follow.

Industry trends

In this section cover issues such as: the ownership and size of successful and unsuccessful companies, moves toward vertical or horizontal integration, returns on investment and general financial performance.

Also in this section explore the impact of technology and possible substitution threats.

Economic trends

What is the economic trend in each major market? What is the range of economic forecasts? What other economic factors could have an impact on the company's operations?

Political

Are there political issues facing you in any of your main or intended targets? How can you protect yourself from unfavorable outcomes?

Social

Consider the impact of any changes in demographic features or social attitudes.

Stakeholder requirements

Some of the information will come from the business values chart and other requirements will have emerged from general discussions. This section should cover the requirements of investors, employees, the pension fund (if appropriate), and others who are seen to have a stake in the company's future. This can be as broad as the strategy team decides.

Competitor analysis

This is developed from the competitor analysis matrix explained in Chapter 5. Usually it is best to give a brief summary of the competition and then include the matrix in the synopsis.

Business values

Again, prepare a brief summary of the business values chart, outline its potential impact on future strategy and include the chart.

Culture

Outline the current and desired culture. Emphasize its importance to the execution of the strategy. Include the culture map.

Organization structure

Consider if the structure that will be implemented is the most effective in delivering the organization' products and services to customers.

Capabilities

Summarize the main capabilities of the company as generated in the workshops.

Differentiation

Outline the main differentiation themes that have been discussed. Relate these to the market analysis.

Resource priorities

During the workshops it may have become evident that you need urgently to develop some key resources whatever strategy is chosen. Make a list of these resource priorities.

Efficiency

Is the whole strategy efficient? Is it at least as efficient as that of the major competitors? What efficiency initiatives need to be taken and why? What opportunities are offered to take costs out of the business by e-business and by developing external linkages?

Generating options

Having completed the synthesis, compare it to your emerging embryo strategy and check that there is a strong logical fit between the two.

From the synthesis produce a range of options around the basic strategy that has been generated. If there is an option that can now be identified that has not previously been considered, ensure that this is highlighted. This work needs to be done either by an individual or by a small working group. It is sent to the members of the strategy group before the strategic options workshop.

THREE GENERIC STRATEGIES

In simple terms, there are three generic strategies a company can follow:

- lowest cost producer;
- differentiation;
- niche.

There is evidence from a number of studies that profits are closely related to the chosen strategy. In general it appears that companies that adopt a high relative quality approach at higher prices achieve greater profits (measured in terms of return on investment) than companies offering lower quality and lower prices.

However, companies that are clearly perceived as offering either of these strategies – high quality and high price or lower relative quality and low price – performed better than companies that were not perceived as offering either extreme. The most profitable companies were those offering high relative quality at low relative price.

The implication might be that companies not recognized as being either high quality or low cost will be less profitable. It could also be that companies that have a sharply defined image in the market place are more profitable.

The purpose is to ensure that the operating model delivers the lowest product/service cost possible within the business model and target market requirements. The leadership team should be asking:

- Does the operating model and structure ensure the company's costs are as low as possible, and lower than the main competitors'?
- Does it differentiate the product/services and the company enough for your customers to want to buy from you on factors other than price?

- Does it enable you to project a sharply defined image to your customers?

The following section is a primer to help think through the lowest cost/differentiation equation.

Lowest cost producer

The lowest cost producer can provide the product or service at a lower cost than any competitor. The company does not have to do so. It may have unique processes, or sole access to cheap raw materials, or special government subsidies. The cost of production may be less, but the selling price may be as high as or higher than that of competitors.

Its strength really shows with the new e-commerce 'b to b' online auctions. For instance, with FreeMarkets.com bids, even for engineering items priced in the hundreds of thousands of dollars, are undercut dramatically. There was a recent example of some specialist engineering that started being bid at over US$600,000 and ended up at US$429,000, for an eventual reduction of 28 per cent.

To be able to bid in this type of situation, which will become ever more common, a company has to have low costs, be able to go lower when necessary even than firms who are desperate for the business and will bid without a profit margin. With price transparency there will often be companies willing to cut margins to the bone just to survive. In order not to lose business to these companies even a strong business will have to be super-efficient. Not only will it have to know its base costs, but also the opportunity costs, spare capacity position, potential orders in the pipeline, their margins and probability of success, the possible impact of price reductions on other business proposals and competitor intelligence – how desperate are they to win the business?

In the past companies with this attitude to low cost would be characterized by tight controls, efficient production and standard products. They would preferably sell to large accounts and the focus would be on 'tonnage', the volume shipped per day or per week. Since overhead control is usually a feature of this operation, then offices will tend to be sparse, the R&D budget low or highly focused, and training and other staff investment kept to a minimum.

This used to be the typical description of a lowest cost producer. However, companies that were low cost and differentiated usually achieved high margins, and they have quite different characteristics.

The biggest threat to this type of company used to be technical innovation. For example, Timex was once the world's largest manufacturer of mechanical watches. Its production technology was unsurpassed. Both the product and market changed with the arrival of quartz watches, an innovation that Timex initially ignored because it thought quartz watches would only be marketed at the top of the market. It lost its market share as a consequence and has never recovered its former position.

With this exception, a low cost position can yield good returns even in competitive markets. Because the company can reduce its price below that of any competitor and still make a profit, it is usually in a position that can be defended in hard times.

Differentiation

A differentiated strategy means that customers view the company's product or service as distinct from anything else on the market. This is achieved by having different products or services, branding, high service levels, unique distribution, non-standard terms of business, advanced technology, a skilled sales organization, better guarantee or warranty conditions, or some other feature of the product or service which enables it to stand out from the competition.

A differentiated strategy could be to focus on delivering service at all levels of the company. Hence quality, marketing and service all become important in creating the total offering to the customer. Buying a BMW car, for example, does not just involve taking delivery of a quality vehicle. It includes the advertising, the sales approach, the service support, the owner's manual, the resale value, and the image that owning the car projects.

Such products are not overly price sensitive either in consumer or commercial sales. However, they must remain fashionable and keep their image and reputation. Some companies, like Wedgwood, remain fashionable without changing the product, but other aspects of the company strategy ensure that the image is maintained.

Niche

A niche strategy involves concentrating on a particular buyer group, geographic area or segment of the product line. Whereas the previous two strategies involve market-wide competition, this approach targets a section of the market and serves it very well, developing all the company's functional policies to meet the specific needs of the selected group.

The MPS concept is effectively niche marketing on a company-wide basis. Often the same basic product or service will be supplied, but it will be customized to the needs of the MPS niche.

Franchising and licensing agreements encourage niche strategies. They allow companies to expand with less capital and concentrate on a very tightly defined market.

There is another aspect to MPU niche marketing. Over the past five years there has been a greater emphasis on meeting customer needs, on customizing products to improve competitive advantage with identifiable buyer groups. Part of this is the ability to understand a customer's needs and have the flexibility to engineer a solution from the shop floor. This form of niche marketing is oriented to rapid change and requires particular skills and attributes:

- fast-paced innovation;
- rapid identification of customer needs and response to them;
- the ability to manage short-run production profitably;
- flexibility;
- a customer-focused attitude;
- a clear operational focus on what the company is trying to achieve.

COMPANY STRATEGY

Figure 9.2 illustrates one of the key roles of strategic business planning: to obtain a balance between an operation's cost base and the value it supplies to the customer.

To state the obvious, a cheap product or service that has little or no value to the potential customer will fail. Equally, a product or service that has huge appeal to potential customers but which they cannot afford will also fail.

A product that is highly priced but affordable in times of economic boom may die in times of recession unless the price can be reduced. For example, Christie's and Sotheby's, the United Kingdom's two most famous auctioneers of precious items and pictures, made record profits during the second half of the 1980s, but during the early 1990s their business slumped. Even as boom times returned in the run up to the millennium neither organization became hugely profitable. Eventually

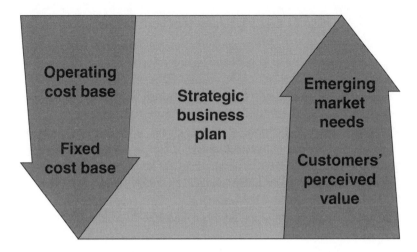

Figure 9.2 Strategic alignment of cost base and differentiation

it became known that they were rigging commissions in order to maintain margins, and still they were not making significant profits.

Hence the first objective of all strategy is to ensure that the company has a cost base that the customer can afford. Since all companies are in a competitive situation, any extravagance in the cost base can only be justified if it provides special value to the customer. All other costs have to be reduced to a minimum.

At the same time as ensuring that the organization does not incur any unjustified costs, you must also ensure that you are always focusing on customers' needs and on what is value to customers. It is fair to say that customers, both consumer and commercial, have unlimited needs. Most consumers would like to take another holiday or would like a high definition television with a 60 inch screen, but they do not buy one immediately because they see other items as having more value for them. In the commercial sector, most managers would like a better IT system, or a corporate jet or helicopter to whisk them wherever. They are stopped by the fact that at present the perceived value is less than the known cost.

The function of the strategy is thus to ensure that there is a balance between the organization's costs, the prices it can charge, and the perceived value of its products or services in the market place. Two imperatives should always be at the forefront of directors' thinking: to keep the cost base appropriate to the business and to know their customers' perception of value.

FIXED COST BASE REDUCTION

As companies grow, there is often a tendency for the fixed cost base to grow faster than sales. In fact, it should be the aim of every management team to ensure that the fixed cost base does not increase as fast as sales, and if sales decrease, then so should the fixed cost base.

This might sound an arbitrary rule and one that cannot be applied to every business in every circumstance. This is true. The problem is nevertheless that in many businesses the fixed cost base has been growing as a percentage of sales over a number of years and this will eventually lead to a major problem.

The rate of change in our society means that the future is not predictable. As we have seen in the case of the electronics company Philips in the mid-1990s when managers admitted that they were 'astonished' by the company's decline in profit to almost nil, even the present can have some nasty shocks. The events of September 11, 2001 have taught all of us to expect the unexpected and be able to react rapidly to a different environment.

Companies must therefore minimize their obligations and commitments and maximize their options. Collaboration with other companies can be an effective means of achieving this. The aim has to be to stay slim and flexible, which means keeping the fixed cost base low: lower than for other companies of the same size in the same industry, and much lower than most managers – staff and line – would like.

Low fixed costs give managers tremendous flexibility. They are able to respond to rapidly falling sales without resorting to the crisis measure of making staff redundant. The remedy is always the same: stop fixed costs growing in the first place. Buy in these extra services you need, preferably as a variable cost, and encourage all staff to think creatively about other ways of operating, so that fixed costs do not increase. Encourage creative frugality.

PROCESS COST BASE REDUCTION

Manufacturing industry possesses an almost unlimited ability to reduce costs. Recently one company reduced scrap from seven per cent of production volume to under four per cent, with a lot more potential for cost reductions in the pipeline. And this was achieved with a simple, commonsense idea that was generated in a workshop.

Kawasaki has applied its own brand of cost reduction across its industrial companies, which range from motorcycles to shipbuilding, aircraft, railway rolling stock and construction. There are numerous examples of how its approach has worked. In one small engine plant crankshaft manufacture was improved to the point where seven men operated 22 machines, producing 2,700 crankshafts per week with a total work in progress of 60 pieces.

Compare this to a British factory where 37 men operated 25 machines on two shifts. Crankshaft production was 1,400 crankshafts per week, with a lead time of three weeks and work in progress of 6,500 pieces. Work in progress in the British plant was 4.6 weeks of output, in Japan it was one hour. British productivity was 38 crankshafts per person per week, Japanese was 386 per person per week.

This was not the result of new machines and high technology. It was mainly achieved by a philosophy of identifying and eliminating waste and of continuous improvement – the drive to keep improving, to keep making things better day in, day out as a way of life.

With high employment there often seems to be a feeling among managers that work should provide variety, change and high job satisfaction, as a priority goal of the business. Having done something for some months, or possibly years, the view is that the management is entitled to a change. They are not. Management earns a living and pays its way by plugging away at the basics, year in year out, decade in and decade out. Process cost reduction is a basic requirement.

DIFFERENTIATION

Mass customization has been discussed before and it will be again in later chapters. The point to make here is that mass customization is becoming its own differentiator.

Differentiation can come in many guises. Brand names differentiate and make a product distinctive, although the name is not necessarily tied to the product. A brand may survive through numbers of products, providing the name stands for enduring characteristics such as design, superior manufacturing quality, reliability or service.

Differentiation is also achieved by having a unique product. The uniqueness can be in the price/performance ratio, flexibility, location or a special characteristic that cannot be matched by the competition.

Many companies are trying to differentiate on their level of service. As more companies improve their service levels and customers expect higher levels, differentiation will only be achieved at the highest levels of service, and only if they are noticeably higher than the competition.

The best customer care programs focus on two attributes of service. One is operational customer care, where the type, level and range of customer interactions are analyzed. Checklists are then produced to evaluate performance against these criteria. The other attribute is the attitude of professional concern required to build up a customer relationship based on trust. A trusted supplier tends to act as a general adviser beyond the particular services the company is offering. When this happens the supplier is effectively acting in a consultative capacity. An organization that succeeds in selecting and developing staff with this capacity has a unique advantage in most marketplaces.

For instance, one large financial organization redesigned its clerical offices and equipped them with 'hub and spoke' desk layouts. The original design had assumed that teams would tend to have between 10 and 12 members. In fact, the organization discovered that working teams, whose members support and cover for each other, are much smaller, generally three or four members. The office design and the furniture that had been purchased actually stopped these small teams from working together. A furniture salesman from another supplier looked at the problem and used his knowledge of office furniture, and his company's office layout facilities, to re-plan the office using the original furniture but meeting the customer's needs. He also obtained a large new order some weeks later.

His role with that company is no longer just that of salesman. He is also a consultant in facilitating teamwork through office design. He now has a unique and distinctive relationship with that customer. When he starts talking about new furniture requirements, he no longer asks 'What are the criteria?' the general question in the furniture trade, but 'What are your requirements, what needs do you have to meet?'

Building this kind of differentiated capability is possible for all companies, whether they are in a commodity, specialist or custom business.

Differentiation is also achieved by continual product/service improvements. One hundred individual one per cent improvements can achieve the same result as a single 100 per cent improvement, often at much lower risk and cost. The 100 one per cent improvements have to come from across the company and be contributed by as many employees as possible. This approach builds a differentiated company, a distinctly recognized business: a company that stands out from the crowd.

Customers can only make a decision to buy on the basis of perceived differentiation. Lowest price is one differentiation. Any other differentiation must be made obvious to the purchaser. This applies whether the product is baked beans – whether to buy a branded can or the store's cheaper own brand – or accountancy services.

For instance, think about buying the services of an international accountancy firm. Some factors are neutral in their impact, such as, 'We have 160 offices in the USA, 20,000 staff, a major tax practice'. All the major accountancy firms will have similar numbers, and they will not be the differentiating factor for a client making a decision on which firm to employ. Differentiators will be factors such as 'We have the world's recognized tax authority on international oil and gas exploration. She would personally manage your account.' This will differentiate that accountancy practice from its competitors.

Differentiation could be described as a measure of a company's creative ability. If it cannot identify how to differentiate itself, based on the strengths it currently has or on strengths developed from its current base, then not only will it be in a commodity business, it will deserve to be.

A reduction in product life cycles and the enhanced ability to copy competitors means that differentiation today is of a new order. Today a company produces a calculator to show your biorhythms, tomorrow a competitor produces a calculator that tells you what you will excel at that day. Whatever one company makes, another can usually make better and cheaper. Even in the aero-engine market where there are just three major companies, Rolls-Royce, GE and Pratt and Whitney, there are minimal profits in the sale of the engines. The profits are in the sale of the spares. The skill is therefore not only to produce the first jet engine with over a 100,000 lb thrust, but also to do it at a price the competition cannot promise to undercut substantially. It is a combination of innovation, design and cost minimization. The eventual profit will be in future years when the spares, services and repairs are sold. It is important, therefore, to achieve the highest possible base of installed engines and thereby maximize the future market for spares, services and repairs. Long-term profit could be in conflict with short-term profit.

Differentiation is not just concerned with product or service, but often also reputation. Wedgwood china cannot be superseded by a technical change tomorrow. IBM had to be significantly beaten in terms of product performance before losing its market dominance in certain market sectors. However, this type of differentiation is built up over years, even decades, of constant high service.

Sony has a reputation for product innovation. However, in the electronics industry almost any product can be reverse-engineered and the patents circumvented within six months. Since worldwide product launches can often take six months or more to complete, this means that competitors can hit some markets with their version of the new product at the same time as Sony.

COMBINED LOW COST AND DIFFERENTIATION

As stated earlier, the best strategy is to combine low cost with differentiation. Some business theorists believe that a company has to be either a lowest cost type of operation or a differentiated organization, but not both, because they represent two totally different cultures. For many companies, doing more with less means that they have to differentiate their products and services and also reduce their cost base.

Few companies admit to following a lowest-cost strategy. When asked why, their answer can be summed up as 'it's not much fun.' Yet many companies say they have to compete on price just to enter the race. And that is the point. To use a motor racing analogy, 'to be on the starting grid, you have to be within the qualifying time.' You can't win if you're not in the race.

It is therefore not an either/or choice between low cost and differentiation. The strategy recommended is about performance improvement; many actions can lead to performance improvement, which might either come from reducing operational costs or from improving the product or service and thus the gross margin.

Japanese corporations, for example, are recognized for their ability continually to reduce costs, yet many of their most successful cost reduction ideas require the same thought processes as differentiation ideas, and many low-cost Japanese manufacturers are highly innovative and differentiated. Cost reduction and differentiation strategies are compatible and are both necessary if a business is to remain successful in the long term. The balance between low cost and differentiation is a key element in the business strategy.

PRINCIPLES FOR A GENERAL COST REDUCTION STRATEGY

Implementing cost reduction should begin with the financial analysis approach outlined in Chapter 20. Some guidelines for the process follow.

Start with a product or service that meets a real customer need

Ensure that your product or service genuinely meets that need. Products that are cheap because they are shoddily made or provide low-quality service will not enable a business to grow, or even survive, in the long term. Cost reduction is achieved by manufacturing a product or supplying a service that meets the requirements of the customers who purchase it. It is not over-engineered, it does not have superfluous quality, but it will perform to the standard that a customer has a right to expect and will give satisfaction, or better still, absolute delight.

Understand and control the cost drivers in your industry

In electricity generation, for example, 70 per cent of the cost is in fuel. Therefore control of the cost price of fuel is essential if electricity costs are to be controlled.

Study the competition; cost is relative

This is not to suggest a return to the era when in some well-known companies every designer had a cost accountant at his elbow, comparing the cost of manufacturing the part being designed to similar parts produced by the competition. But do study your competitors and observe how they run their business. From the competitive financial analysis already conducted you will have a reasonably good idea of the gross margin percentage they are obtaining. Compare their overhead to your own as a percentage of sales. If it is less, test to see if it seems genuine and if you believe it is, consider how you might equal it, or improve on it. Look for all the areas where competitors might be saving money. Copy any good ideas.

Keep pricing and costing of products or services separate

Ideally have different staff or departments carry out pricing and costing exercises. If the gap between the two is large and positive, there is no problem. If the gap is small or negative, and you still want to proceed with the project, then bring the pricing and costing groups together to resolve the problem.

Draw cost advantage from many sources

Sources of cost reductions include sales, financing and new business approaches. Do not just concentrate on product manufacture or operational efficiencies.

Manage costs down, consistently

Make it part of your culture to manage costs down consistently. However, ensure that it is cost that is being managed down, not quality. It is in this area in particular that the strategy has to link cost reduction with the simultaneous creation of customer value.

Cost reduction is not something you put in a box and bring out when needed; it is a way of life, a method of management.

PRINCIPLES FOR A GENERAL DIFFERENTIATION STRATEGY

Identify the needs that the buyer perceives as valuable

When customers buy, what is it they buy? Why do they buy that particular make and model?

Remember the costs involved

Differentiation usually increases costs. Using the separate pricing and costing procedure, will the differentiation enable a higher price to be charged? Extra costs can only be worthwhile if extra margin can be earned on the product or service.

Ensure extra cost is only incurred where it meets the buyer's needs

To be able to obtain a premium price, the product or service must have perceived added value to the customer. Costs incurred that do not increase the perceived value to the customer are wasteful and may even be counterproductive.

In all other areas reduce costs to the minimum

Where differentiation does not add value in the customer's perception, consider removing it from the product or service. For instance, many types of organization need to have plush offices in the centers of major cities; advertising agencies, management consultants and computer organizations come into this category. However, do all the staff need to be housed at these locations? Often it is possible to keep only key customer contact staff at these expensive offices, while other staff can be housed in cheaper locations, perhaps in areas outside city centers.

Differentiation always has to have an element of the unique about it

This uniqueness must always be maintained even when your competitors copy your product or service.

In banking it is claimed that any new product or service can be copied by the competition in six weeks or less. Competitors can also imitate new products in other sectors more quickly than even two or three years ago, thanks in large part to the increased use of computer-aided design and manufacturing systems.

This means that companies cannot use a differentiation strategy on a 'stop-start' basis. Once you have embarked on a differentiation strategy, you have to stay at the forefront of new product development.

Make differentiation total

Whatever the aspect of differentiation, try to develop it through all your company's activities, the way the product or service is marketed, sold, priced, delivered and serviced. Do not just concentrate on product or service differentiation.

Create value for all users and all levels of buyer

Value needs to be perceived to be created by the customer's decision-making group. However, sometimes the focus on this key group obscures the importance of creating value at all levels of the customer's organization, or in the buyer's social group.

For instance, an office furniture group decided to create value for all its users in an interesting way. Seminars were organized for all members of staff in customer companies. These explained how to set up chairs to avoid backache or pain in the thighs or arms, and how to position VDU screens to eliminate eyestrain. Fitters with spare parts were available to repair or maintain any furniture that was not in perfect condition. This program showed all users of the equipment that the furniture company was interested in them and was prepared to invest money to ensure that they were pleased with their desks and chairs.

Ensure all potential customers perceive the benefits of differentiation

To obtain the benefits of increased sales from the differentiation strategy, customers must be easily able to perceive that the product or service does have greater value to them and that this value is worth more than the higher price being charged.

One of the problems with new product launches is that often they focus heavily on features, rather than on helping customers to realize the benefits brought by those features. This often slows down sales of the new product or service.

Communicate the differentiated benefits

Communication of product and service benefits is itself part of differentiation. Clever communication can indeed be the differentiation in some circumstances. However, in all cases, unless the benefits of the differentiated product or service are communicated to the potential customer, all the other efforts in developing the product are wasted.

ASSUMPTIONS

By the time the embryo strategy has been examined and tested against the principles described, it should be stronger and firm in the mind of every member of the strategy group. Now the assumptions made in the strategy need to be explored.

The first step is to clarify all the assumptions that have been made about the future of the business and its markets. The SBP process involves making decisions about events and circumstances that are outside the company's control.

Many of these assumptions will have been discussed in the opportunities and threats session. What you now need to draw up is a list of the key assumptions, indicating the probability of their occurrence. This can be done in the form of an assumptions sheet, as shown in Figure 9.3.

It is important that these assumptions are borne in mind during each year's planning process, and signs of an assumption being or becoming false need urgent attention. The assumptions are also inherent in the development of the business model.

Assumption	Probability assumption is correct	Impact if assumption is wrong
Five major customers will continue to order at least current volumes	High	1 customer stops - survivable 2 customers stop - major problem
Exchange rate will not move beyond £1 = US$1.60	Medium	60% of sales in USA. At rates above US$1.70 not competitive. Strategy reduces this problem in 3 years
Quality labor will continue to be available	Medium	Wage rate will rise. GM% might decrease

Figure 9.3 Assumptions

STRATEGIC OPTIONS SUMMARY

Having outlined the assumptions, and tested the robustness of the strategy against the assumptions, summarize the strategy using either the growth vector model or the strategic focus model.

The growth vector model

There are only four basic approaches a company can follow. These are summarized in the growth vector model (see Figure 9.4).

The model implies that a company pursues one of the following options:

- It stays in its existing markets with its existing products and harvests the product to extinction, or tries to maintain the share it has, or tries to grow within the market with existing products.
- It sells new or modified products or services to its existing customers.
- It sells existing products to new customers.
- It diversifies by selling new products to new customers.

The fourth option carries by far the greatest risk.

It should be possible to summarize your strategy in a way that fits primarily into one segment of the matrix. However, this is not always the case. The more complex the strategy, the more segments it will be

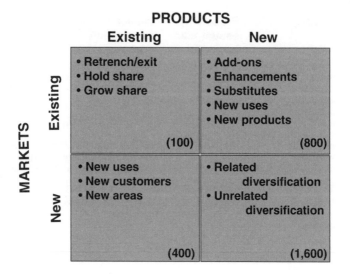

Figure 9.4 The growth vector

in. This model can, however, be useful in summarizing the general strategic thrust.

Strategic focus model

If there is still a lack of clarity within the team about exactly what you are trying to achieve with the strategy, or if a simple summary is required, the strategic focus model can be helpful.

For the purposes of this model, assume that all companies have an implied objective to maximize long-term profitability. The strategic focus model shown in Figure 9.5 is useful to focus the team's attention on profitability and helps to clarify the route you are taking to achieve that profitability.

This is a tool to refocus the team's attention on fundamentals, by taking them through key questions such as whether to increase volume, and if so how. Or how to improve efficiency. Its value is as a summarizing mechanism to clarify the strategy at the end of this session.

Strategic thrust

Having finalized your strategic options, it is useful to write a short summary of the strategic thrust – between one and three pages. This focuses on what the strategy is, the results you expect and the considerations that lie behind the decisions. Without this short summary some

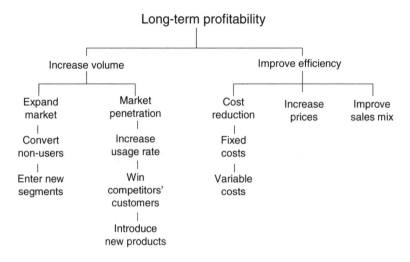

Figure 9.5   Strategic focus model

of the thinking will be lost. It is also useful for ensuring that every member of the strategy team agrees on how they see the strategy.

SUCCESSFUL STRATEGIES

There are a number of key points to be aware of when developing a strategy.

Changing or implementing a strategy will take time. The results might take years, rather than months, to become visible. Consistency is the key to making a strategy work and to improving the performance of the business.

When evaluating the success of the strategy, measure not only the financial performance or market share, but also the underlying performance of the company, such as:

- customer satisfaction, using market surveys;
- cost basis compared to competition, as outlined in Chapter 13 on MPS prices and costs;
- understanding of product/service performance compared to competition.

Continually probe and test the strategy, and be prepared to refine it. Always think twice before deciding to make a significant change in strategy.

10

Completing the strategic business plan framework

The process of developing the first draft of the strategic business plan is now nearly complete. The company purpose will be reasonably clear; it might need some rephrasing but in essence it is established. Everyone knows what the business exists to do and what it stands for. There may also be a slogan or tag line that employees and customers alike will remember easily and around which the company communication can be built.

The goals have been virtually completed. The wording might still need to be polished, but this can be left until later. The evaluation process, which will follow the completed first draft report, will help in refining the details.

The key values, what your company stands for and the driving value that keeps it going have also been agreed. They should shine through the wording of the SBP framework to be sure that everyone understands them.

DEVELOPING THE PERFORMANCE TARGETS

Performance targets are critical to implementing the SBP process. Now the company purpose and the goals have been agreed it is time to generate them.

Depending on the process used to develop the strategy, performance targets can be developed in a number of different ways. If an initial two-day workshop approach is used, then the first draft of the performance targets is generated at the end of the workshop. By then the strategy team is becoming tired and time is often running out. The approach then is to develop an initial list of performance targets that can be reduced before the next workshop.

Often in this session there will be 20, 30 or more performance targets produced, which is for virtually every company in every situation, far too many. Performance targets generation needs a disciplined approach with absolute clarity about what the business wants to achieve.

The important part about performance targets is that they represent an outcome that moves the business in the direction of the goals. Therefore the critical question with all performance targets is: if they are successfully executed what will have been achieved and is that a major step in the development of the business?

For instance, working with one client there were over twenty performance targets, including three that were allocated across two goals. One of these was to increase the ratio of MDs to projects, another was to develop new project management processes and the third was to train project managers and project staff. Arguably all three of these are actions, even if phrased as performance targets.

The outcome from these three is relatively easy to achieve, given the budget and resource. More MDs can surely be recruited who will meet the job specification. New project management systems can be bought or developed and then implemented. A training program can also be devised to meet agreed objectives and delivered to appropriate employees.

The result of achieving these three performance targets will be a lot of activity and targets that are achieved, a tick on the page so to speak. Yet these are not the outcomes the strategy team actually want.

The clear objective of these three performance targets is to improve project effectiveness and efficiency. This is a common requirement in many software, construction, clinical trials and similar type operations where the projects that fail often eliminate much of the profit earned on the successful projects. The performance target could be stated as: 'reduce project completion times by 10 per cent compared to current methods, reduce costs by 15 per cent and achieve specification, time and budget projections in 90 per cent of cases with no project overrunning budget by more than 15 per cent.'

The way to achieve this performance might be to increase the ratio of MDs to projects, implement new project management processes and increase training. It might also be a totally different set of procedures, such as changing the structure of the project management function, recruiting more experienced project managers from outside the company and being prepared to pay them high rates, it might be examining the way projects are sold and ensuring there is a reality check on the contract before it is finally signed.

The real objective here is for the performance target team to understand what the strategy team require and then creatively develop an action program for achieving it. Because of their focus and more detailed understanding they will usually produce a better solution to achieving the required outcome than the management team specifying quasi actions as performance targets.

The action program developed by the performance target team can be quantified in terms of the financial benefit and the cost. The performance target and action program can be subjectively evaluated in terms of other advantages, customer satisfaction, reputation in the industry, ability to negotiate better deals and increased attractiveness of the company to recruit the best employees. A decision can be made on whether this meets the required investment threshold. If it does then it can be compared to the other performance targets and triaged into the priority list.

The performance target that now exists represents a significant strategic initiative, with measurable outcomes and an agreed project cost. The business is also achieving a target that will match with the other targets to improve the overall performance of the business.

An example of more meaningful performance targets could be with increasing the rate of innovation. Bureaucratic thinking could develop a number of performance targets to increase the rate of innovation, such as recruiting more scientists, starting suggestion boxes or using external consultants. However, a performance target could say: 'increase the rate of totally new product introductions so that every year 20 per cent of total revenues come from new products that have been developed in the last two to three years.' One response could be similar to that of 3M, who famously encouraged their scientists to spend 15 per cent of their time on areas of research and invention of their own choice. This policy has now been expanded to other areas including manufacturing and marketing. Hence the performance target effectively becomes how to encourage employees to work on areas of interest to develop new products. This is a totally different approach to increasing innovation than previously considered.

Reducing the number of performance targets increases the sharpness and focus of the strategy. It ensures that the targets have outcomes that really impact on the company performance and that they are clearly not actions dressed up as targets.

In establishing performance targets another useful approach is to think that within the direction set by the goals, what are the three key areas of business improvement that need to be achieved this year? For example, in one particular year the priorities could be to improve the quality of products, to increase efficiency by increasing revenues without adding to fixed cost and thirdly to increase the cohesiveness within the organization. Establishing these priorities at the start of the performance target generation process will help to define the immediate areas of improvement or development.

This will not preclude 'out of the box' or blue sky initiatives, as these will have been identified during the goal development process at the start of the strategy teams thinking.

This approach of thinking of the long term initiatives through blue sky thinking and immediate initiatives to meet more current business needs ensures that there is balance in the overall strategic plan.

Once the performance targets, their outcomes, budgets and resources are all agreed, there is one final test of congruity and cohesiveness. When all the performance targets are reviewed together, as a vertical list on the strategic business plan, they are mutually exclusive, there is no overlap between them, and collectively exhaustive, they address all the areas the business needs to achieve in the next period of time.

The other check is to review the horizontal logic flow, from performance targets through to goals. The question to ask is 'Are the performance targets moving the company towards achieving the goals at a fast enough rate?'

THE DRAFT FIRST REPORT

The purpose of the whole strategic business planning approach is to ensure that the strategy team has ownership of the strategy. The first draft report is a key element in giving this ownership. When the eventual strategy is developed this report can almost be thrown away, its job done, but at this stage it marks the thinking of the group, how they arrived at the present embryo strategy and helps their thinking on what can be improved in that strategy. The draft report should adopt the following layout:

- cover sheet;
- list of participants, date and location of workshop;
- introduction (general overview of the workshop; picks out the key data generated; usually on one sheet of paper);
- financial performance (analysis of the company's financial performance over the period discussed in the workshop, with financial data generated from the base data forms and during the workshop);
- internal analysis (includes feedback on the management team, including the Belbin team report if available, but not the individual reports; also includes the business values of the group, the culture map, organization structure and the output of key strategic strengths and weaknesses);
- external analysis (the key strategic opportunities and threats are described plus any other relevant external analysis such as competitor analysis, market trends and drivers, technology changes and entry into new market segments);
- strategic thrust (briefly outlines the key strategic thrust the company will follow);
- the strategic business planning framework (in the format of Figure 10.1);
- immediate actions (list of immediate actions the company has decided to follow before completing the SBP process);
- appendices (including the Belbin team analysis, the base data output, the analysis of the base data output, results of the brainstorming on strengths, weaknesses, opportunities and threats, analytical data and any other relevant information).

REFINING THE PLAN

The draft strategic business plan produced after the first workshop is refined in subsequent discussions and workshops until the directors are satisfied it will deliver their goals.

By the time the final strategic business plan is completed the assumptions, synthesis of strategic options and other sections that are relevant to the company will be included. The strategy will have been viewed from so many angles that it is unlikely a major strategic mistake will be made unless the leadership team decide, deliberately and in full knowledge of the dangers, to take a high risk strategy dependent on a few factors and based on unfounded or untested assumptions.

Company purpose	Goals	Performance targets
	Distinctive capability	
	....	1. .... by 8/1/2002
	....	2. .... by 2/1/2003
	....	3. ....
		.... by 6/1/2003
	Market/product/service	
	....	1. .... by 6/1/2002
	....	2. .... by 10/1/2002
	....	3. ....
	....	.... by 4/1/2003
	Identity	
	....	1. .... by 2/1/2003
....	....	
....		
....		
....		
	People	
		1. .... by 8/1/2001
	....	2. ....
	....	.... by 3/1/2003
	....	3. .... by 10/1/2003
	Efficiency	
		1. .... by 10/1/2002
	....	2. ....
	....	.... by 3/1/2003

Figure 10.1 The strategic business planning framework

Goal:

	Key performance targets		Action program	Completion date	Executive responsibility	Person days required
1.		1.1				
		1.2				
		1.3				
2.		2.1				
		2.2				
		2.3				
3.		3.1				
		3.2				
		3.3				

Figure 10.2 Action program resource analysis

When the leadership team develops the strategy it will also identify the key actions to achieve each performance target. Against these actions will be a completion date and executive responsibility. Many of these actions will be at a macro level and will need detailed action lists of their own if they are to be successfully implemented. For this reason responsibility will be assigned to an executive, who will often be a department head. Eventually this executive will be responsible for developing the detailed action program. This first cut at generating an action program is usually sufficient to conduct an initial resource analysis to ensure that the strategy can be implemented within the time frame required by management.

The action program resource analysis (Figure 10.2) is used to establish the initial resource analysis. A similar form serves to monitor progress on a regular, usually monthly, basis.

11

Evaluation

TEST THE LOGIC

Having developed the strategic business plan and obtained agreement and commitment to it, the first step in evaluation is to test that it is logical; that is, that it all makes sense and that it is congruent.

The easiest way to do this is to have the company purpose, goals and performance targets on one sheet of paper and the action programs that refer to each performance target on another. Draw the lines on each sheet so that the plan can be pinned to a wall, or laid out on a table, in the SBP framework format.

First check that the company purpose and each of the goals relate to each other. Do they all make sense and are they pointing the company in the same direction? Next check that each performance target relates to the relevant goal and that there are no clashes, where one performance target cancels out or duplicates another. Ensure that the whole plan is compatible, congruent and has a feeling of tightness about it.

TEST THE SOUNDNESS

After making any corrections that are agreed to be necessary, test the plan to see that it is strategically sound.

There are 11 principles of strategic management. Understanding these principles is the key to thinking strategically, which is one of the ultimate objectives of the SBP process. The strategic business plan now needs to be evaluated against these strategic principles, as follows.

1. Differentiation

- The strategy is significantly different from all your competitors' and will offer real value to your target customers.
- It will favorably influence customers in their choice of suppliers, products or services.
- The value of the differentiation will remain for at least three to five years.

2. Defense against competitors

- No competitor can realistically adopt the same strategy.
- No competitor can interfere with, interrupt or stop you, in implementing the strategy.
- Competitors will not be able to undermine the value to the customer of the competitive position the strategy achieves, by using tactical or simple (ie low-cost and quick) strategic initiatives.

3. Concentration of resources

- The resources of your company (marketing, technical, financial, experience, skills) are effectively concentrated on achieving a consistent direction and a limited number of goals.
- The concentrated resources of your company are large enough to ensure that the goals can be attained and that as far as can be foreseen; no competitor will be able to concentrate greater resources on stopping you attaining your goals.

4. Building on strengths

- The strategy builds primarily on strengths that already exist in your company.
- If other strengths are required for the successful execution of the strategy, you must be able readily to acquire and retain them. If these strengths are easily acquired and retained, is it also easy for competitors to obtain them?
- If the acquired strengths are crucial to the success of the strategy, then do you have a secure defense against competitors? Review your position if there is any doubt in this area.

5. Timing and speed

- The timing of the strategy's implementation must ensure that you will obtain and retain the initiative over your competitors.
- If there is a well-defined window of opportunity, then the actions required to attain the goals must ensure that the window is open to the greatest extent at the time of your entry and that it will ideally not remain available to your competitors once you have started to exploit it.

6. Simplicity and unity

- The strategic plan must be as simple as possible. The potential for misunderstanding must be eliminated.
- The strategy must be easy to communicate to employees, suppliers, customers and stakeholders.
- The strategy must enable responsibility, authority and accountability to be assigned clearly and consistently.

7. Flexibility

- Flexibility is an essential element in the reallocation of resources. It allows managers the freedom of action necessary to exploit success and reduce vulnerability.
- Your information and control systems must be able to identify when and where changes in resource allocation are necessary.
- The experience and skills of your managers need to be adaptable to meet different circumstances to those envisaged under the planned strategy.

8. Efficiency

- The available resources need to be allocated to best effect. This means attaining the goals with the minimum resources and expenditure commensurate with attaining the result in the specified time.
- Your operational efficiency, measured in terms of how you can best meet your goals, must enable you to perform better than the best of your competitors.
- It must be possible to measure the efficiency of the firm, both in terms of efficiency targets set for key operations and the company as a whole, and also, if possible, its relative efficiency compared to its main competitors.

9. Coordination of aims and means

- All performance targets and action programs must contribute to attaining the goals and the company purpose.
- All the goals must be mutually supportive and collectively cohesive. Put simply, the goals must all relate together in a way that makes sense to the leadership team, the board of directors, and can be communicated to employees.
- All the goals must combine to have a greater impact as a set than if presented as individual goals.

10. Exploit emerging opportunities

- The strategy must identify any substantial new opportunities and exploit them if they are consistent with your overall strategic thrust.
- It is essential that these opportunities are properly researched and understood. If they are incorporated into the strategy, then the confidence placed in them must be well founded.
- There must be confidence that a competitor is not also able and ready to take advantage of them.

11. Cultural fit

- Is the strategy fully consistent with the norms, values, experience and expectations of the managers, employees and stakeholders of the company?

Use the strategic evaluation, Figure 11.1, to test how well the team believes the strategy meets the evaluating criteria.

Depending on the number of people in the SBP team, it is sometimes best if they split into groups of two to complete the strategic evaluation form. The whole team then meets to discuss the evaluation, exploring and explaining differences between the various assessments.

Complete this form by putting a cross against each strategic principle indicating the degree to which you believe your SBP conforms to the criteria.

If the overwhelming majority of the SBP team members believe that the strategy is good or very good against all the strategic principles, it should be an excellent strategy. If this is not the case, explore those areas that are making people uneasy and what can be done to rectify the situation. There are few hard and fast ground rules to cover what could happen, but some possibilities follow.

	Very Weak	Weak	Neutral	Strong	Very Strong
Differentiation					
Defense against competitors					
Concentration of resources					
Building on strengths					
Timing and speed					
Simplicity and unity					
Flexibility					
Efficiency					
Coordination of aims and means					
Exploit emerging opportunities					
Cultural fit					

Figure 11.1 Strategic evaluation

For example, if the whole team is completing the form together, see if there is a team fit problem. It can happen that a team loses one member, especially if the majority of members feel they are making real progress. This one member might go along to the workshops, but not feel involved in them for some reason. This might be his or her first chance to make this isolation known, or, at worst, to sabotage the project

Or there might be a factional split. Usually this will have emerged before, but completing the evaluation form might be the rallying point for the faction to make their feelings known. It is rare for this to happen at this late stage in the process.

Then again, the program might be too ambitious and would put too much strain on the company. There might be misunderstandings about how the strategic principles are defined. Or the plan might really have some weaknesses that have to be corrected.

It is unusual for a SBP to be completely off course at this stage. What may be required are minor alterations in performance targets or action programs. The most frequent change here, especially if it has not been considered already, is a reduction in the number of performance targets and action programs. If there are too many there will be insufficient resources to carry them all through.

FINANCIAL ANALYSIS

The SBP leads naturally into the budgeting process. The strategic framework is analyzed to establish the revenues and costs of the program. This should be easy to calculate directly from the performance targets and action program. As responsibilities for all actions are clearly identified, allocating budgets is also straightforward.

Because the timing of performance targets is specific, and the periods when costs will be incurred is known, cash flow projections can be made using the framework as a guide.

Finally, once the financial performance from the strategy is projected, the leadership team can decide if the performance meets their expectations and is within their resource capabilities.

PART TWO

Strategic concepts

This part reviews a number of strategic concepts, including how strategy development varies over phases in a company's strategic cycle, the role of the hypothesis in developing new strategies, particularly ones that change the future market/product stance of a business, and how business strategy needs to start from a simple base and then respond to the complexities in the business environment once this basic strategy has been developed.

Developing strategy is an iterative process. Depending on the business situation of the company so the type of strategy event needs to be different. Chapter 12 encourages thinking about the type of strategy session that is appropriate each year.

At the start of a strategic planning exercise, there is often a need to clarify and expand the thinking of members of the leadership team. One approach is to develop a hypothesis (see Chapter 13). The definition of a hypothesis is 'a proposition made as a basis for reasoning without the assumption of its truth'. From the research, competitor analysis and general readings, about the industry and business trends, the aim is to stimulate thinking about the future, to start the strategic development process with some ideas on the potential for the business. Hypotheses are useful as walls against which to bounce other ideas. The rule is that when the hypothesis has served its purpose, or is proved wrong, it is discarded.

The second approach is to think through what strategy is. Chapter 14 seeks to create the thought that a robust strategy is initially developed from clear and simple thinking about the major objectives of the business. Considering too many complexities before developing the bones of a strategy leads to it being convoluted and difficult to understand. Implementation becomes difficult if not impossible.

This can be considered a part dealing with mindset. It is designed to help constructive thinking and use the most precious resource any company has, the time and talent of its leadership team, effectively and efficiently.

12

Degree of strategic change

The degree of strategic change is dictated by a number of factors. As discussed in the next chapter, manufacturing technology, huge computing power and the Internet are leading many companies into dramatic change. 'Paradigm shift' is not too powerful a description of what is occurring. This will lead many companies into making an industry-transforming change.

Understanding the strategic cycle helps leadership teams decide the type of strategy session that is appropriate each year.

The Sigmoid curve

When companies start on a new strategic direction they follow a path that is similar to a sinusoidal curve. This phenomenon is called the sigmoid curve. It demonstrates the process of change, renewal or development of a new vision and strategy through to its abandonment.

All life goes through this cycle. Effective change means starting a new course of action while the existing cycle is still strong. It is part of the axiom that 'whatever made you successful in the past won't in the future'. Companies, organizations and institutions that do not renew will die. The leadership skill is to start the renewal process before peaking on the existing business cycle.

At point A on Figure 12.1 the leadership team would think the company was doing well and there is little need to change tack. Only ever with hindsight can we know this is absolutely wrong. And hindsight we only have about yesterday. And yesterday is too late

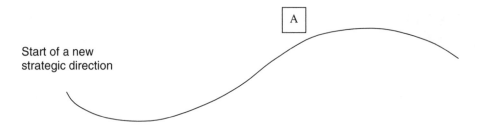

Figure 12.1 The sigmoid curve

tomorrow. With hindsight we can see that the strategy or market was just about to decline.

Whilst no one knows in advance where the peak is, to start too early and be ready for the change is a small sin; to start too late can be fatal.

When growth is plateauing, margin vanishing or the instincts of the leadership team are that something new needs to be planned: this is the time to start considering a new and probably radical strategy. In Figure 12.2 the leadership team have started on a new strategy at A1. For a period of time this new strategy will probably depress results and there will be a period of worry and uncertainty while it is being proved.

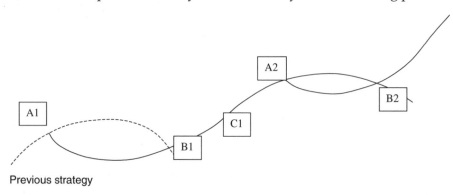

Figure 12.2 The strategic cycle

At point B1 the strategy shows signs of being successful and the strategic business plan will be about refining and developing the master strategy. At point C1 it will be concerned with maximizing the impact and benefits of the strategy. The main impact will be on the types of performance target that are developed and the action program the company will invest in for the next year or more. At point A2 the cycle repeats itself. The total cycle could last ten or twenty years, though with the rapidly accelerating rate of change it is likely to be shorter and become shorter still.

This thinking leads directly to the idea that strategy is not an annual repeat of the same process. There is a strategic cycle that varies with the change in the industry, the market it serves and the position of the company. The type of strategic planning needed each year is different, and leadership teams need to think through the type of strategy they need. This does not radically change the strategic framework or the process the first year SBP is used but it does change the type of strategy that is produced.

The type of strategy at A, B and C can be summarized in Figure 12.3, the degree of strategic change model.

The strategic planning cycle chart shows the types of issue that arise in different stages of the process.

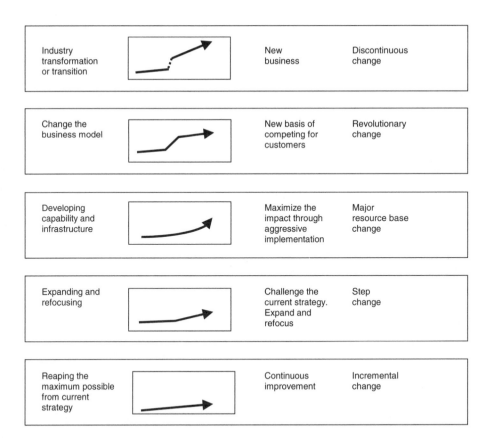

Figure 12.3 Degree of Strategic Change

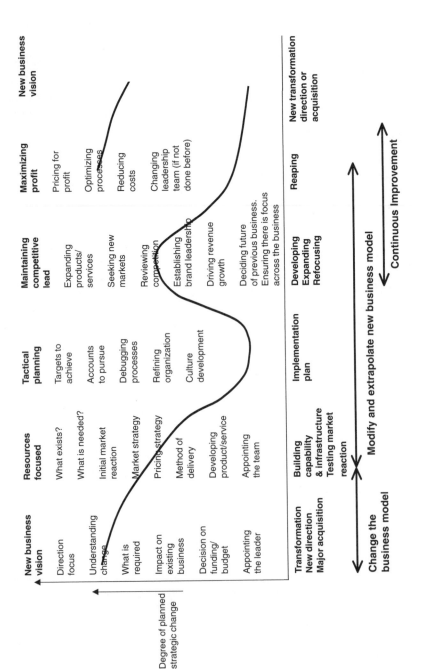

Figure 12.4 Strategic planning cycle issues

Transformation strategy

It is rare for a business to go through an industry transformation, totally abandoning the industry it is in, to enter a new sector. There are examples, such as Nokia under Jorma Ollila, which divested all its electronics and rubber operations in 1992 to focus on mobile telephones, a business it had only been in since 1987, with the development of the original hand portable.

More common is a major diversification into new business sectors that may eventually transform the company out of its original business or there will be a radical change in the business model. A current example is the Boeing company. Deciding that competition, tough unions, especially in the Seattle area, and other pressures were squeezing growth in its two core business lines – commercial aircraft and weapons where growth is believed to be less than five per cent annually – Boeing is rapidly moving into new markets. Chief among these are Internet services for air travelers, air traffic management, aircraft servicing and space communications. It is refocusing itself as the 'biggest and most profitable space company in the world'.

To emphasize this shift in its strategy, Boeing has moved its headquarters from Seattle to Chicago. Nothing could demonstrate more the degree of strategic change than this move. Boeing and Seattle have been almost synonymous for 80 years.

Currently over 60 per cent of Boeing revenues and 74 per cent of operating income are generated by the commercial aircraft division. Announcements from its CEO, Alan Mulally, further amplify the corporate strategic thinking. Boeing will not compete in the super jumbo category, one it has owned since introducing the 747 in the early 1970s. It has effectively abandoned the market to the Airbus A380, a super jumbo capable of carrying 550 passengers. Instead Boeing will focus on developing a new twin-engine jet, named the Sonic Cruiser or 20XX, which will fly about 20 per cent faster than today's jets. This will save about one hour for every 3,000 miles traveled. Whether this aircraft will be manufactured in Seattle will not be decided for a number of years.

Almost simultaneously with these announcements, Boeing announced that it will seek to reduce the cost of its aircraft manufacturing business and will begin by transferring fabrication of fuselages from Seattle to Wichita, Kansas. Along with this there is open discussion of outsourcing more manufacturing to specialist producers, as Airbus Industrie has done, and even manufacturing wings in Japan.

Boeing is an example of a business following a transition strategy, not quite leaving one industry to enter another, but investing heavily and betting its future on new industries in some of which it has only limited experience.

A number of factors can drive a transformation strategy. The leadership team can decide that the existing business is now reaching a mature stage, and even though it might produce respectable profits for many years, it will not continue to provide the performance investors expect.

Change the business model strategy

Many businesses seldom or ever go through a real transformation strategy. Many more companies change the business model. Those companies that adapt e-commerce to their existing business – into a 'clicks and mortar' operation – will change the business model rather than transform the company.

The starting point for a business model changing strategy is usually the hypothesis. It focuses the leadership team on the opportunities and threats facing the industry.

There are three organizational skills required to be able to change the business model:

- being able to construct and use a hypothesis to sense the opportunities and threats in the competitive environment. This means that the leadership team must be able to understand such a hypothesis and should have a leading role in preparing it;
- for the organization to be a self-adapting organism rather than a hierarchical structure. Once the need to make radical change is recognized the company understands the implications and can implement the required changes. This requires involved leaders at all levels of the organization;
- the changes can be made without disrupting the ongoing operations ability to generate profits and cash flow to the extent it seriously damages the company.

Owning the hypothesis

- A creative, far-sighted hypothesis leads to a strong new strategy. The process of developing the hypothesis is crucial.
- Consultants can be useful to prepare a hypothesis. However, the risk is that having prepared it, probably as part of a strategic development assignment, they have a strong influence over the strategy development. The leadership team reviews the output but because their own input is usually limited, and top strategy consultants are very persuasive and highly paid for their advice, the leadership team often does not intuitively grasp the full implication of the hypothesis. They have not worked, argued, discussed and created the hypothesis and the resulting strategy. Because they do not own it in this sense, the implementation is more easily flawed.
- Swissair is an example. Until the late 1990s Swissair was one of the most admired airlines in the world. For those of us who traveled regularly to Switzerland it was the airline of choice. Now it has been liquidated and restructured after incurring huge losses.
- Advised by McKinsey, its long-term consultants, Swissair followed an expansion program, developing its aviation services group, particularly its catering business, which was second only to Lufthansa. To obtain customers for its aviation services Swissair invested and partnered with a string of 10 second-tier carriers, including Sabena and three small French airlines. In return for the investment these airlines used Swissair's catering and aviation services.
- The problem is that nearly all the airlines invested in had serious problems. These deals have now been terminated but at a huge cost to Swissair.
- Swissair have had a solid management group for most of the last 30 years. They would know the problems of turning round these underperforming second tier airlines in a tough and competitive industry.
- The usual process when top strategy consultants design a company's strategy is that the company chairman or CEO, the recognized leader of the company, invites them in. At huge expense they gather vast quantities of data, review similar situations to the client's in other industries they have worked

in, analyze the data using complex models and then present a hypothesis or scenarios. From this they develop the strategy and present it persuasively to the chairman or CEO. Once he endorses it the consultants present it to the rest of the leadership team. With the chairman's or CEO's backing, the intellectual firepower of the consultants, supported by the reams of data and information they have gathered, it is difficult for other members of the leadership team to effectively challenge the consultants' strategy. It is often more a rubber-stamping presentation than a genuine review. Mistakes that experienced managers would identify in a strategy development workshop go unheard.

- Because there is no high-level ownership of the strategy, implementation is not as effective as it could be. The result is a Swissair situation.
- This is not to say that strategy consultants do not develop successful strategies. But the suggestion is that strategy development is hard work, but work that should be done by the leadership team, perhaps facilitated by a strategy expert. This ensures the leadership team has ownership of the strategy and a sound understanding of what is required for effective implementation.

The 'change the business model' approach involves rethinking how the competitive basis can be changed to such a degree that the company obtains huge advantages in the market. The auto industry example described in the hypothesis in the next chapter is an example of this.

Only the best management teams ever seem to think like this. One of our clients had a business that was growing at over 35 per cent per annum, many of the elements of the strategy planned over four years earlier were just starting to generate significant revenues and improve margins, when the CEO said he wanted a completely new strategy developed. The current strategy would produce good results for at least another three years, but he knew that the competition was narrowing the leadership gap, reducing the margins, spoiling the market for his company, and that now was the time to plan for what would be the new business. This new business was still rooted in the same industry supplying services that met a similar need. It was the approach to meeting this need that was totally different and changed the business model.

One of the huge drivers of change now is e-commerce and the types of issue discussed in Chapter 20. This is the value of the hypothesis.

Part of its function is to identify the forces of change and the impact they may have on the existing business. More businesses will have to change the business model strategies in the next 10 years than in the whole of the period since World War Two.

Cannibalization has become the fashionable word. If a company does not cannibalize its business someone else will own it anyway. E-commerce is changing the way business operates. It reduces costs and in the process eats at the main business. The classic successful example is Charles Schwab. In 1996 Schwab established a separate online business to its main discount brokerage. The unit was called e-Schwab and had its own offices, staff and operating structure. e-Schwab charged US$29.95 per trade and started to boom. The full service discount brokerage charged an average of US$65 per trade. Customers rapidly understood the value proposition and used Charles Schwab for advice and e-Schwab for trade. The tensions between the two businesses can be imagined. Eventually the decision was made that all trades would be at US$29.95. The stock plummeted at the prospect of losing an estimated US$125 million of revenues.

The new price structure was introduced in January 1998. The stock price collapsed by a third of its value. However, the number of accounts grew from three million to over six million and the stock price recovered.

The strategy Schwab adopted was industry-changing. The reverberations are still being felt as players like Merrill Lynch decide and implement their e-commerce strategy.

Having established the new strategic direction, reorganized the company, and marketed themselves the Schwab strategy will not need another major change for a period of time, perhaps two, three or more years. The intervening strategy sessions will be concerned with developing and expanding the basic offering, staying ahead of the competition, reducing costs so that when necessary they can reduce their price per trade, trying to increase customer loyalty and ensuring their systems are hacker proof.

The timing of events will vary with each organization. With acquisitions the process will be accelerated and much of the work on resource allocation and the tactical planning will be completed in one year.

However, with strategic transformation and change the business models the first year is generally spent developing the ideas, creating a business vision and deciding how and where to compete. This is true even in the Internet age. Mistakes made at Internet speed are still mistakes. Contemplation of the new business is still a key to success.

Another example of a change of business model is British Airways. It had pursued an alliance with American Airlines and at one stage the two companies believed they could reduce the return price of a transatlantic fare to US$160. Now from looking at being able to win a huge share of the coach class market, BA has been thwarted in its attempt to join with AA and is reversing its strategy on coach class.

The new BA business model is focused on business and first class customers. It is now ordering smaller-sized 777 aircraft and will have almost as many of these as the 747 jumbo aircraft in three years. In catering to business travelers it has introduced the flat bed, a seat that lies down into a completely level surface, into business class. This change of business model has huge risks. If there is another major recession, as happened in the 1980s, then firms will cut back on business class travel. Having a large coach class at least helps maintain cash flow if not profits.

It is interesting how the BA business model, announced in 2000, gels with the Boeing Sonic Cruiser concept announced in April 2001. The Sonic Cruiser will also be aimed at the business traveler and will be capable of flying a passenger directly to their destination rather than to a hub, which super jumbos will still have to do.

The BA strategy is also open to competitive reaction. American Airlines is increasing the legroom in coach. If an airline could design an economical way to manufacture a seat that has a leg rest and reasonable tilt back angle, similar to current business class, so that executives on long flights can arrive reasonably refreshed, then many companies would opt for such a service. When low season flights across the Atlantic from New York to London can be purchased for US$350 return, including taxes, and a business class fare costs US$6,000, sheer cost control often makes using coach a reasonable choice. It does not take much for the BA model to fail, and with all those smaller aircraft it is not a model that can be easily reversed.

This is not considered as a criticism of the BA strategy. They have a problem and are addressing it with a different business model. They must have considered the risks and probably have contingency strategies for changes in the economy. What is interesting is that in changing their business model, they create opportunities for rivals to change their business model. This will be assisted by the introduction, albeit many years away, of the new Airbus A380 and the Boeing Sonic Cruiser.

Developing capability and infrastructure

This particular type of strategy development often follows after a new strategic direction has been established in a previous strategy session. It seeks to further develop the strategy, put flesh on the skeleton, ensure proper resources are allocated and make changes in the light of the experience gained so far.

It can result in a reasonable degree of change, especially if the new strategy planned earlier, either transformational or business model change, is not being implemented as expected or not showing the results expected.

In particular this type of strategy session will review if the implementation is aggressive enough, the level of market acceptance, the pricing level strategy, start planning further developments and ensure the right team is in place. One particular change that sometimes occurs at this stage is a change in leadership of the new project.

Expanding and refocusing

Usually two or more years after the radical new strategy has been agreed and implemented, the strategy sessions focus more on how it can really be expanded and refocused. New market opportunities will be explored and the strategy will focus on how revenues can be increased out of the current business model/product range/production resource/service capability. This is also the session in which competitors start to be analyzed and ways sought to maintain or achieve domination of the market.

Reaping

Many strategy sessions often do little more than review the current strategy, ensure it is on track and make modifications. This is a valuable process. Its real function is to challenge all the assumptions on which the existing strategy is based and ensure that the plan being implemented is the most effective for achieving the goals of the company. When strategy sessions start reaching this stage it is time to consider having a transformational or business model change type strategy event.

Process

The leadership team will know where they are on the strategic planning cycle. Using the chart for degree of strategic change, they decide the type of strategy session they need to hold. This helps with planning the workshop structure and where the emphasis needs to be placed.

If the leadership team decides they either need a transformational or business model change it has to be the leadership team who decide if they have the drive to make this change.

One client, a division within a large business, decided they would focus almost exclusively on one part of their business. At that time the total business only had revenues of US$40 million and was stagnant. This one element could grow to over US$100 million in revenue and good profits in two years. To make the change a number of staff would have to be released and new staff with different capabilities hired. The whole approach to operating would have to change, offices would be closed and the business totally transformed. The plan was achievable, but not, in my opinion, by this management team.

According to its business values chart (see Chapter 7), the team collectively was risk averse and neutral on growth. (This exercise is undertaken without thinking overtly about the strategy and helps to reveal the drives of the leadership team.) The Belbin analysis indicated that the team was good at discussion but poor at implementation. Ideas were not turned into action. They themselves agreed this was true.

On these two factors alone I was concerned that they might start the process, weaken the current business but fail to build the new business. The final confirming factor was the attitude of two of the main members of the team. They had to fly from California to the East Coast for the meeting which was planned to start at 4.30 pm. Their plane landed at 4.00 pm and it was 30 minutes to the meeting. They rolled-up at 6.00 pm, having showered and changed at the hotel while the rest of us waited to start. When they arrived there were no apologies. Their total attitude was very relaxed, non-urgent, life is too short to rush. One of them would have to be a key driver of this transformation.

The strategic intent was, I believe, correct. The window of opportunity was present and the timing was perfect. The business had most of the key resources to make the transition and would have been the industry leader. The flaw was that the leadership team would never have successfully led the change.

Going to the senior person in the company, who was in the workshop, and suggesting they had an excellent strategy but the wrong team was not easy. However, recognizing the strengths of the team and its match with the planned strategy is essential for success.

This indicates part of the interlinking between the strategic development process, the strengths of the leadership team, developing a hypothesis and recognizing where in a long strategic cycle the company might actually be positioned.

13

The role of the hypothesis

In strategic consultancy there is often a need to develop a hypothesis about the factors and variables impacting on a business. This can be useful at any stage in the strategic process, though its structure will tend to change according to where the business is in the strategic development cycle.

Its role in developing transformational or change the business model strategies can be crucial; it can be the catalyst to generate new thinking. This type of hypothesis will be similar to the example 'death of a salesman', given later in this chapter, though this is not company or industry focused but issue focused, because for this purpose it is more instructive and general in its approach. My hope is that you will also find it interesting.

Definition

The *Oxford Dictionary* defines hypothesis as 'a proposition made as a basis for reasoning without the assumption of its truth'. The aim is to stimulate thinking about the future and to start the strategic development process with some ideas on the potential for the business. It is based on technical and economic research, competitor analysis and general readings about the industry and business trends.

Hypotheses are useful as walls against which to bounce other ideas. The rule is that when the hypothesis has served its purpose, or is proved wrong, it is discarded.

During other stages in the strategic development cycle the hypothesis will focus on more immediate issues, such as development of the strategy, modification and improvements, and explore various scenarios relevant to the particular situation.

E-commerce

For many organizations, at least one element that will impact the business model will be the e-environment, especially e-commerce.

E-commerce is driving down costs, particularly selling and other costs of doing business. For many companies it will be a paradigm shift.

Examples are everywhere. Buying plane tickets, hotels, flowers, books, engineering parts, computers, insurance, stocks: you name it and it can probably be purchased over the Internet.

This change is also reducing the role of the salesperson. The most obvious example is in financial services, where increasingly business is being transacted over the Internet. The sales forces might still be required but the cost structure will make it impossible to continue working as they do now.

This hypothesis explores the potential impact of technology and the Web on three industries, pharmaceuticals, automobiles and sports shoes, with the claim that over the next few years, these forces will put an end to the need for the majority of salespersons in these industries. It was originally written in December 1999, so the errors are already apparent. This probably makes it a more valuable hypothesis example than a more recent one. (References to 'this year' etc should be read as if it were still 1999.)

DEATH OF A SALESMAN

The convergence of new manufacturing technology, increased computing power and the Internet is leading to huge change in the way industry operates. Mass customization will be possible as never dreamed of before and will occur in totally different industries. As new distribution channels develop, sales forces will become less influential and in some industries the role of marketing as it is currently understood will also decrease.

Understanding these forces and how they might impact on business will be critical to the survival of many companies. These forces must be factored into the strategic planning process. The following three examples for the pharmaceutical, automobile and sports shoe industries are intended to outline the drivers of change and what the future industry structure might be.

Pharmaceuticals

There are 60,000 medical representatives in the USA. Pharmaceutical company sales forces have grown 40 per cent in the last three years and in 1999 they promoted sales of $86 billion. According to IMS Health, revenues will increase to $143 billion by 2002. Much of this increase will be driven by a surge of new blockbuster drugs, an ageing population and intensified marketing by pharmaceutical companies.

The total promotional spend directed towards physicians and patients is now over US$6 billion per annum. Of this direct to consumer (DTC) spending is set to increase by 54 per cent this year to US$2 billion. The cost of the industry sales force is estimated at some US$4 billion per annum, nearly five per cent of revenue.

Medical representatives are different from most other sales people. They do not directly take orders for product or service. They make presentations to physicians, explaining the benefits of their product over other products for a specified illness or indication. The pharmaceutical company then tracks if that physician is prescribing more of the promoted product through the prescriptions he writes. If it increases the reps visit was worthwhile, if not it can be judged a failure.

The medical rep is part of the whole marketing effort to physicians. It includes peer meetings, telemarketing, advocacy hotlines, educational programs, direct mail and journal advertising.

This entire marketing and sales effort could be about to become redundant.

Forces impacting the pharmaceutical industry

Drugs used to be identified by screening thousands of compounds to see if they had a potential medical use. If they did they would be tested in tissue culture, then animals and then people to see if they had any adverse effects. The next test would be if they offered a new or better treatment for a medical condition. It was a hit or miss affair, very much like a roulette wheel. Discovering a new blockbuster treatment could generate billions in revenue and guarantee a pharmaceutical company's success for many years.

Over the last few years the process of drug discovery has become more scientific. There are four main drivers of change: combinatorial chemistry, high throughput screening, genomics and drug development moving from the laboratory to the computer screen. (See the layperson's guide to biology etc later in this chapter.)

These new approaches and many others will result in more drugs being available that can be tested for impact against specific proteins.

Genomics

Mass-marketed blockbuster drugs that are not differentiated across patients have driven the traditional pharmaceutical business. Blockbuster drugs are generally going to successfully treat only a percentage of patients with a given condition; drugs that are effective in curing one patient are ineffective or even dangerous in another. For example, Clozaril, a schizophrenia drug made by Novartis induces a life threatening blood disorder called agranular cytosis in about two per cent of patients.

In oncology, Bristol-Myers Squibb are developing drugs that are more molecularly defined and would affect only those cancers with the same genetic mutations. Part of the impact of this could be that clinicians will change from defining tumors according to their locality – such as prostrate, colon or liver – and define them as a category of cancer according to the genetic mechanism at work. According to BMS there are more similarities in certain subsets of colon and breast cancer than across other cancers of the same organ.

Patients' sensitivity and or resistance to a therapy are often genetically pre-determined. Currently physicians cannot distinguish in advance the responders and the non-responders.

Presently response rates to oncology therapies are in the 20 to 30 per cent range. By testing for the genetic construction of a tumor it will be possible to prescribe specific therapies. The potential result is to increase response rates to the 30 to 80 per cent range.

The information in the box below is a layperson's guide to human biology, how drugs work, and advances in drug development. This again was written in 1999 and references to 'within five years' and the like should be read accordingly.

A layman's guide to human biology, how drugs work, and developments in drug development

Molecules

The human body is made of molecules. Drugs are molecular compounds. A drug works by its molecules interacting with a human molecule to change the operation of a cell.

Organic molecules and lead compounds

Organic molecules are formed by the ability of carbon atoms to link together to form branching chains and interlocking rings of infinite variety. They can also link with atoms of hydrogen, oxygen, nitrogen and sulfur.

Chemists rearrange molecules to form new compounds. These compounds are stored in libraries. A few years ago a normal sized library for a big pharmaceutical would have been a few 100,000 compounds. Now it can be over a million and it is possible to hire an exclusive library of 100,000 for US$1 million from a specialist organization.

Under the old system a chemist could produce 50 to 100 compounds a year. Under the new approach, named combinatorial chemistry, they can produce up to 50,000 compounds per year.

Libraries are then screened to see if they have any potential medical properties. This means exposing the compound to a tissue culture to see if there is any impact. If there is some impact then chemists add or subtract atoms to increase the potency. A compound that appears to be effective is called a lead compound. Pfizer has estimated that its entire library of 1.1 million compounds could be screened against a single molecular target in six months at the normal rate of throughput.

Generally it is reckoned that only 1 in every 10,000 compounds makes it through to becoming an approved drug.

Drugs and humans

Protein molecules are essential to the structure and function of all living things. They comprise amino acids, which can form into innumerable chains that enable the protein to perform its huge number of different tasks.

Cells are the fundamental structural unit of all living things. On the outside of a cell is a protein membrane. Human (and animal) cells contain a cytoplasm, a jelly-like substance in which all the parts of the cell are suspended. The most important part of the cell is the nucleus, which contains the DNA, including the chromosomes and, within the chromosomes, the genes. The chromosomes that each person gets from his mother and father comprise about 3 billion unique letters of genetic code that effectively define a person physically, emotionally and mentally.

Cells are specially adapted to carry out a particular function. They are operated by interacting with a specific molecule in the human body. On the outside of cells are receptors or recognition sites, which are generally proteins. Receptors react to very specific chemical (molecular) signals. The cells only perform their function when instructed to by interacting with these specific molecules. All other signals are ignored. When a drug can mimic exactly the chemical signal of the body it can block or change the action of the cell. This is what leads to curing the condition.

The ideal drug will only interact with a single protein. If the target is a pathogen or parasite, viruses, bacteria, fungi or worms that live in the human body, the drug will not interact with human proteins at all. If the drug is metabolic, which means it acts directly on the molecules that comprise the human body, then it will only interact with proteins that are produced in the target tissue. If it interacts with other proteins it may cause side effects. Tissue is a collection of cells specialized to perform a particular function.

The more targeted a drug, the more effective it will be. However, because of our genetic differences the best drugs only work on about 60 per cent of the population and it is not unusual for a drug to only work on one out of three people effectively.

Genetics

The human genome has been decoded. Within five years it will be possible to categorize people into sub-populations where the similarities in genetic code will make it possible to have almost personalized medicine. Knowing our own genetic code will enable us to know our propensity for a certain disease, the lifestyle that will result in us having the best quality of life through exercise, eating and vitamin supplements. It will also inform our doctor on the best treatment regimen for any illness that we do contract; prescribing drugs that will be effective for our particular genetic make-up.

Computer modeling

Currently all drugs have to be tested in clinical trials on humans. This is a slow and expensive business. In future it will be possible to 'model' humans with different genetic codes and test their interaction with certain drugs. This modeling will become so sophisticated that it will be possible to feed the model other drugs and combinations of food and see if the trial drug has any adverse effects when combined in the human body with other substances.

It will still be necessary to test drugs on humans for some time, but the modeling will identify potential problems and will also help to determine those drugs that will be most effective with different genetic sub-populations.

For instance, there may be 10 different types of prostrate cancer, which is why some people taking a particular drug are cured and others don't respond.

Understanding how the individual genetic fingerprint impacts on the effectiveness of drugs is known as pharmacogenomics, and it is pharmacogenomics that could lead directly to the end of the pharmaceutical sales forces.

A future scenario

With physicians knowing the genome of patients and their predisposition to particular diseases, and drug characteristics being linked to disease and gene types, prescription will become more scientific and accurate. Physician IT systems will identify the most effective drug for a given indication in a patient with a known genomic fingerprint. Once this is known and approved by a medical authority, perhaps a role for the FDA, it will change the drug commercialization process.

Patients' sensitivity and or resistance to a therapy are often genetically pre-determined.

Imagine a huge database containing all the genomic sub-populations. For each sub-population there is a list of diseases for which the subgroup has a predisposition. This would be complete with a list of indications and tests for each condition, continuously updated as new medical knowledge becomes available and new drugs are approved. For each of the main diseases for the genetic group there is a recommended medical regimen complete with the specific drug or combination of drugs. With the ability to rapidly increase drug development it will be possible to target drugs at genetic sub-groups.

The current estimate is that a simple genetic test will be available in 2004. With individuals knowing their genomic fingerprint, which illnesses they have a predisposition towards, and knowing where to find information on lifestyles and treatments that will improve their particular quality of life, they will become a true consumer group. No longer will they blindly accept the diagnosis of the physician nor the prescribed course of treatment. They will be untrained, but very knowledgeable in a narrow segment of medicine, that which affects them and their immediate family.

The knowledgeable consumer/patient will move from the periphery of medicine, where others knew what was best, to an informed decision-maker who can discuss the best therapy treatment and regimen.

This will be combined with a daily or real-time medical check-up. Matsushita has already built a prototype 'smart' toilet. This will provide a check-up on weight, fat content, vitamin deficiencies, etc. But this is just the start.

Once the genomic fingerprint is known it is only a matter of time before a simple test kit is installed in the bathroom of our homes. Each morning we poke a finger into a hole and put an oral probe under the tongue. This device will record our temperature, cholesterol, blood pressure, vitamin intake, nutritional analysis, viral antibody reading, and the need to increase or decrease any medication being taken. While standing on scales our weight is automatically recorded.

All this data will be transmitted to a health coordinator; a data warehouse that stores our personal medical data and notes changes over time. The co-ordinator has the technology to assess the data, review it against the individual long-term health records and make suggestions. Speaking to us, like a virtual doctor, it will recommend changes in diet, exercise routine and vitamin supplements. It will warn of problems, like the onset of a slight cold and automatically order medicines and supplements, effective for our genetic grouping, and have them delivered to the home or workplace.

This virtual doctor is available 24 hours seven days a week. In emergency or serious medical cases it will search the database for the best specialist practitioner with a record of successful outcomes for the medical condition and automatically make a date for an appointment or summon an emergency service.

In high-risk patients, the daily monitoring could be combined with a patient implant that would constantly monitor the health state. Data would be transmitted over wireless networks to the coordinator. This would be particularly valuable for people with a potential for strokes and other conditions where rapid medical assistance is vital to recovery.

With both the 'finger in the hole' and real time information implants, consumers will be capable of monitoring a huge range of conditions. It will be possible to give people timely advice on their physical condition and what they should be doing to improve their quality of life.

In this scenario there will be fewer blockbuster drugs and a greater range of drugs focused on meeting genomic sub-group requirements. This will change the entire approach to medicine and to the drug commercialization process.

The US population, with their huge thirst for health knowledge, will want to know what they have a predisposition for and what they can do to avoid such diseases. The results will be positive for some industries, such as the cigarette industry, because it may be that only people with certain genetic characteristics will have a propensity for lung cancer or emphysema. For some it may be safe to smoke while for others it is an almost certain killer.

This information capability will be crucial to the payers, the HMOs and insurance companies. For them to be able to monitor high risk and high cost patients, advising them on effective life styles and ensuring patients are following recuperative regimes, could save them millions of dollars. It is probable that discounts will be given to people who have an implant or who follow a prescribed course of treatment or lifestyle. This maybe the condition that health insurers impose in return for providing normally priced insurance to potentially high-risk people.

This sounds Orwellian, but escalating health costs, in the United States and the developed world, will force radical solutions.

Whatever the eventual outcome is, there can be little doubt the healthcare industry will undergo significant change and unless the genomics forecast is completely incorrect, it will be a major driver of the change.

With the ability to discover and develop huge numbers of new drugs, target them at population sub-groups and treat patients for exactly their illness or medical problem, the role of the medical rep trying to convince physicians will no longer be necessary. In the longer term the role of primary physician may itself greatly diminished. But even in the shorter term, say up to 2005 or 2010, physicians will know when a patient/consumer is becoming unwell either through daily testing or the implant sending data via the health coordinator (data center) to his computer when there is a change in condition. Patients will also know when they are becoming unwell before significant symptoms manifest themselves.

Health and an ageing population

*With an ageing population living longer, the means to keep them healthy unto death will become ever more vital.*When a patient visits the physician they will both know the probable problem in advance of the meeting. The physician may need to conduct some specific tests to verify the condition, but generally the course of the cure will be prescribed over the computer system. Where there are options these will be defined by the computer system.

Under this scenario the power rests with the authority developing the database of genomic sub-groups, disease predisposition and recommended therapy. In virtually all cases they will be the deciders of which drug is appropriate to each genomic sub-group for each medical condition. There may be a number of drugs that are available and have equal efficacy, in which case cost will be the decider.

This suggests the entire medical profession will change within 15 years, and that significant change will happen within seven. The argument is that understanding ourselves and our individual genomic fingerprint will enable consumers to obtain personalized healthcare. The correct drug for each patient with a specific genomic fingerprint and medical condition will be available to the physician online. Once he has verified the medical condition, the cure is already prescribed. The health coordinator will keep physicians informed on the new drugs and their use. There will be no more need for the medical rep or marketing once the transition to the new prescription method is established.

Targeting drugs

The power to sell more product will be in targeting drugs to be effective for the maximum number of genomic sub-groups. Success will go to the most scientifically effective pharmaceutical companies.

This primarily describes one channel for accessing healthcare. In practice there will be a number of channels. One will remain through primary physicians and will be essential for the poorer members of society, the elderly and those who do not want a virtual doctor. The primary physician's approach using genetics and recommended protocols via a database will be similar in output to the virtual doctor.

Another possible channel is for pharmaceutical companies to own disease categories. They will achieve this partly through having the best-recognized portal on the Web for a therapeutic area. This will attract patients/customers. Using Novartis and its schizophrenia drug, Clozaril, as an example. MDs will petition Novartis to be a recognized Clozaril and schizophrenia specialist in their locality. As part of their appointment Novartis would expect them to stay current on all schizophrenia developments and on the new drugs introduced in the therapeutic area, especially their own drugs. Novartis will access patients through its portal and when appropriate pass patients onto the Novartis appointed expert MD. Well-resourced specialist medical experts would support the local MDs and ensure they were current with the latest knowledge.

With this approach patients would automatically associate the names of pharmaceutical companies, or their brand names, with specific therapeutic areas and know, or rapidly discover, which portal to visit.

Through the Web site they would learn the identity of an appropriate physician for the treatment of their problem.

For all of these approaches the role of the medical representative will decrease once the new modus operandi is in place and both physicians and patients know how to use it effectively. During the period of transition medical reps might be more needed than ever. Their role would be in helping physicians make the change. Once this is achieved and the medical schools have incorporated the new approach in their training, the numbers of medical reps will rapidly decrease.

For all involved in healthcare, patients, physicians, payers and pharmaceutical companies, the paradigm shift in one form or other will occur in the next ten years.

Automobiles

Auto sales in the United States are running at an all time high. Even so, discounts on new cars are still being offered and the margins are tight for all but the most sought-after models.

US auto sales totaled US$350 billion in 1999. There were 22,000 auto showrooms and General Motors alone had 7,700 independent dealers. Auto retailing is huge business and a big employer. It has proved almost immune to change in the approach to selling vehicles. Most are still sold belly to belly, as the saying goes. The car salesperson, perhaps not a well-liked figure, is still the most important shifter of metal. The transaction negotiation, including the discount from the sticker price, trade-in allowance and financing program, is usually unsatisfactory in that the purchaser of a vehicle never knows if he has obtained a good deal or been taken to the cleaners by the dealer's salesperson. Approximately four out of five customers dislike the current auto purchasing process.

Efforts to change the system have not proved successful. Wayne Huizenga, who made himself a billionaire at Waste Management and Blockbuster, has been selling new and used cars for three years using a different formula. Every car has a fixed sticker price which cannot be changed. The concept is similar to that pioneered by the Saturn division of General Motors. The format looks attractive, one that consumers would jump at. Yet Huizenga's auto group is making a pre-tax profit of only 1.9 per cent, which he hopes to increase to 3 per cent by the end of 1999.

The Internet is of growing importance in car retailing. Firms such as Autobytel.com, Autoweb.com, CarPoint and CarsDirect.com have become customer identification portals for the auto dealers. The power of the process is indicated by the fact that Autobytel.com learned that 64 per cent of its customers buy a vehicle within 24 hours of using its service.

Now online car sellers are quoting fixed prices and selling cars over the Internet. This allows buyers to purchase a car without having to haggle with the dealer's sales personnel. The vehicles are still supplied through a local car dealer.

A major problem for the Internet companies is that state franchise laws make it virtually impossible for anyone to buy a car except from a dealer. Some experts think this will change in the next five years, the time frame that will apply to the changes predicted here.

Both GM and Ford have announced initiatives to buy out some of their dealer network. Originally GM planned to buy as much as 10 per cent of the independent dealer network, though they now claim to have abandoned this plan. Ford already has five Auto Collections in the United States, where it has bought stakes in several dealerships in an area and consolidated the operations.

Dealers have fought moves by the automakers to move downstream into retailing. Through lobbying and argument they have managed to tighten laws in several states limiting manufacturer ownership. Ford has promised that they will only add two or three more of Auto Collections in the next few years.

Even as it promises to limit its direct growth of owned dealers, Ford is using the Internet to increase pressure on dealers. In parts of Arizona, Ford is giving Web shoppers information on the transaction price; this is lower than the sticker price. The scheme works by calculating the actual vehicle transaction prices derived from dealers' financial statements. This is called the 'e-price'. A customer configures his specification over the Internet and afterwards is given an 'e-price' for that specification. Participating dealers agree to sell the vehicle for the e-price.

The result is that prices are declining and dealers are losing control of their margins. An average transaction price is a mixture of high price and low price deals. Once a potential customer knows the e-price he will not pay above it, so over time the average price will continue to drop. The old sticker price was once the starting point for price negotiations. Now the e-price becomes the starting point.

The dealers are unhappy about the entire distribution strategy of Ford and GM. And they are probably right to feel threatened. From the basic facts it appears that the manufacturers are following a long-term strategy. Over the last decade they have sought competitive advantage from cost reduction and new model development. After pursuing lean manufacturing and quality initiatives the leading car and truck makers have squeezed out most of the costs from production and warranties. They have also ended up with similar product lines.

During the next decade the big car manufacturers want to achieve two main objectives, to improve the efficiency of the distribution system and to become closer to the customer. They are working to the date when the state franchise laws that mean only a distributor can supply a motor vehicle are repealed.

A future scenario

The ideal situation is for cars to be built to order, just like Dell computers. The public needs to be educated that car prices are fixed, just like computer prices. The variable is really the trade-in price. However, there is a known market value for a trade-in vehicle, depending on the model, specification, age, mileage, location and condition. This value does not change with the price of the vehicle being purchased.

Equally, finance charges can be calculated for each buyer on a basic information set.

This is the process Ford is following now. Working within the existing regulatory framework Ford is educating the public to change the buying patterns that have ruled the industry since its birth. By giving potential customers detailed information, including transaction prices, they are hoping to obtain the same result as Autobytel.com, whereby the majority of inquiries are turned into purchases within two days of visiting the Web site.

The Internet is a growing force in car retailing. The manufacturers want to control this information and purchasing channel and use it to restructure their dealer network. The key is for them to be able to quote the lowest price for any model and specification in their range. Once the public recognizes that they offer the lowest price they will become the source of virtually all Internet referrals for their range.

If the aim of the auto manufacturers is to maintain sales volume through the existing dealer network while being able to restructure it and establish direct sales through owned distribution, then stage one is to gain control of Internet pricing and referrals.

Stage two is to enter into agreement with those dealers who can see the future and establish a new working compact. This will envisage the end of huge lots of unsold cars and the move to made to order supply. (The time scale is still 2005 to 2010). The exact procedure, pricing and selling costs will be agreed and the margin on new car sales tightly established. Over 90 per cent of the profits associated with a new car occur after the initial sale so there is negotiating space for the manufacturers and dealers.

Stage three is to develop manufacturing plants that can make cars to order in five days, produce a number of different models down the same track and be capable of being economically mothballed or switched off when sales are slack.

Once the regulatory environment is changed, and the auto-buying public has become more willing to accept fixed prices, the whole structure of the industry can change.

The manufacturers can organize owned or partnered showrooms and test centers where buyers can see and test-drive models. Advisers will explain the features of the car and generally facilitate the showroom and test drive operation. Around the showroom will be computer workstations for anyone who would like to order online from the showroom, though this could equally well be undertaken from the buyer's private computer. The showroom advisers could operate and explain the system to anyone who is not comfortable using a computer. As each part of the specification is agreed a virtual car could be displayed on the screen together with the price.

The auto manufacturers need owned distribution for three reasons. Firstly, the current 'product push' allocation system is inefficient and dealers spend considerable energy in hiding from manufacturers what is happening in the market. It is the logistical stockpile of unsold new cars that enables dealers to exploit the market. The dealer network is not a partnership with the manufacturers, but an antagonistic pairing where the dealers will misinform the whole system to create more profit for themselves

Secondly, for manufacturers a much better system would be to have an integrated order input system that will enable them to manufacture against a confirmed customer order. It is possible a car could be manufactured within five days of the order being placed. In order to stop cars being pushed into the distribution pipeline during sales slowdowns the manufacturers need the ability to economically mothball plants or reduce production. This will enable capacity to be kept in line with demand and lead to an orderly market.

Thirdly, the current dealer operation is inefficient in terms of marketing, distribution and administration. A lot of cost could be taken out of the system. This would give the manufacturers the ability to increase margins in good times and offer buyers a better value proposition in hard times. With the over-capacity in car production facilities this ability will become a survival factor. Owned sales outlets combining the Internet with bricks and mortar will give this capability.

While at the showroom the buyers existing car could be viewed by a vehicle expert who would grade it for condition. This is the only variable that is subjective in calculating the trade-in price and a simple 'excellent' to 'poor' rating system should suffice. Provided the condition of the car has not deteriorated since the evaluation and the mileage is within say, 250 miles of the quoted price, the trade-in allowance is known.

At this stage the manufacturers would control the viewing, test drive, new vehicle pricing, trade-in allowance and financing. The order input is for a specific build of car they should be able to manufacture within, say, 5 working days, perhaps less. GM and Toyota are already dreaming of the 'five day car' built to order.

The manufacturers will have driven so much cost out of the ordering system: reducing marketing and distribution costs by approximately seven per cent, and, more importantly, cutting the vast stocks of unsold cars that jam the distribution system. The buying process can now dovetail with the highly efficient internal systems into which the manufacturers have invested huge capital.

Equally, buyers can obtain exactly the specification of car they want in a reasonable time frame. Compromise, between what the customer would like and what the dealer can supply, will generally be a thing of the past. Of course, there will always be hot models where demand exceeds supply, but under this system manufacturers will be closer to the market and with flexible manufacturing will be more able to meet such surges. More companies will follow the BMW and Honda manufacturing model whereby their factories can make eight different models on one assembly line.

The manufacturers will also have a stock of used cars. Used car sales are generally more profitable than new car sales. The manufacturers can now begin to control the high end of the used car market, opening up a whole new profit stream to them. With their guarantees on the condition of the vehicle, buying a good used car will be no more of a risk than buying a new car. Again, used car prices will have fixed sticker prices so salespersons will not be required. Customer facilitators are all that will be needed, and they will cost less to employ and be trained in different skills. Potential customers will be able to view used cars over the Internet, entering their ideal specification and receiving details of the nearest location of a vehicle that meets their requirements.

This is not to suggest that there will be only one distribution channel.

Even for the same manufacturer there will be owned and partnered retail operations and a dealer network. The dealers will compete with the factory-controlled outlet and when sales are slack might still stock vehicles. They will have a different value proposition to the manufacturers operation. They may still be prepared to haggle over price and/or trade-in allowances, offer special deals on servicing or a guarantee on the trade-in price of the new car at a future date. Because more than 90 per cent of the profits associated with a car are achieved after the initial sale, he has the flexibility to vary the offer.

For manufacturers to control the system, over-production of vehicles to maintain high utilization of high fixed cost facilities must cease. Perhaps within 10 years it will be possible to economically mothball production units in times of low demand. An alternative is that the big auto manufacturers will outsource a percentage, say 10 to 30 per cent of their production. BMW is considering outsourcing the development and entire assembly of its latest SUV, the X3.

If generally the auto industry outsourced a percentage of its production, then the outsource manufacturer would be able to balance reductions by one manufacturer against increased sales by another. This assumes the outsourced facility is able to manage the production of many different models down the same production line. Over time an approach on these lines would be able reduce manufacturing over-capacity, currently estimated at about 25 per cent, to, perhaps, 5 per cent, without a manufacturer running the risk that if they develop a number of hot models, or their sales increase dramatically, they would not be able to satisfy demand.

This would not eliminate market swings when the total registration of cars drops by 10 per cent or 15 per cent, but it would make it easier to manage by spreading the pain in a more even fashion and still leave plants operating at 80 to 85 per cent utilization where they are still profitable.

It will be interesting to see if Ford, GM and DaimlerChrysler, who have joined together to create the world's largest online purchasing company, Covisent, would be willing to establish a manufacturing outsourcer who could help all three companies to improve profitability within a reasonable time frame.

This only leaves servicing in the equation. This could be done through manufacturer-owned service centers, but because there is a huge investment in excellent service centers, conveniently located, this could be left to third party suppliers. This would also ease the blow of the dealers losing a major part of their business.

Besides the competitive advantage of being closer to the customer, controlling the retail operations will make it easier to introduce the new fuel cell technology. This is costing the auto industry a fortune in R&D and is even said to be the reason for the recent spate of auto company mergers.

The new vehicles will also be more expensive, at least initially. The consumer will need convincing to pay more for a car that probably has a lower performance, in terms of acceleration and top speed, and uses a technology that will not be understood. Unless US gas prices increase significantly, the improved fuel economy will not be enough enticement to change. Auto makers who control the retail market will be in a much stronger position in a changing market.

The truth is that just as with the Dell business model, the manufacturers want to move into a direct relationship with the customer. The auto makers want to take the 'shady' element from the buying process and make it a clean transaction between a reputable supplier and a loyal customer.

The result will be an industry where the retailing end is as efficient and professional as the manufacturing and consumer finance operations. Car salespeople in the role they occupy today will become almost extinct in selling the products of the main auto makers.

Sports shoes

About 12 years ago I had a dream of a new business model for the sports shoe industry. Three separate events created the idea. Ours is a sports-mad family. Both my sons play almost anything with a ball, and in particular they played rugby. My younger son used to have pains in his legs after every match and would need his legs massaged for some time at night before he could go to sleep. After trying a number of doctors I took him to a sports specialist who said that he ran with his feet and ankles twisted inwards. This put strain on the inside lower calf muscles. The solution was simple, felt pads had to be put on the instep of every one of his shoes, including his rugby boots. This cured the problem.

Rugby was the Michaelmas term sport. The Easter term's was hockey, which they played on an outdoors artificial surface. The boys said that the surface put a strain on the knees. At about this time the idea came to me that it should be possible to design sports shoes that individually fitted every athlete. In fact I became aware that top class sports people have their shoes individually made for them, and one told me they were wonderfully comfortable.

Finding shoes that are really comfortable is difficult for some people, especially those with broad feet, high insteps or other anomalies with their feet.

The idea was simple. Our customers would visit a small retail center located in a mall, high street or a concession in a department store, and have their feet analyzed on a special machine. At that time I envisaged people wearing special disposable stockings and standing on a platform with a grid of studs that would compress under pressure of the foot. The compression pattern would give the exact size of the foot, the degree of arch on the instep and the main pressure points on the foot itself. I even thought that in time this could become a dynamic system with customers walking on something like a treadmill so that pressure points could be analyzed while walking. This equipment would also analyze any physical disorders of the feet and recommend a local medical specialist who could give advice. The company might even make a contribution towards the cost of such advice.

With current technology it is probable that a combination of studs for pressure points and 3D imaging for size and fit would be used to record the foot dimensions and characteristics.

Once the measurements had been made the customer would choose the style of sports shoe required, and would then have the ability to customize this shoe by having different colored stripes or names put on the shoe. As the technology improved the customer would have the ability to customize the shoe more and more.

Once the design was finalized by the customer they would pay at the shop and delivery would be guaranteed within, say, three days. The information from the measuring center would be fed to manufacturing plants that would have special machinery that could adapt basic styles so that every shoe was tailored individually to each of the customers' feet.

Whether the technology to do this on an economic basis could be developed I do not know, but I am told that it can. Again the aim would be to have 48-hour manufacturing and delivery within three days of placing the order.

With adults, once the initial shoe pattern is known then within reasonable time spans, say two years, the customer can place orders directly over the Internet, again styling the shoes to meet personal tastes and paying with the order.

The beauty of the approach is how it simplifies logistics, stockholding and speeds up cash flow.

For an example take a sports sneaker. It will come in half sizes from 6½ to 14, a total of 16 sizes for men. If both medium and wide width fittings are available there are 32 variables for one style of shoe. If a sports shop carries 70 styles of sports sneaker and a stock of two pairs of shoes for each style it will have a total of 4,480 pairs. At an average stock price of US$18 this amounts to US$80,000. Add women's sneakers, from size 4½ to 12, medium and wide, 50 styles (there are fewer women's styles) and two pairs of each, and at US$18 cost each there is just under US$60,000 tied up in stock. Juniors might add another US$40,000 of stock. Of course, virtually no shop carries a stock that comprehensive. The result is that it loses customers and loyalty to the store when a customer's requirement cannot be met.

The current approach is so inefficient that eventually someone will either use this or another approach to bring it into the 21st century.

The original idea was for sports shoes. But the real market for this innovation might be in shoes aimed at the 50 plus age group. They are not only an expanding market demographically, but comfort is even more of an issue for them. Once the technology exists to make sports shoe, then it can be developed to manufacture any type of shoe.

One implication of this approach is that it would require local manufacturing. The cost of production would be higher than current approaches using mass manufacturing in low cost countries. The savings on logistics and on the retail margin would offset this. Equally, because the shoe is tailored to the requirement of the individual, returns should be very low.

I never took the idea forward. In November 1999 Nike announced that it would be possible for customers to customize either the Air Turbulence or Air Famished styles by choosing their own base and accent colors and add a personal eight character ID to the product. Initially the program is limited to 400 orders per day.

Whilst this is not as complex as the approach I envisaged, it is never the less a step along the same road.

The main drivers and enablers

The demise of the salesperson in many industries will be caused by three main factors.

First is the drive for efficiency. The information and order-taking processes that salespersons perform can be carried out more efficiently over the Internet. Nobel prize winning economist Ronald Coase has estimated that the interaction costs – the time people and companies spend searching, coordinating and checking whenever they exchange goods – account for as much as a third of all economic activity in the United States. This cost will be slashed. Contributing to this will be greater accuracy, direct input to the business systems and 24-hour operation. Along with this is the saving in cost of maintaining sales operations. There are various estimates of the cost of making customer contacts, but generally they are something in the order of US$200 plus for a salesperson, US$65 for a call center and less than US$5 for the Web. A retail salesperson obviously costs less but is still an expensive resource.

The Internet and other change drivers will reduce the number of order takers – which is the greatest proportion of people involved in selling. Salespeople who make contacts, creatively structure deals and seize opportunities will always be in demand.

The second factor is putting the customer at the center of the process and meeting their specific requirements through mass customization. The enablers for this are manufacturing and service technology, increasing computer power and communication through the Internet. In our three very different industries this pattern is clear: personalized medicine and quality of life recommendations in healthcare, the exact specification of vehicle ready in a reasonable time frame for the auto industry and customized design in sports shoes giving the customer individual expression and comfort.

In the pharmaceutical industry the saving in R&D will be huge. Instead of drugs failing to obtain registration because they have an adverse effect on certain patients, perhaps only two per cent of the population, they will be approved for the correct genomic groups. Blockbuster drugs will be fewer but the success ratio should increase dramatically from the one in 10,000 compounds that is the current norm. Because medication will only have to be prescribed once, there will also be a saving in prescription costs.

In the second two cases the logistical cost savings potential is enormous.

The third factor is customer loyalty. The new approach to business using the Internet requires huge marketing expenditure if it is aimed at the consumer. The cost per new customer is still high. Retaining customers will be important, especially in the second phase of the new business, when positions are more established and the next efficiency drive will be in reducing marketing expenditure. Low price, customized product, easy to deal with, a good track record of past buying will create customer loyalty. That must be established during the early part of using the Internet as the main sales approach.

Dell is the example of both cost reduction and mass customization as discussed earlier. It should also be a leader in customer loyalty.

What happens to the sales force?

Salespeople will still be needed. Charles Schwab says that 90 per cent of customers use two or more channels to contact the firm, such as the Internet and call center. This may be a transitional development but it will be necessary for most businesses.

Increasingly it may be possible to combine the Internet order with a discussion with a representative. Company representatives will be accessible during and after the ordering process and will appear on the consumer's computer screen via a small camera on the top of their computer if required. Hence they will not even be anonymous. Since all the data will be available to the company representative they will generally be able to resolve any queries quickly. Just knowing this facility is available will be enough for many users, especially once they have experience of ordering and receiving satisfaction.

This will only require a few salespeople, and the number will probably decrease with time. The rest the company will have to release. The efficiency drive of the new business environment will force companies to minimize all costs. Using figures from the Occupational Employment Statistics for 1997 there are over 14 million people in sales and related jobs with an annual wage bill of US$338 billion. A rough estimate indicates that over 4 million jobs could be lost, with a saving of over US$100 billion including all employment costs. (See the box at the end of this chapter.)

The immediate strategy is for companies to ensure they have excellent information on all their customers. Debriefing sales forces and maintaining the information is critical.

Next they have to decide their Internet strategy. Will it be to set up a new division and cannibalize the existing business, to make the Internet part of the current business or some other path? Once these decisions have been made they then have to start educating existing customers on how to use the new procedures. Keeping current customers is going to be vital during this process.

Table 13.1 Sales occupations in USA, 1997

Category	Number of jobs	Mean annual wage	Total annual wage	Jobs at risk	Wage saving
41002 First line supervisors	1,672,080	33,950	56,767,116,000	300,000	10,185,000,000
43002 Insurance sales agents	248,130	40,850	10,136,110,500	150,000	6,127,500,000
43005 Brokers – real estate	21,020	55,120	1,158,622,400		
43008 Sales agents – real estate	78,270	34,790	2,723,013,300	18,000	626,220,000
43011 Appraisers – real estate	33,570	40,130	1,347,164,100		
43014 Securities, commodities and FS	213,240	58,950	12,570,498,000	150,000	8,842,500,000
43017 Selected business services	247,920	37,940	9,406,084,800	50,000	1,897,000,000
43021 Travel agents	117,000	22,850	2,673,450,000	40,000	914,000,000
43023 Advertising	126,020	36,360	4,582,087,200		
43099 Other services	112,770	32,490	3,663,897,300	20,000	649,800,000
Total services	1,197,940	359,480	48,260,927,600	428,000	19,057,020,000
49002 Sales engineers	77,330	54,040	4,178,913,200	25,000	1,351,000,000
49005 Scientific and related, not retail	391,610	47,090	18,440,914,900	150,000	7,063,500,000
49008 Sales reps, not retail or scientific	1,032,880	39,510	40,809,088,800	150,000	5,926,500,000
49011 Retail	3,842,730	17,970	69,053,858,100	1,000,000	17,970,000,000
49014 Salespersons – parts	293,940	23,930	7,033,984,200	150,000	3,589,500,000
49017 Counter and rental clerks	444,220	15,330	6,809,892,600	100,000	1,533,000,000
49021 Stock clerks, sales floor	1,264,970	15,900	20,113,023,000	300,000	4,770,000,000
49023 Cashiers	3,122,490	14,480	45,213,655,200	1,500,000	21,720,000,000
49026 Telemarketers, door to door	407,850	19,120	7,798,092,000		
49034 Demonstrators and promoters	81,310	18,160	1,476,589,600		
49999 All other sales and related workers	488,730	25,740	12,579,910,200	100,000	2,574,000,000
Total products	11,448,060	291,270	233,507,921,800	3,475,000	66,497,500,000
Grand total	**14,318,080**	**33,457**	**338,535,965,400**	**4,203,000**	**95,739,520,000**

This is a hypothesis. In many businesses salespersons will still be required, but their role in the total selling mix will probably have to be redefined. However, in other industries salespeople as we know them today could disappear completely.

Every article on the Internet and business suggests some kind of paradigm shift. There is the real possibility that the demise of salespeople as we currently define them is that shift. In terms of cost reduction, increasing efficiency, and in a contrary way, becoming closer to the customer, it could be the big change.

14

Simple strategy in a complex world

Business is fundamentally simple. For most commercial companies its real objectives are relatively clear. Two factors make it complex: people and the business environment.

With people their individual objectives and aspirations are myriad, confused, emotional and often illogical. This statement is true for those on the leadership team or on the shop floor, particularly if those on the shop floor now sit at intelligent terminals and create new concepts and knowledge.

The business environment, with legislation, taxation, complex financing and controls, national interests and continually moving currency exchange rates, to name only a few, takes away the basic simplicity. Consultants with ever-new fads add to the fog and confusion. It is perhaps amazing that business does as well as it does in delivering the requirements of its customers.

With all this diversion it is important to remember the goals that are implicit in the aims of most commercial businesses. I have called them the implicit goals of business. The list can be extended or reduced but it forms a basis for simple strategy.

Business strategy is about how to achieve these simple objectives in an increasingly complex world with rapidly changing technology, legislation and competitors, with an organization of people: employees, partners, customers and suppliers, each with their own agendas.

The implicit goals of business are:

- making a real (perhaps cash or EVA) profit that will satisfy the investors and enable the company to invest in its facilities and people and so develop a continuing competitive advantage;
- controlling the corporation and deciding its destiny. For the leadership team this is often of crucial importance;
- building/maintaining a business that is reasonably secure and will be able to continue offering employment to those it wants to keep. If a market sector can be dominated it is excellent. Occasionally a visionary or entrepreneur, or a board of that mindset, will want a high growth business and this will change the dynamics of the other points to an extent;
- being in an organization that offers a challenge to leadership team members and key employees, particularly to their business acumen, drive and intellect;
- if possible, enjoying working in the business.

The good strategists never lose sight of the simple while planning through the complex. When one reads interviews with John Brown of BP, Jack Welch of GE or Lawrence Bossidy at Honeywell, amongst many others, it appears they have an approach to planning the business. They understand the broad picture and major issues, they can factor into this understanding the complicating factors and then establish clear goals which provide a corporate direction that is understood by employees. Establishing the strategic business plans and how they will be executed throughout the organization then becomes far simpler.

To sum up so far: implicit business objectives are simple, the environment within which to achieve them is complex and often causes managers to lose sight of what they are trying to achieve. The job of leaders is to understand the main opportunities and threats, allow for and incorporate the complex factors, and establish a direction that will enable the business to thrive. This is expressed in terms of goals and targets that employees can comprehend and will enable them to develop and implement business plans that will deliver the required results.

The business direction will often be stated in terms of revenue growth, profit growth, technology, customer focus, customer service, differentiation, time, reduced delivery cost and quality. Sometimes it will be expressed in terms of a real vision, a concept of the future the business can achieve. The strategies to deliver the business direction or vision include market and product/service development, better business delivery systems, more effective marketing and selling, more efficient use of resources and an acquisition plan. Sometimes the strategy will include techniques such as TQ, empowerment, re-engineering, decentralization, culture change and customer intimacy. These are purely enablers to achieve the strategy, they are not of themselves strategy.

In arguing that the objectives of business are simple and have not changed much this century, I am not denying that life is more complex or that business is generally tougher. Many businesses claim that margins are being eroded, life cycles are shortening, everyone seeks good staff and legislation is forever adding new hurdles and complexity to life.

If we accept that the fundamental objectives of business, the 'what', are largely unchanged, we can only conclude it is the 'how' which has become harder. The 'how' is closely linked with that other word loved by management consultants and authors of business books: 'change'.

Business has always needed to change, and has always depended on people to make the change. From hunters in the Stone Age, in the business of feeding their families, to the engineers of the industrial revolution, to today's biotech and IT knowledge worker, change is as natural as breathing. The keys to successful change are implementation and execution. A strategy that is not implemented is useless; implementation of a number of good ideas can produce improvement in performance. Execution goals therefore, such as building core competencies or developing employees, can have a positive effect on the business, especially when they are developed as part of the strategic planning process.

So if business is fundamentally simple, why do companies go bust while others thrive? Businesses always had to make products or provide services that are demanded by customers, sell them at a price they are willing and able to pay, provide them through accessible distribution channels and thus generate the revenue to make the business profitable.

Let us look at an anonymous example. A high tech corporation, quoted on NASDAQ, has a p/e ratio of nearly 60:1. To maintain this, the CEO believes it has to grow every year at 35 per cent compound. For some parts of the business this is possible, but in one core part, which produces the majority of the revenues and profits, a strategy of specialization is being pursued. This is a high cost strategy and requires the corporation to employ scarce, and expensive, people. To achieve high revenue growth the company cannot charge above the market rate, already it is at the top of the market price range. Because of the pressures and stress this strategy causes the rate of staff turnover in this key division is already unacceptably high. What it needs to do is improve margins, accept a reduction in the growth rate if necessary, and recruit the specialist staff.

Alternatively it could stop being a specialist and become more of a generalist in its approach to the market. Within these two positions there is obviously a range of options.

Such an approach is deemed unacceptable, heresy even. The CEO says 'if the profits doubled and we only grew at 25 per cent the stock price would halve'. This comment stops any debate about reducing the revenue growth. He has sold high revenue growth to the security analysts and would not change his stance because of the risk of them downrating the stock.

The champions of specialization are in the political ascendancy and the operations managers are trying to make the numbers in an impossible situation. Something will crack soon.

The analysis is simple; some of the solutions are simple. What makes it complex is the high p/e rating for the stock on NASDAQ, the growth through acquisition drive of the CEO and founder, the stockholdings of the top executives, some of whom have most of their wealth tied up in the corporation, and the fear that a collapse in the stock price might damage the company in the eyes of its customers as well as the financial community.

Simple analysis, complex situation; what strategy should this corporation follow?

In this case the first objective of the implicit objectives of business does not totally apply. The corporation has never paid a dividend and has stated it has no intention of doing so in the near future. Growth and market share are the drivers of the stock price, not profit – though an acceptable level of profit is important the market knows that fast growing organizations are often not very profitable. Logic says that one day the rate of growth has to slow, that there is a finite market. The executives in the company will say the market is growing at a rate that will not inhibit its growth, and besides, it already has plans to expand into another, related, market.

Analyzing the situation further, this business can, and does, use its high p/e ratio to acquire other businesses. These are usually privately-owned companies and the payment is with stock, which can only be sold over a period of years. This stops dumping on the market and a collapse of the stock price. Acquisitions are generally planned so there is no dilution of earnings per share. Hence growth can be maintained through acquiring private companies whose revenue will help maintain the revenue growth of the corporation.

No real effort is made to integrate these acquisitions into the business. They are left as stand alone businesses and given the objective that with a new powerful parent they should now grow at 35 per cent per annum. In practice the new powerful parent makes demands on the executives of the company. It makes them attend various meetings that add no value to their business unit, report more information to the staff departments at head office that adds no value, and look after the visiting senior executives from the parent company, whose comments, advice and addresses to the staff again usually add little or no value. This can take up over 30 per cent of the executives' time in the acquired company, for no added value. The difference is that the new corporation expects its acquisitions to grow more rapidly just by being in the corporation. It is nonsense comparable to the South Sea Bubble. Being more sophisticated, more complex, it is harder to spot and can last much longer. A persuasive and believable CEO also brilliantly sells it. It is probable that the CEO believes his own analysis and story.

In this case the strategy, rapid growth at lower prices or specialization at high prices is simple. The environment in which to make the decision is very complex. The first implicit goal of business, to make a real profit, has been partially put in suspension. This creates tremendous possibilities to acquire companies at no real cost. A new measure, growth and market share, has been substituted for profit that is fed by cost-free acquisitions.

If the acquisitions were integrated so that the whole became greater than the sum of the parts this would still be a viable strategy. When the whole becomes less than the sum of the parts it becomes a potential disaster.

Standing back from the hype the solution is fairly simple, and has now become inevitable anyway. It is almost the classic conglomerate solution. The corporation has to stop and consolidate its position, start generating profits and accept a reduction in the p/e ratio. Doing this now will be less painful than leaving it. That is the simple strategy. The clever part is in the implementation so that the p/e ratio decreases by the minimum possible, stockholders are not made to feel too bitter and employees can begin to believe in the corporation again. Once they stop leaving at the current rate the profit performance will start improving and customer satisfaction will increase.

The above piece was written over three years ago. In the fall of 1999 the stock price crashed to a p/e ratio of 17:1. The chaos and personal devastation was great. The basic rules of business always apply in the long run. The company has now focused back on the fundamentals, taken some tough actions and the stock price has started to revive.

Simple strategy is not easy strategy. Tough decisions are still tough. But sticking to the implicit goals will have to be the route forward eventually.

To be successful a big business needs a clear purpose and understandable goals, and a strategy that plots how to achieve them in a complex environment. Most of the business visionaries and entrepreneurs I have met can explain their goals, and 'grand strategy', within fifteen minutes. The strategic planning hours are in the detail required to make it happen: deciding the methods of business development on a global basis, developing a price structure, building the operational resources, creating the culture, retaining customer loyalty, looking after investors and achieving the required financial performance in the necessary timescale. Often the visionary does not want to attend these detail sessions, believing they tend to obscure the grand vision, that they block the big new ideas.

In most large corporations there is no visionary. In our experience Bill Gates and Steve Jobs are rarities in large organizations, but often there is a 'vision', a word picture or graphic of the direction the organization is moving. This is usually supported by a grand strategy, the main strategic initiatives that will make it happen. The vision and grand strategy can always be succinctly stated. One of the initial objectives of corporate strategic planning is to clarify, update or develop a vision and grand strategy.

Corporate strategic planning

Corporate strategic planning integrates the vision and the big new ideas with the strategic detail necessary for them to be successfully implemented. It is designed to put the corporate board in control of the business and ensure that all parts of the business are moving in the direction established by the board. It will also, within agreed limits, give the strategic business units their own operating autonomy helping to foster creativity, employee allegiance to the unit and the strengthening of management.

The approach does involve the corporate board in gaining a new understanding of the business, both at the corporate board and strategic unit level. This includes developing data on the key revenue and profit generators, customer needs and customer loyalty, the values of the organization and the total resource capability of the corporation. Many multinational corporations rarely completely understand the extent, nature or potential of their full corporate resource.

The process puts the corporate board in control of the entire enterprise without diminishing creativity and drive in the strategic business units. The whole process is iterative and it is at the heart of becoming a learning organization.

Ideally the process should start with the corporate board and then move to the subsidiary business units. This way the view from the top is clearly communicated. However, I have started with subsidiary units and worked back to the corporate board and the approach is still successful. Either way the process has to be iterative with regular feedback to the corporate board on the strategic business unit plans and what is emerging from them.

Divisional, operating and service function strategic business plans

The SBP process serves to convey the corporate strategy plan to the operating units, ensures that it is understood and that key requirements of the plan are incorporated in the unit's strategic business plans.

It is a common occurrence amongst multi-divisional corporations to find that two divisions fight against each other more ferociously than they compete with third party corporations. There are many cases where one division has co-operated with an outside competitor to help damage a 'sister' division. The structure and operating credo in many multi-divisional corporations encourage this behavior.

The strategic business planning process properly implemented stops internal fighting. It encourages the strategic business units to demand and use their own operating autonomy within the parameters of a common corporate direction. It fosters creativity, allegiance to the unit and calculated risk taking. With a clear corporate strategy establishing the parameters and expectations, the business unit managers are able to use their skills to build high performance businesses.

Each operating and service unit will develop its own strategic business plan. These plans become the operating document for managing and monitoring the business performance.

During the process considerable information is generated. This includes:

- data on each operation;
- financial, investment and productivity information;

- customer data as it applies to each operation;
- personality profile on every participant;
- strategic business unit strengths and weaknesses.

From the strategic business plans and the base data it is possible to identify new corporate opportunities and synergies between business units that will lead to increased effectiveness and efficiency.

Workshops for the key management of the operating units are at the heart of the process. Facilitating the building of the team, ensuring that the most rewarding strategic options are considered and then developing a strategy that can be measured for results has a major, positive impact on performance.

Resource identification and analysis

Many multinational corporations rarely completely understand the extent, nature or potential of their full corporate resource. Developing strategic business plans for each operating and service unit provides an unparalleled opportunity to really establish the key strengths of the company, its areas of strategic weakness and its current distinctive capability. The information gathered across the corporation is used to develop a 'resource and opportunity' model. This includes a summary of intellectual, IT, operational, management and financial resources, the key corporate wide strengths, weaknesses and the existing corporate distinctive capability. The opportunities, market analysis and competitor analysis from each division are collated and explored for corporation-wide opportunities.

This analysis and synthesis is then developed into a number of potential strategic scenarios for consideration by the corporate management team. This approach helps to develop strategies, which are creative and bring new and different products and services to the market.

From all the above you will know that I believe the key to successful strategy is execution. In my experience, execution, not strategy as such, is the prime factor separating the winners from the losers. This is why my approach focuses equally on establishing the strategic direction and on the implementation, the execution of the strategy. It is also the reason it sets a limited number of clear goals and performance targets. This makes implementation much easier.

PART THREE

The strategic business planning process

One of the most difficult executive tasks is to develop and implement a comprehensive strategy that will deliver sustained competitive advantage. The first two parts of this book dealt with the strategic framework and strategic concepts. This part develops an approach to generating a strategy that will be owned, and committed to, by the leadership team and an action program that will be owned, endorsed and implemented by all employees.

15

The development process

In Chapter 1 the purpose and benefits of strategic business planning were discussed. In this chapter the focus is on the process that enables those benefits.

THE STRATEGIC BUSINESS PLANNING STRUCTURE

The structure is outlined in Figure 15.1. This process should be followed closely but not absolutely. One company ran the process internally and used the VP of HR as a facilitator. The chairman of the company made him follow every nuance of the process as outlined in this book. It worked in generating an effective strategy that led to 40 per cent cumulative annual growth. But my understanding is that it was not much fun either for the participants or the facilitator. This company has now been a client for five years but the HR VP took a year to forgive me for the pain he believes I caused him.

My own approach is to think through what the business is trying to achieve with strategic business planning. I then assess how much business data the strategy group already knows. Finally I talk with the participants to discover their expectations and the issues they want to see covered.

From this point I develop a summary of existing data and approaches to presenting it, a list of what additional data needs gathering and how it should be presented, and a written analysis on the current situation. From this is developed a schedule for the workshop and a rough plan

Planning	Data collection	Building the leadership team	Data analysis	Development	Evaluation	Implementation
Project planning	Completing the base data forms	Releasing the emotions and tensions in the leadership team	Internal analysis	Company purpose	Assumption planning	Developing the departmental/functional plans
Writing the terms of reference	Arranging the data in presentation format	Freeing the mindsets	Financial analysis	Initial development of SBP goals	Checking the logic flow	Communicating the SBP to all employees and encouraging them to develop the detailed action program
Selecting the strategy team	Collecting and preparing reports for psychometric test	Developing their motivation and vision	The 10 per cent rules	Sub-group workshops	First evaluation against strategic principles	Detailed resource analysis
	Customer survey and preparation of results	Helping the leadership team to understand each other and appraise the strength of the group	Drafting the initial performance budget	Synthesis of strategic options	SBP resource analysis	The learning organization
	Collection of additional data after workshops		Internal business analysis	Completing the initial SBP framework	The iteration process	
			External analysis	Developing the business model	Final evaluation	
			Deciding on immediate actions			
			Developing a hypothesis			

Figure 15.1 SBP Structure

of the analytical tools that could be used. Most workshops never go completely to plan and to make them 'live' you will have to improvise to some extent.

PLANNING

The absolute essential for success is that the recognized leader of the company, division or department champions and actively participates in the project. The more visible this endorsement the more effective the strategy will be, especially during implementation.

The reason for this is obvious - the process is about leadership. It involves establishing a clear direction for the company and a set of actions to move in that direction. It is about leadership at the strategic, human and resource levels. Without commitment from the top it will not achieve real results.

It also has to be recognized that there is a cost. The SBP process will take the participants time. The plus side of this, though, is that in many corporations the leadership team are already spending hours in meetings talking to each other, often with no clear underlying agenda. That is not to say that an agenda does not exist for each individual meeting and that items and actions are not carried over from one meeting to the next. It is just that for many meetings there is no clear aim, no benchmarks against which to measure progress. Look at the agendas for your company's management executive meetings. Take one from a year ago and the last one. How much progress is really being made? Ask yourself this question even if sales have increased, productivity improved, profits are greater and cash flow has remained reasonable.

Is the market driving your company? Are you controlling the business? Are new products and services available and ready to maintain growth? Have the underlying problems of the previous year been solved or merely put off to a later date with a temporary cure? Above all, did you plan for this growth or did it just happen? What strain has it put on the company and how are you correcting the situation? If sales have not increased, if performance is not improving, then the issue becomes even more critical.

The SBP process should reduce the time required for board and management meetings, although they will still need to be held. Hence the project will entail a cost in leadership team and managers' time and it is better to recognize this before, rather than after, starting the process. On average the time commitment is usually between five and seven days per participant.

It is essential to pick the right membership for the SBP team. Maybe it will only consist of the leadership team, the CEO and VPs, or perhaps, one or two senior managers with the potential to join the leadership team might be invited to participate in the process.

The last question is who should facilitate the workshops. A process consultant will bring a lot of benefits but will be expensive. Internally the best person is someone who is not normally part of the team but is respected by members of the team and has experience of facilitating meetings.

The worst person to facilitate the workshop is the company or division leader. Generally the best workshops are those in which the management hierarchy is virtually eliminated – everyone in the workshop is acting as an equal member of the team. Often leaders tend to assume the role of presenter rather than facilitator. The strategy that emerges will be seen as his and the buy-in from other team members will be limited.

THE TERMS OF REFERENCE

Having decided on the composition of the strategy team and chosen a facilitator, the first task for the leader of the SBP process is to write an outline approach stating the objectives, how the process will be structured, its parameters and completion date. It is similar to a proposal that would be written by an outside consultant. More accurately it is the terms of reference for the project. This is not a long document, but should clearly state the objectives of the assignment, the methodology to be used, the likely time to be taken, and the staff required. Its value lies in helping the leader to think through what he wants from the process and in ensuring every other participant understands what the project aims to achieve and how it will operate. It usually consists of the following sections.

Background

Consider the company's origins, where it had its early success and how it grew to its present position. Describe the issues it now faces, in particular if there is one major issue; describe it in some detail. Sometimes a brief description of the industry and the issues it faces, or changes in competitor companies will be appropriate. The aim of this section is to ensure that every reader agrees that this is an accurate description of the business at this moment in time. As they read it they should be mentally nodding.

This is not the place, neither is this the document, to start discussing or proposing solutions. This comes during the SBP process itself.

This section should also cover the reasons why the leader believes that the strategic business planning project is important to the future of the company and why it is being undertaken now.

There may be some members of the team who will find good reason why the process should not be started immediately and wish to delay it. This may be because of genuine doubt about the value of the process or because they are so overloaded with work that they really do not believe they can allocate the time to a new initiative. However, often the reason for proposing delay is their insecurity. The process will expose those who are no longer contributing and sometimes a leadership team member will move function or even leave a company during the exercise. In one client, the subsidiary of a large multinational, where performance was poor and declining, the workshop exposed a number of leadership team members who were not contributing or worse, negatively impacting on the business. Of the eight who were at the first workshop four had left within three months. Within one year this company was a star performer. In time the non-performing leadership team would have left anyway, but the SBP process was the catalyst for change and accelerated their departure. As a result the performance improved more rapidly and there was job security for the five hundred employees.

My own experience over fourteen years is that if there is a lack of clarity over the direction the business is following or implementation is poor, if performance is unsatisfactory or there is a feeling that some fresh thinking is required, proceed as soon as practical. The sooner benefits start flowing through the stronger the business will become.

Purpose and scope

This will follow on from the background section and define the objectives for the project. It details some of the areas to be covered, the output that will be generated, the framework that will be produced at the end of the process and the timing for the project.

Method of working

This will include how the project will be conducted, the creation of the SBP team, the use of workshops and the use of outside advisers. For some assignments it is valuable to have either a non-executive board member, a partner from the auditors, the corporate attorney, or a senior representative from the advertising agency participate in the process.

In one assignment, where customer partnering was a key issue, the president of the major customer was invited. I was concerned about this approach, feeling it would inhibit open exchange within the client's leadership team. On the contrary, it was a very open workshop and the partnering with the customer became exceptionally strong. It is not an approach I would generally recommend; the SBP process is unpredictable and sometimes there is a need to keep issues within the corporation. However, every company is different and creativity in selecting the membership of the strategy group is one of the keys to developing a challenging strategy.

Staffing, time and costs

With most companies financial cost is not the main issue. Time is, particularly in North America with key employees traveling vast distances, the huge market size and opportunity, and the drive to work long hours. There appears little time to stop and think what we are trying to do; we are too busy doing it.

The development of the strategic business plan will take each participant between five and seven days over two to four months. For the facilitator it will take between 15 and 30 days for the basic process, probably less if a consultant is used.

For most purposes this approximate estimate on times and costs will suffice. If an external consultant is used he will provide an estimate from his firm.

Establish the timescale; from starting the project to completion of the strategic business plan.

The process of writing the terms of reference will clarify what you are going to do and how you are going to do it, both in your own mind and in the minds of your team members.

DATA COLLECTION

Having planned the project, the next step is data collection. There is an unlimited amount of data that could be collected, but if you gather too much it will be difficult to analyze it and produce meaningful output. Therefore start with the forms included at the end of the data collection chapter. If you want more data, be sure of how it will be used before collecting it.

BUILDING THE TEAM

Part of the data collection exercise can include gathering information on personal vision and motivation and completing forms for a psychometric test. When this is done the first evening of the initial workshop is spent uncovering and understanding the personal tensions and issues among the leadership team. The process that we use enables participants to disclose their feelings and beliefs, about themselves and their colleagues, in a low risk environment. When this is done effectively the rest of the workshop process becomes positive and largely eliminates hidden agendas.

DATA ANALYSIS

Data analysis often proceeds in parallel with data collection. The approach proposed here is to gather a limited amount of data and then fit it into analytical frameworks.

The analysis sometimes highlights the need for more information; if possible wait until after the first workshop before gathering it.

Some analysis will take place on the run, during meetings and discussions. New data that changes the perception of cause and effect relationships will emerge during meetings and will be analyzed almost then and there. Action plans to implement some of the ideas that emerge will be developed and implemented at the end of sessions. Hence data analysis will merge with data collection and with action planning and implementation.

THE DEVELOPMENT OF THE PLAN

The SBP approach uses a clear process to guide leadership teams through the project. It is flexible, but follows the structure given in this book. The only failures with the approach have been where the process was changed and too many short cuts were taken. This book outlines the process logically, starting at the beginning with the terms of reference, the leadership team's personal objectives and vision for the future, and data collection. It ends with completing the SBP framework and then evaluation, implementation and continuous improvement.

FORMAT AND PRESENTATION

The format of the plan develops during the process. At the end there may be some discussion over wording, but the basic document should not take long to complete and present.

There is always one golden rule at this stage of the process: do not suddenly produce a document that is a total surprise to everyone in the team. If it is the leader's plan, and team members cannot recognize their own contribution to it, they will not have any commitment to it. In fact they will believe that the whole exercise was merely a sham to allow preconceived ideas to be foisted on the company, and they will resist it. Remember; without team support the plan will go nowhere.

One definition of leadership is taking a group of people where they want to go. An analogy can be drawn with Canada geese who, when they migrate, fly in a large V formation. The flock heads in a constant direction, but their actual flight pattern is in a series of S-shaped loops. This, so the story goes, is so that the leader can see that the flock is actually following him all the time. All leaders need to take their followers with them.

It is similar with strategic business planning. The process is about people: their attitudes, relationships, styles of management and working, perceptions, knowledge, personalities and insecurities. It is therefore extremely complex, as anyone who has managed people will recognize.

Leadership in the SBP process does not involve handing down decisions. It is leadership that builds commitment, listens to individuals and creates a company that will enjoy real competitive advantage through having a united team following a clear, thought-out and considered direction that they own.

At the end of the day you bet on people not strategy. Strategies are intellectually simple; their implementation is not. To ensure successful implementation requires a focused team effort. The team that owns the strategy will make it work.

EVALUATION

Any plan or recommendation needs testing against some criteria. The SBP process includes strong evaluation criteria against which the eventual plan can be compared. Do not rush this phase of the process. Ensure that the team both believe in and are committed to the strategic business plan that has been produced. This part of the process must never be omitted, or left to a small sub-group of the main team to complete.

IMPLEMENTATION

The key to implementation is to ensure that everyone in the company is given sufficient opportunity to contribute to the strategy. The leadership team develops the company purpose, goals and performance targets. The process is then driven as far down the organization as practical by allowing staff to contribute to developing the action program. This passes over ownership of the active part of the process to them.

In a knowledge-based organization this might mean taking the process right down to the most junior employee. In companies where there are a large number of unskilled employees this may not be practical. Driving the process too far down the organization can also create confusion because the language of strategic business planning is not always easily comprehended by those totally unfamiliar with the concepts.

It is important to judge carefully at what level in the organization there needs to be a change from participation in the process to communication of the plan. However, even where employees are not involved in contributing to the main action program, ensure that the plan is communicated to them and that at the appropriate departmental level they are enabled to make input through suggestions and discussion.

THE PROCESS OF STRATEGIC BUSINESS PLANNING

The SBP structure therefore consists of:

- planning;
- data collection;
- building the team;
- data analysis;
- development;
- evaluation;
- implementation.

In his book *Making It Happen* (1988) John Harvey-Jones, former chairman of ICI and a successful business consultant, describes the direction-setting process used in ICI. He discusses the need to dream of tomorrow's world, to be aware of social conditions, to consider young employees in the industry, to imagine the technical visions of tomorrow and to understand the financial markets so that ICI are prepared to take advantage of changes. He says:

> The sharing of all these things can only be accomplished by hours and hours of talk. We have found that this sort of discussion requires a certain amount of structure, but a great deal of flexibility, and is best carried out in environments other than our normal working environ-ment. We seek to make such discussions as different as possible from the normal way in which we work. We wear sweaters and jeans, we do not keep minutes of what individuals say, we do tremendous amounts of work on flipcharts, we form a lot of our conclusions 'on the run'. The outcome of three days' work is often no more than 10 points on a flipchart, and we would consider that a good rate of striking.

The reason it takes so long is that there will be, and needs to be, conflict. Ideas need to be discussed and developed or dismissed. Alternative approaches to implementing agreed ideas need to be generated and the best selected and implemented. If everyone agrees with all the ideas put forward it is easy to go up the proverbial creek.

ORGANIZING A WORKSHOP

Workshops are best held away from the office and its distractions. There should be at least two flipchart boards and lots of space to stick flipcharts around the walls.

The workshop facilitator needs to be able to explain the objectives, facilitate the sessions and structure the output.

A leadership team can run the workshops without a facilitator and the results will still be excellent. The advantage of using a facilitator, whether from inside the organization or a consultant, is that he or she will tend to reduce the time taken to produce the plan and also help to eliminate any sense of hierarchy in the team. This will lead to more open and constructive discussion. The method described throughout this book assumes a facilitator is being used, but even if this is not the case the process remains exactly the same.

The main requirement of a facilitator is to be able to act as a catalyst for the group, to stimulate their thinking and critical faculties, but without taking over. This involves being able to ask questions, summarize what has been said and agreed, and break the group out of circular discussions. Other qualities required are generating enthusiasm, managing the mood of the meeting, maintaining the pace of the discussion without rushing through important issues and having enough back-up material so that the process never stalls and the group loses track of where it is going.

For this facilitation role it is useful to have experience of running group decision-making meetings, to be used to standing in front of a group or running training sessions.

Often during the workshop sessions some aspect that has not been considered at all at the start becomes critical to the discussion. The ability to be flexible adds to the value of the workshop. Some groups believe that offbeat discussions are the most valuable part of the exercise. If they happen it is often because the team is communicating properly for the first time. The role of the facilitator is to incorporate such discussions into a meaningful analysis of the company.

In their book *In Search of Excellence* (1982) Peters and Waterman talk about simultaneously loose-tight properties. A similar approach is needed when running workshops. They have to be loose enough to ensure full discussion and the emergence of new facts, ideas and points of view. They must be tight enough to maintain progress, keep momentum in the group discussion, and ensure that the outcome will eventually contribute towards producing a high quality strategic business plan that improves the performance of the corporation.

STARTING THE PROCESS

To repeat an earlier comment, the value of SBP is not in the production of the plan; it is in the process of producing the plan. This is not to suggest that a written, well-documented plan is not part of the final output from the process; it is, and producing it focuses on achieving an end result to which everyone is committed. But the plan is not engraved in stone. As soon as it is produced it can be overtaken by events. Strategic business planning is an iterative and ongoing activity, which has to take account of both internal and external changes.

The order in which items are dealt with in the workshops is as follows:

1. introduction and committing the top team;
2. data collection and data presentation;
3. financial analysis;
4. business analysis;
5. external and competitor analysis;
6. goal generation including specific exercises – a major part of the workshop;
7. company purpose;
8. human resource planning;
9. synthesis of strategic options;
10. completing the strategic business plan framework;
11. evaluation and implementation;
12. continuous improvement.

The objective of the first workshop is to obtain an initial draft strategic framework that covers the company purpose, goals and performance targets. This draft will change, perhaps radically over the following months, but it provides a solid base from which to start the process.

As already explained, the process begins with the chief executive writing the proposal and obtaining the support of the executive team. This is something most chief executives will know best how to do in their own organization. However, the proposal document will need to be discussed briefly at the first workshop session, unless this has already been done at an earlier leadership team meeting.

In between workshops the output from the workshop is collated into a clear summary of what has been agreed, and preparation done for the next workshop. It might also be necessary to collect more data and information.

The facilitator usually performs data collection, presentation and analysis. The chief executive should always see the input and discuss the structure of the next workshop to ensure that there are no factual mistakes and that potential problem areas are considered.

One final point before finishing this chapter. Think through what you will tell employees. If they notice that the leadership team are involved in a new process that is looking at the company in depth, they will usually think the worst. So consider putting up a notice explaining that their input and assistance may be required from time to time and that the overall objective is to make the company stronger and more competitive.

16

The reasoning and psychology of strategic business planning

ROBUST STRATEGY

The key objective of SBP is to produce a robust strategy that will be implemented. 'Robust' means that it sets a clear strategic thrust that can be pursued through disruptions in the marketplace and in the economy, whilst flexible enough to adjust to these changes, be they opportunities or difficulties.

Starting from this base it can be clearly seen why the data collection that starts the strategic planning process is limited. The leadership team members who will be at the workshop should know all the key information to plan a robust strategy. The details, extra corroborative or informative data can be gathered when it is identified as being required to develop the strategy. Until then the base data, the financial analysis and the leadership team knowledge and experience are enough to develop a robust strategy.

The strategic plan of one major corporation used to consist of one page of description and several pages of unrelated actions and financial analysis. It was detailed but it did not work. It added little, if anything, to the budget. This company now has a strategy document, with an SBP framework and performance targets that are implemented each year. This correlates with the budget but is separate from it. It has been robust enough to maintain the strategic thrust even through events such as the 1991 Gulf War, which severely affected this organization.

As soon as the SBP is completed it starts to become obsolete. External and internal events create the need for the plan to be modified. However, the strategic thrust itself should not change. Performance targets might be modified and priorities changed, but the goals should be constant throughout the changes.

The other strength of the process is that when changes are necessary the leadership team may well disagree on how the strategy will be modified, but they all start from the same base and know the overall direction in which they want the business to move and progress.

The approach is similar to that used by major Japanese corporations. They have a 10 to 20 year global strategy. When they negotiate with Western companies (and other corporations from anywhere in the world) they are only interested in working together if this co-operation furthers their global strategy. Knowing the strategy and how it fits together gives them great strength during negotiations.

IMPLEMENTATION

One of the keys to the success of SBP is that all levels in the organization are involved in the process. The result is that decision-making at all levels is based on strategy.

There was a US study some years ago that indicated that the number of companies that based their decisions on the business strategy was as shown in Figure 16.1. From our experience there is no reason to believe these numbers will have changed significantly.

It indicates that 38 per cent of fundamental decisions are made without reference to the strategy. Some 67 per cent of medium decisions and 95 per cent of minor decisions are made without considering their impact on strategy. Effectively this means that the strategy is only impacting a few of the decisions made in the company, and that the possibility that the company will achieve its strategic objectives is close to zero unless these are very modest objectives or the business is very, very lucky.

A strategy cannot be implemented when most of the decisions in a company are made without reference to it. It is for this reason that the SBP process involves employees at all levels in developing and having ownership of the performance targets and action program that affect them in their work.

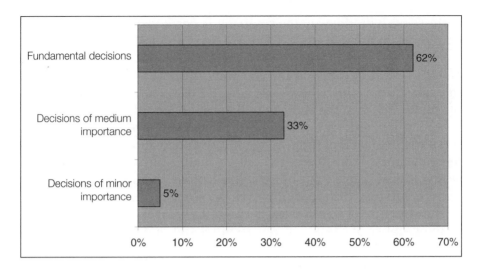

Figure 16.1 Percentage of decisions based on strategy

THE SBP PSYCHOLOGY

Underlying the SBP methodology is the psychology of remembering and acceptance. Understanding this process will help to ensure that the plan is implemented successfully.

The company purpose and the goals constitute what might be called a mission statement. While many companies have mission statements, with most of them there must be a doubt that they actually affect the performance of the business very much. The main problem is that often the mission statement has not been developed as part of a total strategy program, and it has often been developed for the wrong reason.

An effective strategy, one that leads to an improvement in business performance, must affect not only the major decisions made by the leadership team, but also the daily decisions and actions of every employee. To achieve this the strategy – the purpose, goals, performance targets, action programs and individual responsibilities of each employee – must be firmly fixed in both their conscious and subconscious reasoning.

For this to work two things have to happen. Firstly, there must be a match between the strategy of the company and its culture. To have a high service company requires employees to have the right attitude and display the appropriate behaviors. If the overall strategy, and particularly the high level statements on company purpose and goals do not correspond with the way the company is perceived by the majority of employees, it will not work. There are two options the leadership team can follow: adapt the strategy to the existing culture or change the culture. When developing the company purpose and goals, the most important one is often the people goal. If this rings false to the majority of employees, then the strategy will never be totally successful.

Secondly, in order for employees to remember the total strategy easily, it is structured so that it can be readily absorbed and recalled by short-term memory. From there it is only a matter of time, repetition and seeing it visibly lived out by senior executives, before it becomes part of the credo by which that employee operates.

The structure of the strategy is based on the fact that there is a limit to the number of ideas you can comprehend and hold in short-term memory. Try the following test.

The cars named below were all available on the American market in 1999. Some are just brands, others specific models. Read through them, then close the book and see how many you can remember.

Cadillac, Jaguar, Porsche, Jeep, Ford Taurus, VW Golf, Toyota Camry, Ford Explorer, BMW, Lamborghini, GMC Jimmy, Honda Accord, Dodge Status, Ferrari, Mercedes, Suzuki Vitara, Pontiac Firebird.

Now try grouping the cars into a logical framework. You will probably end up with something similar to that shown in Figure 16.2. Using this structure you will probably remember every car.

Of course you could have grouped them in a number of other ways – by price, for instance: less than US$15,000; US$15,001 to 25,000; US$25,001 to 30,000 and over US$30,001. They could have been classified as of US, Japanese or European manufacture. The method of classification depends on the objective but however it is done it is far easier for the mind to store and recall a logical pyramid structure than a list.

Short-term memory can only hold a limited number of distinct items. Depending on the person this ranges from five to nine items. If we therefore group every list so that it never contains more than five items, the chances are that it will be remembered, especially if it is of interest to the reader or listener.

All mental processes follow this process of grouping and summarizing. Concepts, thinking, solving problems and remembering are all grouped in our minds in a sequence that is logical to us. The mind can be thought of as a giant mass of pyramids, each with its own logical grouping. The SBP framework is, of course, a pyramid turned through 90 degrees.

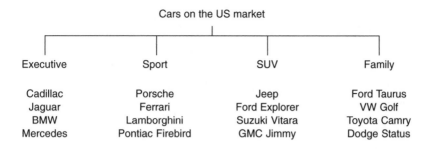

Figure 16.2 Cars on the US market

In the SBP process we want to create a pyramid within each employee's mind. It has to fit with other pyramids concerned with work, business, career and company. That is why the culture aspect described above is so important. Providing there is a degree of fit, the structure of the SBP framework is easy to absorb into short-term memory and from there into the consciousness of each director, manager and employee. This linkage of pyramids is shown conceptually in Figure 16.3.

By starting with company purpose, whether it is a high-level statement or a basic statement of the product or service, the market and the level of performance, the strategic business plan starts with a statement

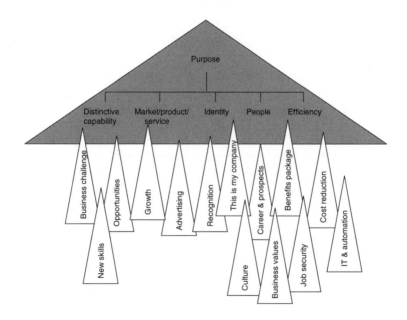

Figure 16.3 Linking of company and individual pyramids

that must ring true to all stakeholders. Each person should be able to recognize and buy in to it. Then, by working through the goals in a logical order within the structured framework, the clear relationship of the purpose, goals, performance targets and action programs becomes apparent. It is also possible to start implementing parts of the program before the whole is completed, as long as it does not run counter to the culture of the organization.

The combination of company purpose and goals effectively creates a clear overall mission statement. In large organizations this composite statement, perhaps with some changes in certain goals to meet local needs, becomes the glue that keeps the whole organization together.

LEARNING THROUGH THE SBP PROCESS

As developing children try to acquire the faculties of an adult, they adapt themselves, and therefore the people they will become, to the conditions in the world around them. They absorb the world, it becomes part of them and all that they see and hear transforms them. They have a special kind of memory, which does not consciously remember but absorbs images, in their entirety, into the consciousness.

One example is language. Developing children do not remember sounds, but rather absorb them and can then perfectly reproduce them. They are able to speak their language according to its complex rules, with all the exceptions, not because they have studied it but because they have absorbed it.

There is a similar phenomenon in most adults. Adults can relate to and remember a diagram or structure and almost intuitively understand how to use it. A description would not give this understanding.

The structure of SBP and the workshop process is designed to achieve the same result. Much of what happens is absorbed and is sometimes difficult to put into words immediately. That is why the process takes time. Every leadership team, every group of managers and employees can learn the grammar, with all its exceptions, but they must be given time to absorb it before it can become part of them and them of it. Given this time they will speak the company 'language' fluently and communicate it to others with conviction.

John Peterman in talking about the failure of his company, J Peterman Company, says that initially there was not a lot of strategizing. Intuitively to him it felt right. The company grew and prospered. Revenue in 1989 was US$4.8 million; in 1990 it was US$19.8 million. Staff numbers grew from 15 in 1989 to nearly 80 in 1990. As he says, everyone was working well together towards a common, if unstated, goal.

With hindsight he sees that his problems started at this time. All the thinking about the brand, the niche, the target market was intuitive. The ideas, the concepts were not written down. The business concept was only in the heads of John Peterman and his creative director, Don Staley.

There was a general philosophy that everyone knew, 'People want to live life the way they wish they were.' The problem is that such a broad statement did not give the staff, especially the new staff joining the rapidly growing organization who had not worked alongside John and Don and had the opportunity to absorb the culture and business philosophy first hand, anything like enough guidance.

John can now sum up the concept of the business in six words: 'unique,' 'authentic,' 'romantic,' 'journey,' 'wondrous,' and 'excellent.' He could demonstrate what he visualized. He could show his staff clothes items that fit the concept and those that did not, explaining why. Using images such as cowboys and some from the film *Titanic*, he could show directly the lifestyle concept that John Peterman represented.

Of course, during 1997 and the rapid expansion into retail there was no such articulation, no process of communication, no time for absorption. People worked at tasks, not to achieve a vision. They worked to achieve targets, which is important, but without understanding the purpose. Even worse, John Peterman himself was swept along with the momentum of the company. He lost part of his original vision, not consciously, but in making many decisions without a clear strategy the vision became clouded.

It is exactly for this reason that strategy development takes time. It has to be articulated, but it also has to be absorbed. It has to become part of our natural, everyday language, one that is spoken with fluency by every member of the company.

Similarly, it was the absorption of ideas that made IBM so strong culturally. The strong philosophy expounded by Tom Watson formed the basis of the culture. But the real power, the performance improvement, lay in the effective way it was transmitted. Employees always used to join at the junior level and were given time, even years, to absorb the culture. When they became managers they could then radiate the culture for others to absorb. That culture and philosophy was the strength of IBM for over 40 years. However, the rate of change in the computer industry turned this source of strength into an Achilles heel. IBM became a rigid colossus unable to move into new market segments as fast as its competitors. The answer was to appoint an outsider, Lou Gerstner, as chairman and change the business philosophy and culture.

COMMUNICATING THE STRATEGY

When the SBP process is communicated strongly and clearly to employees, and they are encouraged to contribute to its development, the result is a strategy that lives. It is at this stage that the organization can really start to make rapid progress.

The first stage of making it live is not too difficult. It is ensuring that every employee has the SBP pyramid in his or her mind. The eventual objective is for every employee's mind to be open to the plan.

In developed societies everybody is exposed to massive amounts of information. If every item was to register in our brain then we would go mad with information overload. Therefore we have a 'gate' that effectively decides what information to pass through to the brain and what to block out. This 'gate' is called the reticular activating system.

There are plenty of examples of the 'gate' in action. Suppose you are interested in buying a new music center. For years the 'gate' has effectively blocked out most of the information on music centers from your mind. Now, however, it lets it flood in and the world is full of news on the product. There are special offers, new technical breakthroughs, at a party you hear from across the room that someone has just bought a new music center and you cannot wait to talk to them about it. The reticular activating system is now open to all information pertinent to our proposed purchase.

Another example concerns parents with young babies. They can sleep quite soundly at night with noise all around them: airplanes flying above, cars driving down the road, noisy teenagers coming home from a party, even thunderstorms. However, if the young baby in the next room starts crying, even slightly, one of the parents will be out of bed before they hardly know they are awake to see if the baby is all right. Their 'gate' is open to the soft cry.

A major part of the SBP process is to open the 'gate' of each employee's mind to what the organization is trying to achieve with the strategic business plan.

A construction company based in Scotland succeeds by identifying new ideas in foreign markets and being the first to bring them to the United Kingdom. The managing director's fear is that the flow of ideas will dry up. His fear makes it unlikely to happen. He is always talking to all his employees about how vital new ideas are to the future of the company. When his employees travel abroad, on vacation as well as business, if they see something that could be of interest to the company they will note the details and feed them back to the company. So this company does not have just the new product people looking for new ideas, it has every employee. Their minds have been opened up to what to look for over many years, all ideas are appreciated and the information flows in.

Developing the strategic business plan and making it live will for all employees 'open the gate' to the organization's goals, performance targets and actions. They will suddenly understand the relationship between their daily actions and the goals, and see purpose in their job. Once this occurs they will start helping to improve the organization, almost as volunteer consultants.

A division of a major British company had been through three months of the SBP process and was ready to start implementation. At this point the managing director, who had been the driving force in the organization, fell ill and was away from work for two months. On his return he could only work part time. He thought nothing would have happened in his absence. He was really surprised, indeed pleasantly shocked, to find when he returned that implementation was far advanced, that employees were enjoying work and that he was no longer required to manage the daily business of the company. He could now start thinking about plans for the following year and the future.

The objective of this chapter is to understand why the process works and why it takes time. It has to enter into the consciousness of all employees.

Time is the key to the process being successful. Most members of the leadership team want to work quickly. They want to produce the plan and get on with managing the business. To have the SBP framework produced on paper becomes the objective of the exercise. Yet if the process is done really well there should be no need for the framework to be written on paper. Everything has been so well discussed, argued, agreed and committed to that everything that is important is already in the minds of the leadership team and can be communicated to the entire organization. It is at this level that the SBP process becomes a means of thinking and managing strategically. Of course, executives will want to commit a framework to paper, but this is not the object of the process.

There is one further point to consider. Are the company purpose and the goals purely for private use within the company, or are they to be made public? Goals that are made public often tend to be blander and more focused on the market than private goals. Because of this they often have less credibility within the company itself and may therefore prevent the SBP process achieving the strategic fit with the culture that is needed for a successful strategy.

17

Building the leadership team

EMOTIONS AND TENSIONS

The process really starts with releasing the emotions and tensions in the top management group. For the purposes of this book the term 'leadership team' is used to identify the group of people who can direct and control the business. They may be a board of directors, the executive team, the senior management group in a division or the owner and his main advisers and managers in a small company. Whatever title they have, they are the decision-makers, the allocators of resources, within the business.

For any business to succeed it is important that the leadership team has some cohesiveness. Decisions must reinforce each other, not be in contradiction with one another. Messages given to customers, staff, financiers and all stakeholders must be consistent from all parts of the company and from all the senior executives. The thinking processes of all members of the leadership team have to be understood by the other members of the team. Ideally each one of them should know how the others would each react under certain circumstances.

Too many of the groups with which I work have individuals who effectively fight each other. I knew one group where the VP of marketing and the VP of operations literally hated each other and never spoke directly to each other if they could avoid it. In leadership team meetings they spoke through third parties and outside of these meetings they did not speak, though they might send occasional bullets, memos as they are sometimes called, pointing out a mistake by the other party. These were widely circulated.

No strategy will be successful unless the group has the ownership of it. The first task is to ensure there is a group, a team, who can take ownership. Hatred, which is extreme and rare, cannot be removed easily. The objective in SBP is to ensure that everyone can work together and take ownership of the plan.

Whether a leadership team is a true team is a moot point in many companies. Managing a business is such a broad task that it is difficult to create the specific focus that enables a real team to form.

The management group might not want to be a team. There are CEOs who have plainly said that they did not believe their executive had to be a team to be effective. They had to work together in effective decision-making, be able to run their functions productively and report back to the executive, but these CEOs believed the group members did not have to be a team to do this. Our experience is that most boards and executives are not teams, but can manage their companies to deliver superb performance if they can find a process for working together.

Therefore building the leadership team means ensuring there is a group to develop, take ownership and implement the agreed final strategy. With most organizations that situation fundamentally exists. The purpose of this part of the exercise is to reinforce it and dispose of some of the emotional garbage – a client's phrase – that exists in any organization. Where the group is disunited the process will be continued throughout the whole strategy formulation process, using exercises to promote recognition of each other's contribution and a willingness to work together.

Often an executive will profess to believe in teamwork. It will be included in the set of values and behaviors that guide their work approach, and be part of the culture of belonging to an organization that allows members to achieve more than they could elsewhere or on their own. But that does not necessarily mean that they are a team.

The best definition of a team is that it is a unit of superb performance. It has a clear target for what it needs to achieve and will single-mindedly pursue that target. The SBP approach will, over time, help create a leadership team that becomes a unit of superb performance.

THE ROLE OF THE LEADERSHIP TEAM

In many companies the role of leadership team members is still unclear. The size of a company will often determine how they operate. In small companies two or three working executives will spend much of their time actually making sales, keeping or checking the accounts and organizing operations and quality control. These small teams of executives often work well together, spend considerable periods of time in each other's company and do become a team in pursuit of their overall goal.

In medium-sized companies, executive VPs are functional managers for 80 per cent or more of their working time (90 or even 95 per cent is not uncommon). They often relate more to their function than to the other executive VPs. They become the champion of their function or division and make decisions according to the impact on their own domain rather than on the total business. This can create a situation where executive meetings become a forum for battle rather than constructive discussion, agreement and disagreement.

There are two key questions that need to be discussed; one that arises now and one near the end of the strategic business planning process. The question now is: 'How does the way the executive currently operates add value to the company?' This is not intended to be a navel-gazing exercise taking many hours. It is a short exploration by the executive members of their current role and effectiveness as a managing group. The question later in the process is: 'How should the leadership team operate to ensure its contribution is adding the greatest value to the company?' (I am switching terms from executive to leadership team to make a subtle point.)

THE MOTIVATIONS OF LEADERSHIP TEAM MEMBERS

Building commitment to the process in the leadership team and ensuring that they can articulate their individual visions for the business is the starting point.

Many companies, perhaps most, have executives with different concepts of where the company is going, or where they want it to go. The personal ambitions of the executive need to be understood, as well as the different contributions that makes an effective leadership team. Therefore the first and perhaps the most important exercise in this stage of the SBP process is to understand the motivations of the individuals in the leadership team.

At the initial workshop the first item is to state the purpose of the strategic business planning exercise and this meeting in particular. The purpose is to enable the leadership team, company managers and everybody in the company to become committed to an agreed direction for the business that will create sustainable competitive advantage and to ensure that every part of the business is moving in that direction.

Every member of the leadership team completes the personal motivation exercise (see Figure 17.1). The purpose of this exercise is to begin the process of thinking about the business strategically. Some senior executives do this automatically and others rarely think about the future and what they want to achieve. Each participant thinks through their own motivations, what they enjoy about the business and what they don't, where the business is going and how it will have to change.

To use an analogy, the person, the car and the person in the car are three different items. A calm and considerate person can become a Tiger behind the wheel of a car. Driving a Ford Taurus they might be a defensive driver, but behind the wheel of a Porsche might drive fast and become a racer, while driving a Ford F150 truck might make them very aggressive and feel that other road users should get out of the way. Different people driving the same model of car will drive in different ways. Worst of all, they may never realize how they change. The person who comes to work everyday will have different behavior patterns with different work situations. The purpose of this exercise is to encourage them to think through what they want and how they may achieve it.

The second exercise considers personal vision (see Figure 17.2). This looks at how executives see the future of the business, their role in that future and the role of other employees in the company. This form should be collected and analyzed to identify agreement on common trends and split views on what is likely to happen. It is an interesting form, in that it often identifies the strategic thinkers and those with little or no strategic vision.

The starting point for discussion is the analysis of the personal vision forms. There are a number of ways of handling these forms. Participants can complete the form in advance of the workshop, or they can be completed at the workshop. Sometimes, when working in a consultancy role with a client, we lead participants through this form. There was one VP of finance who was clear about what she wanted in three years' time: to be the president. When asked questions about how the company's products would change in the next three years, or how the customer base would evolve, she did not have any ideas. She 'knew' that turnover would increase at 10 per cent each year and she thought that other aspects of the company would remain the same. Hence the

---

Personal motivation

Name ....
Title ....

What do I really enjoy about managing this business?

What do I dislike about managing this business?

If I was to reorganize this business I would:

Why would I do that?

What are the barriers that stop me from doing this now?

What new knowledge and skills will be required in the company?

What will my role in the company be?

What would be my objectives in that role?

General Comments

(Add and delete questions to increase the relevance)

Figure 17.1 Personal motivation

only real change would be the current president leaving, her becoming president and her current controller becoming VP of finance. What she lacked was any intuitive strategic vision. She was actually a block to the company moving forward.

The personal vision exercise often uncovers those who have, and do not have, this kind of either intuitive or analytical strategic vision. The key point of interest is not whether the vision is necessarily one that will prove realistic on further analysis, but how well the vision fits together as a whole. It shows to some extent, even at this superficial level, whether executives can synthesize a number of factors to produce a realistic vision.

Ambition and drive may take those lacking in strategic vision to the top, but if they achieve the position of chief executive they will not be

---

Personal vision

Name ....

Title ....

In 3 to 6 years' time the business profile should be:

Product/services (particularly new
products/services and those that have been
discontinued)

Types of customer

Number and location of customers

Revenue

Margin %

Organization structure (if different)

Organization culture (if different)

What else do you think might
happen in the next 3 to 6 years?

(Add and delete questions to increase the relevance to the particular company)

Figure 17.2 Personal vision

able to create a long-term, high-performance organization unless other executives can create the vision under their leadership.

If the personal vision forms are completed before the workshop, collect them and carry out two brief analyses. Firstly, see which executives have a clear view of the future and how well it fits together. Secondly, look for a consensus of ideas and then those with totally different ideas. Develop an approach to running the session which will discuss not only the consensus but also, which is often more interesting, those ideas that are different. Do this without discussing individual contributions at this stage. If the personal vision forms are completed in the workshop, handle the feedback directly and note key points on a flipchart.

Use the analysis of the personal vision forms as a vehicle to facilitate discussion. Gradually, as the group joins in the discussion, start talking about individual ideas. Do not seek agreement at this stage: you don't want everyone to agree immediately and you should certainly avoid forcing anyone into a situation where they would lose face by changing their minds later. Stress that this is just a first feel for how the group sees the future and that there will be much changing of minds, even on fundamental issues, over the next few weeks.

Next, run through the personal motivation exercise, with everyone keeping their own forms. The first question, 'What do you really enjoy about managing this business?' will often produce predictable answers. Words like 'challenging', 'the people', 'pace of development' will occur. As the answers emerge write them on a flipchart and keep the session moving fairly quickly. Once the session is completed review the flipcharts and probe deeper into the answers they have given. For instance, if 'challenge' is one of the words for what they enjoy about the company, explore how they see the challenge, what aspects particularly excite them. Like climbing Everest because it is there, do they want to do something to prove it can be done, or because it is intellectually or technically challenging, or the group of people is so creative/talented that harnessing them to perform at high levels and deliver real performance is a management challenge?

On what participants dislike about managing the company, explore what is the cause of the dislike; is there a common cause to a number of their dislikes and can it be changed or eliminated?

Sometimes, and it depends on the mood of the meeting, the session can end with four additional questions:

- What do you most value about working for your company?
- What does your company most value about you?
- What single element is most going to need change in the near future?
- What talent or attribute of yours is most going to help your company make that change?

Give everyone five minutes to think and then go round the group for the answers. Sometimes the answers are put on a flipchart or, if more appropriate, the group sits in a tight huddle and shares their feelings in a more intimate manner, without recording the answers on a flipchart.

This second approach can also be used when appropriate with the personal vision and personal motivation forms. It is always a question of sensing the mood of the group and adapting the approach to achieve the most productive output.

The purpose of this session is to establish what the top managers think about where the company is going and to ensure that fundamental differences are at least recognized. There are also sometimes interesting developments when executives begin to question their own role and effectiveness and what they might need to do to change.

TEAM ROLES

One other exercise normally conducted at this stage is a Belbin team role profile. The fundamental concept behind this exercise is that effective teams consist of members with different strengths and attributes. The simple analogy is that a soccer team composed solely of strikers would be unlikely to be successful. The defense would be suspect and not many opportunities to score goals are likely to be created, although if any are there is a good chance of putting the ball in the net.

It is similar with a leadership team. If everyone is a brilliant original thinker all that will result is a competition for whose idea is best. If no one is an original thinker then the company will primarily continue as it is, only developing as ideas are stolen from the competition. Unless there is a coordinator, some implementers, team workers or evaluators, it will not be an effective team to plan and direct the business.

The members of the SBP team should take the self-analysis test included in *Management Teams: Why They Succeed Or Fail* by R Meredith Belbin (1981). By its nature this gives a fairly raw measure of personality and team profile, but it is an initial guide to the role likely to be adopted by each member of the team.

As consultants we usually conduct a sophisticated version of this test, which includes an analysis of data supplied by at least four observers for each person being reviewed. This will indicate strengths and possible gaps in the composition of the group. The findings are discussed with each individual and often with the chief executive of the company.

At the end of this exercise each individual is asked to write down, purely for personal use, what he or she has learnt. This can have a major impact on the way each individual and the leadership team as a whole act. Carrying out self-analysis and writing down the results is often the most effective means of changing behavior.

The other great value of this exercise is in analyzing the abilities of a team. The leadership team members (or any other group) can be analyzed according to their strengths and weaknesses as a team. The best role for each member of the team will also become apparent.

Using the analysis as a guide, the team might want to discuss its strengths and weaknesses as a group before embarking on the SBP exercise. This might result in a decision to invite one or two additional members of the company to the next meeting if there are obvious gaps.

Analyzing the personalities of the top team is unbelievably valuable to the SBP process. With one client, the board of a UK top 100 company, the chairman explained that they had already done a psychometric test and that the managing director of the testing company had watched them working as a board and given them a complete report on the way they operated as a group and as individuals. This part of the SBP process was therefore omitted.

The first workshop for this company was run from 8 am to 11 pm on two consecutive days. At four o'clock on the first day, personality problems emerged as one of the biggest issues to resolve. The rest of that day was given over to 'navel gazing', discussion of the personality issues in the company. Because this had not been included within the structure of the workshop as would be normal it took longer to discuss and the outcome was less satisfactory. The group took the Belbin profile two months later.

At the end of this exercise there is a lot of information available. It will be combined with other data developed later in the process to decide if the group is willing and capable of implementing the strategy it has developed.

ADDING VALUE

Finally, address the question asked at the beginning of this chapter: 'How does the way the executive currently operates add value to the company?'

Seventy per cent of executives see their role as establishing, monitoring and reviewing objectives and strategy. Review how your executive sees their role, as a group not as divisional heads attending executive meetings. Is it broader than this definition or quite different? Having decided this, how effective are you at achieving this role and how could you become more effective? Answering these questions within the context of the leadership team session will usually provide an excellent start to the SBP process.

18

Implementation

Implementation is the hardest part of moving a company in a new direction. This is because the numbers involved are much greater than in the development phase, there might be a need to maintain secrecy about certain elements of the strategy to avoid these becoming known to the competition, and at the lower levels of the organization employees are set in their ways and are more likely to resist change.

COMMUNICATING THE STRATEGY

The following description covers the needs of a large organization. For smaller companies a simpler version of this process will usually suffice providing it covers the key elements of presenting the outline strategy to employees, ensures there is a coherent presentation at the function or department level and that this is sufficient to deliver the performance target and meet the action program completion date.

For employees to be able to understand the strategy and contribute to its successful implementation they have to know what it is. The risk is that if all of them know the strategy in its entirety then when employees leave or have a grudge against the company they may well decide to either tell the competition or leak the strategy. This may limit the effectiveness and impact of the strategy, though often the impact of the competition knowing the strategy is less than top management imagine. However, this is not a risk that is necessary to take.

The company purpose and the five main goals are normally presented to staff at either town hall type meetings or at functional or departmental meetings. I prefer the functional or departmental meetings. This is normally broken down into stages depending on the size of the organization.

The leadership team will present the strategy, the assumptions/hypothesis that underlie it, the business model and how this relates to the distinctive capability, to the senior functional and departmental managers. They will be encouraged to comment on the entire presentation content. Exercises are sometimes arranged for them to work in groups so they can actually work at the strategy and take ownership of it. Often they will want to increase the performance targets, but only do this if you are more than 90 per cent sure they will be achieved. The key to performance targets is to stretch the organization, but to try to achieve success in 90 per cent or more and only fail in 10 per cent or less. Failure in this context usually means missing the completion deadline, though occasionally it will be failure to achieve the target completely. So listen to the managers, but do not let them establish impossible targets. However, some modification of the performance targets as a result of their input is useful as this brings ownership of the plan to those who will implement it.

In smaller companies where the functions and key departments are represented on the leadership team this stage is omitted.

Once all the functional and departmental managers understand the strategy and have taken ownership of it they develop a presentation for their group of employees. This will outline the overall strategic direction, the purpose and goals and the performance targets and action programs that they will be involved in attaining. This will obviously be a subset of all the performance targets and action programs contained in the full SBP. Hence at the lower levels of the company only parts of the strategy will be communicated. This usually also fits with employees' expectations. At senior levels in a company executives want to understand the strategy in detail. At progressively lower levels employees want to know less about the overall strategy and more about how it will affect them. This approach enables them to see the strategic direction to be pursued and then how they as a function or department will contribute to moving in that direction.

Before the functional and departmental managers present the strategy to their staff they gather together and each make their presentation to the leadership team and to each other. This is so that everyone knows what every other senior manager is going to tell his staff. It is all too easy for one manager to tell his staff the strategy and their contribution, another to tell his staff the strategy and their contribution and for both sets of staffs to have conflicting views on the strategy and their role in it. This presentation to the leadership team and the peer managers avoids this happening.

Once all the presentations have been approved a timetable for them is agreed. Ideally this timetable will allow for one member of the leadership team to attend each functional or departmental presentation. This is the second step to ensure that there is no confusion as the strategy is cascaded down the organization.

At each functional or departmental presentation the employees are encouraged to understand what needs to be achieved by the perform- ance target, how the macro action plan envisages this happening and then for them to contribute their knowledge to develop detailed action plans. This way the employees will have ownership of the actions, a key element in the successful implementation of the strategy. Depend- ing on the complexity of the macro actions departments might establish mini-workshops to develop detailed action programs.

Many of the performance targets and action programs will require multi-functional teams. These will be headed by the performance target team leader. Employees who are on multi-functional PTTs attend the functional or departmental presentation first and the PTT briefing second.

This process is less time-consuming than might be imagined and ensures that a consistent message is delivered throughout the organiza- tion, that everyone understands what the company is aiming to achieve by the strategy and the actions they will take to help it achieve them.

THE FIRST YEAR

If your company has done very little strategic planning before, it is best to produce a simple form of SBP in the first year of using the process. This would apply to companies that have just used budgeting, or where leadership team members have in the past each written their own part of the plan and perhaps used some form of strengths, weaknesses, opportunities and threats analysis.

The first time leadership teams use the process they become compre- hensively aware, and have articulated and documented, all the things that need to be done to establish a platform for moving in the desired strategic direction. There is a strong urge to achieve many outcomes in a short time frame.

For such companies it is most productive to focus the process on establishing goals and short-term performance targets. The process is managed by completing the action program: every time part of the action program is completed it is ticked off and the strategy is seen to be on course.

This is a very mechanistic approach but it is highly effective. It produces companies that perform better and that have middle managers and employees who understand what they are expected to achieve and how they will go about achieving it.

It is usually the first time that leadership team members have analyzed their company in depth, starting with themselves as individuals and as a team, and working right through the process. One of the fundamental aspects of making the SBP process successful if your company has not really planned before is to use the techniques sparingly. For instance, you would not use the entire marketing analysis in a company that is not reasonably experienced in strategic planning, but select one or two of the techniques to begin to identify the market/ product goal. Use your judgment throughout the process to select what is crucial to your company now, and remember that there will be another year.

The first year of the process concentrates on improving your understanding of the business through analysis and deciding on the five or six goals. Having done this, there may be a feeling that you need to achieve at least a base operating standard, and performance targets can be set for achievement within one year to bring you up to this notional base level.

Often developing the performance targets for the first time does not take too long, although, as mentioned before, they do need to be kept to a manageable number. The leadership team members will influence the development of the action program, though they should try hard to ensure that the managers contribute to the process and have ownership of it.

In a company new to planning, the strategic business planning framework will usually be very detailed, with all the action programs fully described. As each action is completed it is ticked off and the strategy is assumed to be on target. The type of monitoring document that can be used is shown in Figure 18.1.

At the end of the first year of the SBP process, teams usually experience quite a lot of self-satisfaction. Managers understand how their actions contributed to the performance targets and the goals, confusion is eliminated and progress, both perceived and actual, is made.

Goal:

	Key performance targets		Action program	Completion date	Executive responsibility	Status at ( )
1.		1.1				
		1.2				
		1.3				
2.		2.1				
		2.2				
		2.3				
3.		3.1				
		3.2				
		3.3				

Figure 18.1 Action program monitor

However, there may be a downside in that the SBP becomes a corset, restricting some new initiatives, and the 'ticking of actions' mentality can start to spread. There are some thoughts to keep in mind for achieving success in the first year of using SBP. Firstly, when developing action programs, try to ensure that managers are responsible for most of the actions. It sometimes happens that leadership team members are responsible both for the performance targets and more than 80 per cent of the action program.

In one client the leadership team members were responsible for achieving all the performance targets and over 70 per cent of the action program. This defeats the process. After modification their responsibility was reduced to less than 30 per cent.

Even in the first year, where there is a tendency for leadership team members to be responsible for many of the performance targets, ensure that they are not also responsible for the action program, except where this is absolutely essential.

Short-term performance targets tend to dominate the first year of the SBP process. The reason is that there is usually a need to produce fairly immediate results to assure managers of the efficacy of the process, and to bring the performance of the company to a base level of effectiveness.

In the second year there is much more of a mix between one-year and longer-term performance targets. Longer-term performance targets are organized in a different way to short-term targets. This change has to be made after the first year of the process, before the 'ticking the actions' mentality can take hold. Companies that are already experienced in strategic planning will start with this second type of performance target.

LONG-TERM, FUNDAMENTAL OR COMPLEX PERFORMANCE TARGETS

Performance targets can be structured in a way that subtly changes the organization structure.

They enable companies to move to a project type of structure, away from a functional structure, in a controlled and acceptable manner.

The process described below is effective when applied to long-term performance targets, but is usually too powerful to use for short-term targets. Therefore it is not generally used in the first year of the SBP process, nor is it suitable for all the performance targets in subsequent years.

PRIORITIZING PERFORMANCE TARGET

Every strategic initiative has a cost in terms of financial investment, opportunity and human resources. Performance targets have to be prioritized in terms of their contribution to achieving the corporate goals. Without ruthlessly evaluating the expected outcomes there is a danger that there will be a lot of activity producing too few results and the business does not move forward at the pace that could be achieved.

PERFORMANCE TARGETS

Ensure that the performance targets do not overlap. Performance target projects should be mutually exclusive, so that two teams will not develop different approaches to solving a similar problem, and collectively exhaustive, in that they achieve everything intended under the strategic framework. Ensure they are outcomes and not pseudo actions.

Reduce the number of performance targets to those that will really impact the company. Ensure they define the outcome but not the approach to achieving it. With each of the performance targets ensure there are clear success measures against which the initiative and its management can be judged. It is also possible to produce a cost benefit analysis that will indicate whether the investment in the performance target will achieve returns that exceed the corporate investment threshold.

This approach also improves management performance. A senior manager could now have a major performance target entailing a whole range of actions lasting over a year with clear stretch measures that he would be expected to achieve or exceed.

My aim with all performance targets is to simplify the structure of the performance targets, increase their scope, have meaningful measures to clarify and monitor their attainment and have key managers as performance target leaders with individuals in a team that they head responsible for the action program.

Once the performance targets are rationalized and success measures are established, it is suggested that the following approach be adopted.

Performance target team instructions

Taking each performance target from the SBP framework, a performance target leader will be appointed. They will consider the actions that will be needed to achieve the performance target. There will already be guidance on this from the SBP framework. On the basis of these actions, they will decide the ideal mix of skills that will be required in the PTT.

Once the composition of the team and the allocation of actions to individuals are agreed by the leadership team, they will follow an implementation process similar to the description below:

1. Expand the performance target statement to include definitions of outputs, achievements and benefits. Cost/benefit the results expected against the resource requirements.
2. Develop a performance target plan including interim milestone measures, timing, viability, constraints, alternative options, resource requirements and an action program complete with responsibilities. (This might involve people coming onto the team, and perhaps some members leaving over the life of the performance target. The plan must include how people exit from the project team: their contribution is recognized and they are kept informed of subsequent progress.

The new members joining the project are briefed on the project objectives, current status and the contribution they are expected to make.)
3. The PTT leader develops his or her personal development objectives
   for the project. (This might include developing a particular skill (say,
   cost/benefit financial analysis) and attending an appropriate course.)
4. The plan is presented to the performance target review group for
   approval and resource allocation.
5. Performance is monitored against the milestone measures at regular
   intervals. Real outputs must be achieved, not just a statement that
   the project is 60 per cent of the way to completion.
6. Make proceed/stop decisions at each milestone.

This process may sound bureaucratic. In fact it is very simple. The
strategic plan starts the PTT with what is often a crude objective.
Sometimes this will not even define the parameters and scope of the
target clearly enough to indicate the real outcome expected. This gives
enough flexibility and vagueness for the PTT to make modifications
that will give them ownership and commitment.

The best PTTs spend a great deal of time and effort on rephrasing
and clarifying the performance target so that it belongs to them, individually and collectively. Given time and a good team leader, they will
identify meaningful aspirations in a performance target that will motivate them to want to contribute greater effort to the project. There has
to be a check at this point by the leadership team that the performance
target meets the strategic requirement outlined in the SBP framework.

Successful PTTs are probably the key to creating a high performance
organization. Some of the characteristics of these teams are worth
exploring.

The team will be most effective if all its members make approximately
equal contributions to the project. This ensures that it remains a team
project and is not run by one person with a number of assistants.

In their 1993 book *The Wisdom of Teams* Jon Katzenback and Douglas
Smith discuss the difference between a working group and a team. They
define working groups as relying on the sum of 'individual bests' for
their performance. They pursue no collective work products requiring
joint effort. By choosing to use teams instead of the working groups,
members commit to risk conflict, deal with the problems of joint work-
products, and take the collective action necessary to build a common
purpose, set of goals and mutual accountability. People who call
themselves teams but take no such risks are at best pseudo-teams.

It is interesting how even on short (five-day) strategy and management courses, real teams can emerge from competitive groups, while

others never become more than the sum of the individuals. Just as shown in the team performance curve, real teams seem to start more slowly. They hammer out the real purpose and objectives of what they are trying to achieve. Discussions go on for hours. On courses they are nearly always the last to go to bed. They always eat together as a team and put an invisible wall around themselves, excluding non-team course members. These real teams nearly always excel. Sheer effort and commitment ensure that they do well.

Most groups when they start to work together go through a period of establishing how they will organize themselves. A working group will tend to focus on their leader who will organize the tasks and activities that everyone will complete. There will be a certain amount of discussion, but progress with the task will be the key to making progress. For short-term performance targets this approach is usually the best. The working group will tend to take the performance target as given. They will not elaborate or expand on it. They will achieve the target but no more. The concept is shown in Figure 18.2.

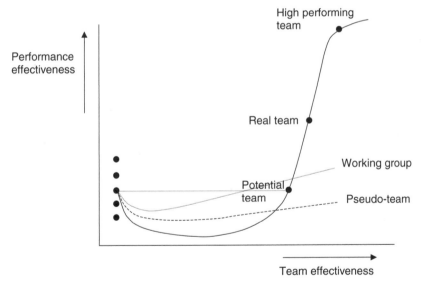

Figure 18.2 Team effectiveness

The pseudo-team and high-performance team will usually form around the same type of performance target. It will be a challenging project that requires understanding and effort. The pseudo-team will start as if it will put in the effort to become a real high-performance team. However, they are defeated by the effort required to become a team and become action-orientated early in the process. Because there will usually appear to be some degree of team ethic within the group they will often not realize their failure to become a team, they will be less well managed than the working group and will lack the commitment of the high-performance team.

For these reasons the pseudo-team is the worst performing of the three types of team.

The high-performance team will start much more slowly than either of the other two, and there will be little to show in the early part of the project for all the time its members are spending together. Managers need to allow them space to create their unit, to make the bonds, to ensure commitment. Rushing a team at the early stages, when they are drawing together, will stop them becoming a real team.

INSTRUCTIONS TO PTTS AT THE START OF THE PROJECT

- Review the performance target, understand what outcomes are expected, and rewrite it, ideally on less than one sheet of paper.
- Define the metrics that will be needed to measure attainment.
- Develop the key action plans and estimate the staffing requirements using the planner. Use the existing action program as a primer.
- Develop the milestone measures and timescale.
- Put names against the action plans. This list of names will form the team. Does this group have the potential to be a high-performance team?
- Decide the method of working – dedicated teams, dedicated leader and part-time teams, totally part-time membership. Think through communications, intranet message boards, meetings, weekend retreats.
- The PT Leader should think through the possible personal objectives he/she would like to gain from the project in terms of personal development and what resources will be required to achieve them (eg attending a course, working internationally, spending time with a particular executive to learn a specific skill or gain specific knowledge).
- Prepare a 20-minute presentation for top management within one week of commencing the project.

ACTION PROGRAM DECOMPOSITION

The action program developed in the strategic business plan is at the macro level, with an assigned executive responsibility and completion date. This is broken down using a similar form for each action into a detailed action list for each PTT, function or department, with completion dates.

From these detailed lists an individual action program is printed out for each employee. This specifies the action, the completion date and the number of days to complete the action (actions requiring less than half or one day are too detailed). This is the document the employee signs up to complete and will be a key element in the performance review. In signing up to these actions and dates every manager and employee should remember they also have a 'day job', obtaining sales, producing accounts and operational delivery for example. The actions specified as part of the strategic business plan are in addition to these normal tasks.

The regular review of actions achieved by the completion date, and those not achieved, ensures that all reviews relate to the strategy and do not become confused with other objectives often set without reference to the strategy.

MONITORING ATTAINMENT

Using the action program monitoring document, each month the leadership team review the macro level actions. Provided these are on schedule there is no need to discuss them. Where an action is falling behind schedule a decision can be made on whether to allocate more resources or to set a later completion date.

There is one rule in monitoring performance: no surprises. If an action program is scheduled over eight months the leadership team expect to hear if it is behind schedule at the latest at month six. It is no good at month seven, or worse month eight, to learn it is not going to be achieved on time. Any functional executive who repeatedly misses completion dates and fails to inform the leadership team long before that date is due is a poor manager whose position should be reviewed.

With that one caveat, monitoring the program is direct and straightforward and provided this is well controlled the strategy will be achieved on time.

19

Data collection

If there is a cautionary message about data collection it is to beware of collecting too much. Follow the SBP approach by completing as fully as possible the base data forms at the end of this chapter and, if you believe it will be valuable, conduct a telephone customer survey. Each survey needs to be developed to meet the needs of the particular company. The output of a well-conducted telephone survey will generate key discussion during the workshops. Apart from that, only gather additional information after the first workshop unless you know certain information will be required during that workshop.

In many of my assignments as a consultant I also have meetings with the client's customers and suppliers. This approach proves effective in gaining an outside perspective on the business and its competitors. It might be something that the members of the leadership team would like to undertake.

THE BASE DATA

For in-house data, the appropriate directors should complete the relevant base data forms. Ideally this should be at least two weeks before the first workshop.

The way the forms are completed can bring out some interesting issues. Lack of information is instructive in its own right. The chief executive has to decide if the information which is missing would help in conducting the SBP project and also if it would be valuable in the normal management of the company.

Each form is quite short and designed to collect the most relevant information. In many cases executives will want to expand these forms so that they are more comprehensive. At this stage of the exercise it is better to leave them as they are. As the project progresses a much clearer view of the value of information will emerge and more can be collected as required.

The base data forms are included at the end of this chapter. They are:

1. Sales history.
2. Sales forecast.
3. Key customers.
4. Competition.
5. Marketing.
6. Key suppliers.
7. Organization structure.
8. Operating facilities.
9. People.
10. Innovation.
11. Efficiency.

There are a number of external sources of data that can prove valuable. The Internet can provide a wealth of information; credit rating organizations such as Dun and Bradstreet also issue reports on specific industries, as do security analysts.

Trade associations, the trade press and government reports may provide sources of outside and comparative information. Again, do not collect too much, but the right information properly presented can change the perspective of a company's position.

Having collected this information it is essential to try and add value to it by thinking how it needs to be presented. This is not strictly data analysis, but data presentation to facilitate the analysis process. Without spending too much time playing with words, if we can identify patterns and trends and understand the business better by changing the way the data is presented, then this has to be a good thing.

Sales

Start with the form on sales history, and arrange the raw data as shown in Figures 19.1 and 19.2.

When completing Figure 19.1, rank products or services by their total sales volume in descending order from the product with the most sales to that with the least. Do not initially try to group them into A, B or C.

Product ranking	Product name	Sales value	% of total sales value	Comments
1		$	%	
2		$	%	
3		$	%	A PRODUCTS
	80% of total sales			
5		$	%	
6		$	%	
7		$	%	B PRODUCTS
	15% of total sales			
"				
14		$	%	
15		$	%	
16		$	%	C PRODUCTS
	5% of Total Sales			

Figure 19.1 Product/service ranking by sales value

Product ranking	Product name	Total profit contribution	% of gross profit cont.	Comments
1		$	%	
2		$	%	
3		$	%	A PRODUCTS
	50% of total sales value			
5		$	%	
6		$	%	
7		$	%	B PRODUCTS
	70% of total sales value			
"				
14		$	%	
15		$	%	
16		$	%	C PRODUCTS
	100% of total sales value			

Figure 19.2 Product/service ranking by profit contribution

Repeat the exercise with Figure 19.2, ranking products or services by their gross margin in descending order. Again, at this stage make no attempt to rank them.

Having drawn up the two lists, group the products or services according to their value to the company. In Figure 19.1, A products are those that provide the major sales. It is not unusual to find that 20 per cent of the product or service lines will produce 80 per cent of revenue. In the example the cut-off point for A products is shown at 50 per cent so as not to overstate the case, but often this percentage will be exceeded.

There are no meaningful rules about the cut-off point between A and B products. When the rankings are reviewed there is usually a point at which there is a step change in sales volume between one product and the next, and this is where to make the change of ranking. B products will usually account for between 10 and 20 per cent of sales, but again look at the list and note where the step change occurs.

All other products will be rated C. It is not unusual to find that 70 per cent of products or service lines account for only 10 to 20 per cent of sales. If the revenue is graphed as shown in Figure 19.3, it becomes easier to identify points where the slope of the curve changes and defines the groups into A, B or C.

Having completed the ranking by sales value, follow the same procedure for Figure 19.2, ranking products or services by gross margin.

When examining the rankings, look for mismatches between ranking by sales value and ranking by profit contribution. If there are any, consider whether revenue is being achieved with products or services that are not making a real contribution to profits.

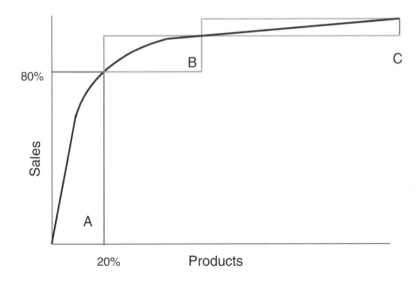

Figure 19.3 ABC analysis

It is rare not to find some surprises in this analysis. However, do not start cutting products or services yet. Instead, look carefully at your costing system, check how overheads are allocated and use a common-sense approach to checking if the costs are accurate.

Activity-based costing

Most companies allocate overhead costs such as the accounting department, engineering maintenance, general management and utilities in proportion to some form of direct cost. For example, a manufacturing company might allocate its overhead burden to production cost centers. The basis of allocation varies but, for instance, the total energy consumption for a company might be allocated to production cost center in proportion to their floor area. The fact that production cost centers using ovens and heat treatment processes will consume far more energy than say, a light assembly cost center, will be ignored.

The energy overhead cost burden will be added to all the overheads allocated against that production cost center. The overhead costs will then be charged to manufactured products on the basis of machine hours used, staff hours used, or the value of materials consumed. Often a combination of these factors will be used in a set formula to provide a basis for cost allocation.

For instance, if a production cost center has a total overhead of US$750,000 allocated to it and there are 20,000 available machine hours, the hourly overhead allocation is US$37.50. Each product that uses one hour of production time in the cost center is charged this amount in addition to the direct cost of manufacture.

When overhead costs represented only 10 to 20 per cent of total costs it was acceptable to allocate the overhead as a percentage of direct costs, since the approximate relationship was near enough. However, it is now possible for overheads to be as high as 1,000 per cent of direct costs. Therefore overheads need to be allocated carefully before any decisions on costs can be made.

This situation can be even worse with service operations. In one business that was project-based the management had no idea of the margin on any one project. It is almost literally true that it was only at the end of a year, and only then with some guesswork on uncompleted projects, that they knew how much profit they had made.

Any system of allocating costs is an approximation. However, there is evidence that indicates that using a system of overhead cost allocation, called activity-based costing, allows more accurate information to be obtained. Activity-based costing seeks to establish product cost on the basis of the resource-consuming activities that are required to design, engineer, manufacture, sell, deliver and service each product or service line.

Based on this type of analysis, Figure 19.4 indicates the type of situation that occurs. The most profitable one per cent of products by revenue contributes 36 per cent of gross margin. The next four per cent contributes another 46 per cent of gross margin. At the other end of the scale, 15 per cent of gross profit is lost on the least profitable one per cent of products. They are making a loss for the business.

Just eliminating the loss-making products from the range will not necessarily increase profits immediately, because it will leave production or operations with a gap in workload. However, in the longer term, considering how these products can be made profitable, either through value engineering or price increases, or making a decision to replace or cease producing them, will improve the company's profits.

The real virtue of activity-based costing is that it forces companies to analyze and understand their real costs and relate them back to products or service lines.

Product evaluation

Information as shown in Figures 19.1 and 19.2 should be presented to the first SBP meeting. It is quite possible that the group will want to take some action to cut out low-selling or unprofitable items. Completing Figure 19.5 will help to move the discussion forward.

'Trend' in this table refers to whether sales are increasing or decreasing. To keep or discontinue is the decision to be made. The distinction between old and new products is an arbitrary one: depending on the business a product might be old after six months or five years, but generally managers can quite easily decide when a product no longer has the adjective 'new' applied to it. There are of course gray areas: modified products, brand extensions, repackaged products and products that may be new in some markets but are old in others. Do not be too concerned about these. As a simple rule, if it is a C product, the trend is downwards and it is thought of as old; it is a candidate for the product/service cull. With A products the basic decision is whether to invest in marketing, product development or process development to increase profits or to milk the product for all the cash possible while it sells well.

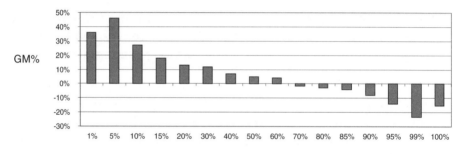

Product margin by percentage of total products

(1% of total product range by product category represents 36% of total gross margin)

Figure 19.4 Gross margin by product percentage

	Trend	Keep/ discontinue	Action/ comments
C Products — Old rank/description			
C Products — New rank/description			
B Products — Old rank/description			
B Products — New rank/description			
A Products	Trend Improvements Investment Milk		

Figure 19.5 Product evaluation chart

The decision to scrap products is a key management task. Drucker in *Managing For Results* (1964) calls it 'sloughing off yesterday'. It has to be done if resources are to be released to tackle new and potentially more profitable tasks.

What might well happen when you propose cutting back on some products is that the sales force will insist that you have to offer a comprehensive product or service line for this or that reason. There may be truth in this, but think of the cost of keeping unprofitable products as well. Arguably, a plethora of services that perform poorly damage profits even more. With many service organizations staff turnover can be 25 per cent per annum or more, especially in a low unemployment environment. The cost of training new staff in a wider range of services, the reduction in utilization this often brings, and the loss of focus that service staff has if trained in too many lines reduces their effectiveness.

While you are examining Figure 19.1 and 19.2 look for anomalies: a product or service that does better than expected, or an old product that suddenly revives. Ask why it has happened. Have new uses for the product been discovered? Is it being sold in a new market? Is it due to one salesperson or one customer? Is there an approach that we can apply to other products and replicate the success?

Cull gently at this stage. As a general rule, do not cull newly introduced products. Concentrate on old ones in the C products that were never successful or ones where the trend has just drifted downwards.

Finally, following the discussion about products and the new understanding that will emerge, review the sales forecast form for the following year and consider how this should be changed.

Some of these discussions and decisions will occur outside the workshop, often because further data collection will be required. At this stage be sure that the strategy process is not becoming lost in too much detailed discussion on specific product issues.

Customers

The customer analysis is similar to that for products and is begun by completing the information shown in Figures 19.6 and 19.7.

Look for similarities between major accounts (do they have the same representative?), between industries or geographical groupings.

Again, look for the exception, especially in B customers. Do these customers come from industries other than those you would expect, which might indicate new markets that could be available, or are there B customers who would be expected to be A customers? Examine the lists for customers who do not fit the pattern and question why they do not. Are there opportunities for other sales?

Finally, are you making a profit from your C customers? Is there a cheaper way of serving this market?

Having analyzed the customer list for opportunities, now analyze it for threats. What customers have dropped from A to B over the last year, and which from B to C? Which customers have been lost altogether? For each customer, or at least the major customers, ask a series of questions:

- Were they previously loyal customers or did they often stop and then start buying from us again?
- Where do they buy now?
- Is our product or service now superfluous to their needs?
- Are they using a different channel, such as the Internet?
- Is this part of a pattern in customer defections?

With the business world changing so fast, the impact of the Internet, the creation and demise of large businesses, this exercise really needs to be conducted every six months. Spotting trends quickly is a key to survival. Our customers are one of the keys to spotting trends. When customers defect always ask them why. The answer can ensure your survival.

The biggest question the SBP analysis process raises is often: 'How can we change our sales operation to provide better customer service and improve profits?' The customer profitability analysis is included to help you to make this decision.

Companies often find that they have a large number of customers with sales of less than one per cent of total sales. This segment of the customer base can take a disproportionate amount of the sales force's time. You need to be sure that there is not a cycle in the way these customers order: for instance, whether they have always placed their orders every second or third year, and in that year become a major customer, while being a C customer for the other years. If a cyclical pattern does not apply, you can start deciding how to sell to these customers.

It may be that a mail order catalogue is one way of obtaining the orders, or that regular telephone calls would be able to pinpoint when a sales call is justified, or that you could organize regular meetings for a number of customers at a hotel to discuss their needs. Thinking through such situations creatively enables managers to do more with fewer resources.

One accounting firm did this type of analysis on client accounts. It discovered that it had 15,000 accounts, and that 14,000 of those had a fee income of less than US$3,000 per annum. Many of them were also showing a loss for the firm. Nationally it culled large numbers of clients, a painful and for some partners a personally embarrassing experience. It was also expensive: to find a new accountant for a client can take up to two days of partner time. To sign off the accounts of a small company may only take two hours, but these small accounts were losing money, tying up resources and dragging down the firm. Once they had gone, staff morale improved. They could now work on the jobs that held greater interest and enabled them to learn and develop. The result was that profits started increasing.

Sometimes the analysis will reveal the opposite, that the largest customers are actually costing the company lost profits. At one large bakery in England, all the directors 'knew' that supermarket customers were the most profitable and specialist shops the least profitable. Detailed analysis proved that the exact opposite was true. After allowing for discounts, payment terms, returns, queries, disputes, stipulations on quantities and specified delivery times to depots, they found that there was almost no profit on the supermarket business. Of course, they could not stop supplying the supermarkets or sales volume would drop by half, but they did review how they structured the business terms.

Research indicates that customer profitability usually looks like Figure 19.8.

A small number of customers could have a negative 11 per cent gross margin. Evidence from clients throughout the world, from publishing to engineering to insurance, supports these findings.

One of the major HMOs was rapidly expanding revenue in the 1990s. In the process it signed up one of the largest industrial giants in the US, a corporation that is a household name.

This industrial giant negotiated a tough contract. It persuaded the HMO to work for very low rates, explaining that its name alone would help the HMO to sign up many other large industrial customers. Once the contract was operational the industrial giant became difficult and unpleasant to work with. The HMO made large losses on the account. After a few years the HMO decided it no longer wanted the industrial giant's business; it could not afford to keep it on the current basis. It negotiated a contract where the HMO did all the administration on a fee basis, while the industrial organization undertook insuring the health risk.

Self-insuring the health risk made the industrial giant an ally to the tough administration of the HMO. The corporation and the HMO in administering the plan had the same objective: to provide good health cover and provision of medical services at a reasonable cost. It is an unfortunate fact that not every medical need, from cosmetic surgery to the most expensive treatment that might be available but is not proven more efficacious, can be paid for by an HMO or insurance company.

The approach between the HMO and the industrial giant became more of a win/win by aligning the administration and cost control skills of the HMO with the risk-taking exposure of the industrial giant.

Ranking	Customer name	Customer revenue	Main products purchased	Representative/ location	% of total	comments
1		$			%	
2		$			%	
3		$			%	
"			80% of total sales value			A Customers
5		$			%	
6		$			%	
7		$			%	
"			15% of total sales value			B Customers
14		$			%	
15		$			%	
16		$			%	
"			5% of total sales value			C Customers

Figure 19.6 Customer revenue analysis

Ranking	Customer name	Customer profitability	% of total profits	comments
1		$	%	
2		$	%	
3		$	%	
"	80% of total sales value			A Customers
5		$	%	
6		$	%	
7		$	%	
"	15% of total sales value			B Customers
14		$	%	
15		$	%	
16		$	%	
"	5% of total sales value			C Customers

Figure 19.7 Customer profitability analysis

Throughout the relationship the HMO has never found there was any value in using the industrial giant's name in winning other business. Large customers are not necessarily profitable, but carefully considering the nature of the relationship can often yield satisfactory results for both parties.

Sometimes it is useful to categorize products or services into groups and relate each group to the customer base. With one injection molding company, examples were collected of the work being produced on each machine. These were then categorized by the level of skill required to produce them. This was a subjective judgment, but the client later confirmed it as substantially correct.

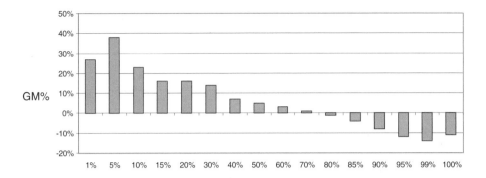

Customer margin by percentage of total customers

(1% of total number of customers represents 27% of total gross margin)

Figure 19.8 Gross margin by customer percentage

There were four categories. Category 1 was complex work for major corporations. A lot of work in this category was done free of charge, such as sampling of pre-production parts, and the margins were not very good. Until the first SBP workshop this was the market on which every director wanted the company to concentrate. 'First division work' was how they phrased it. They had just won their first big order and were targeting their sales force on this type of customer. Category 2 work was highly skilled, but mainly subcontract component work. The volumes were high and the margins good. When the customer base was analyzed this was the type of product most of their biggest customers were buying. Category 3 products were similar to category 2, except the skill requirements were lower. Category 4 products were production line fillers that any competent injection molding company could manufacture and the margins were small.

The directors analyzed the products made, cross-referenced them to their margins, and looked at the customer base and the products purchased by the top six customers, which accounted for over 50 per cent of sales. This led them to query the strategy that they were drifting into (of concentrating on Category 1 products). They decided to refocus the sales effort on the Category 2 products. They did not totally drop the Category 1 customers, because they were high profile accounts that gave the company good publicity. Also they could provide large orders and, owing to the stringent manufacturing requirements they placed on their suppliers, staying with them ensured that the injection molding company remained at the forefront of the industry.

Something that does not show up in this analysis, but which can be useful, is a view of the products each customer buys – an example from a plastics extrusion company is shown as Figure 19.9.

Product sales by value (US$000s)								
Customers	1	2	3	4	5	6	7	Total
A	234	178	155	214	91	62	0	934
B	307	211	154	76	77	32	0	857
C	231	145	0	170	129	74	78	827
D	180	81	97	0	44	12	42	456
E	74	62	58	0	41	36	40	311
F	30	51	52	33	31	0	0	197
G	28	36	12	15	21	20	0	132
Total	1,084	764	528	508	434	236	160	3,714

Figure 19.9 Customer/product purchase chart

As would be expected there is a strong correlation between the biggest customers and the products with the greatest sales volumes. However, even in this simple analysis it is interesting to note that product 7 is not bought by four of the biggest customers. Who is buying it? Is it one customer outside the top seven, or a large number of smaller customers? This type of analysis often produces some revealing insights.

Increasingly my work with clients and the feedback given by participants on my public seminars proves that this kind of customer profitability exercise is one of the keys to rapid profit improvement and freeing up of resources. The story is the same whether in Europe, North America or the Far East: this simple exercise can be extremely worthwhile and rewarding.

Other base data forms

Usually, unless something really strange is identified, it is sufficient at the first workshop to present the base data forms for competition and marketing without changing the way the data is presented. There are plenty of areas for discussion without doing any further analysis.

With the suppliers form, a similar analysis can be performed to that done for products and customers. However, be sure why you are doing it. If you think that increasing awareness of what is spent might concentrate the buying decisions in those areas where there is greater pay-off, then that is fine. If it highlights areas where the company is exposed to risk through a supplier ceasing business, then it is worthwhile. But if you do not expect any of these factors to be relevant, then do not bother to analyze the output too much. The real value of this data is when you come to plan your ongoing relationship with suppliers and what more you will expect from them. Nevertheless, this form does highlight how supplier relationships are handled, and with one company the analysis led to a complete change in the system used by the purchasing department.

The reason for the base data form on organization structure is to ensure that there is a formal chart of the organization. Check that obvious problem areas are not present in the structure. These include issues such as quality assurance reporting to production, new product estimating reporting to sales, and design and development isolating themselves from production and marketing.

The form on operating facilities needs some discussion at the workshop, especially if poor equipment is leading to loss of competitive edge.

The people profile in the relevant form needs nothing more than presentation of the facts. The key issue, which is also included in the leadership team vision form, is if a lack of knowledge or skills is holding back the company's progress or prospects. Generally this form will identify any statistical personnel problem, such as unbalanced age profile in the company or in a key department. The real issues concerning people in the company will emerge later in the process.

The innovation form is a record of performance in this area, and if lack of innovation is a problem it is usually easy to spot.

The purpose of the efficiency form is to check if the efficiency of the entire operation is improving each year.

Further action

Data collection is at the heart of developing a robust strategy. In some large corporations the forms described above have been completed with a lot of care and the analysis has revealed many areas of immediate improvement with a high pay-off. Medium-sized companies usually go into less detail, but the output is simpler to use. In both cases the forms nearly always identify immediate improvements and give a clear base from which to view the future. Such benefits derived so early in the SBP process usually also create a keenness to work harder.

Try to keep the discussion on the output from the data collection to half a day in the workshop. The benefits emerge fairly quickly and detailed action can be delegated to subcommittees. Keep the project on course to have a first draft SBP by the end of the second day of the workshop.

The rules for the discussion are as previously outlined: use flipcharts to record the input, pin the sheets up on the walls and summarize the discussion and progress made at the end of the workshop.

There will normally be a number of actions that the group wants to take immediately. This may be anything from culling some products, changing the sales organization, launching a recruitment drive, changing the organization – though not restructuring at this stage – to increasing the spend on research and development.

Providing none of these actions will diminish the company's overall capability, or change it radically before the new strategy is developed, then it is good to take action because the benefits of the process will be flowing through quickly into improved performance, which builds confidence in the approach and commitment to it.

BASE DATA FORMS

Complete the base data forms using information that is readily available within the company. Generally clients complete between 50 and 70 per cent of the information. If there are existing management reports or print-outs simply attach these to the relevant form. Some general data as listed below would also be helpful.

General data:

- most recent accounts;
- advertising or promotional material;
- articles or publicity on the company or individuals in the company;
- product descriptions or information;
- photographs of the location.

Other sources:

- other sources of data: government, industry, specialist reports, etc;
- existing information gathered on competitors, major markets, previous studies undertaken by the company.

NB The point of this page is to be aware of all the data that already exists within the organization.

Base Data Form 1: Sales History

	2000/01			1999/00			1998/99		
	Sales Value	Gross Margin	GM%	Sales Value	Gross Margin	GM%	Sales Value	Gross Margin	GM%
Product/ Service									
Total									

Group products into groups with sub-totals as appropriate. Dating assumes company has completed year 2000/01

Base Data Form 2: Sales Forecast

	2000/01			Next Year's Forecast
	Budgeted Sales	Gross Margin	GM%	Budgeted Sales
Product/service				
Total				

Base Data Form 3: Key Customers

Name	Location	Representative	Industry/Application	Sales Revenue 2001/02 Forecast	2000/01	1999/00	Main Products Sold

Base Data Form 4: Competition

Name Size   Location   Key Strengths   Key Weaknesses

Indirect: Companies who meet the same customer need with substitute products/services

Base Data Form 5: Marketing

Definition of Target Market

Key Messages to Customers

Media used to communicate messages

Promotion Budget   Next Year's Budget   2000/01   1999/00   1998/99

Advertising
Literature

PR

Exhibitions

Other

Total

Base Data Form 6: Key Suppliers

Name	Type of Agreement	Products Supplied	Purchases 01/00 99/00 98/99	Budget 01/02

Base Data Form 7: Organization Structure

Chairman
CEO
President
Vice Presidents
Departments or Functions (Include number of staff in each)

Base Data Form 8: Operating Facilities

Plant by Type Comments	Age	Number of Units	Maximum Capacity	Current Utilization	Break-even Utilization
Value of plant and equipment		Budget 2001/02	2000/01	1999/00	

Does the facility need new equipment to maintain competitive production or operations? If so what is required and what is the capital cost?

Base Data Form 9: People

Personnel Profile

Age	Number Employed	Years of Service Average Total	Staff Turnover % 2000/01 1999/00 1998/99	Comments
<20				
20–29				
30–39				
40–49				
50–59				
>60				

Total Number of employees with qualifications

	Relevant to Job	Not Relevant to Job
Post Graduate Degree		
First Degree		
Professional		
Technical		
Other		

Training given to staff in last 12 months

Total number of employee days training	Average number of training days per employee	Titles of main training courses/events

Knowledge and Skills

Are there any deficiencies in knowledge or skills that are, or might in the future, restrict progress

Base Data Form 10: Innovation

How many new products or services have been launched in the last 3 years? (Only include enhancements or product extensions if they are major)

Description	Last 12 months	13–24 months	25–36 months

How many of these products/services were:
- Developed in house?
- Developed with others?
- Factored in?

Of the new products/services introduced in the past 36 months how many are in the following categories by sales value?

Top 10%	11%–20%	21%–30%	31%–40%

List any marketing or business innovations in the past 36 months

Innovation	Date of introduction	Is it successful?

How many new products/services are planned to be introduced in the next 12 months?

What is the process by which new products/services are developed?

Base Data Form 11: Efficiency

Efficiency performance:

Revenue/Employee	Cost/Employee	Income/Employee	Improvement % On Previous Year			Inflation %
			Revenue/Emp	Cost/Emp	Income/Emp	
$	$	$				
2000/01						
1999/00						
1999/98						

If there is an improvement over and above inflation, what has driven the improvement?

What are the comparable numbers for the 3 major competitors?

Revenue/Employee	Cost/Employee	Income/Employee	Improvement % On Previous Year			Inflation %
			Revenue/Emp	Cost/Emp	Income/Emp	
$	$	$				
Competitor 1						
2000/01						
1999/00						
Competitor 2						
2000/01						
1999/00						
Competitor 3						
2000/01						
1999/00						

What initiatives are currently in progress to improve efficiency and what is their expected impact in improving efficiency?

Revenue/Employee	Cost/Employee	Income/Employee	Improvement % On Previous Year			Inflation %
			Revenue/Emp	Cost/Emp	Income/Emp	
$	$	$				
Initiative 1						
Initiative 2						
Initiative 3						
Cumulative impact						

20

Financial analysis

INTRODUCTION

The objective of this chapter is to give a real understanding of the financial performance of a company and to target those areas where a performance improvement will yield maximum results. From this analysis the leadership team needs to establish the financial parameters that the business must achieve. These may include achieving certain levels of profitability, cash generation, revenues, earnings per share or stock price. The financial analysis suggested here will help to clarify the thinking on the financial goals the business needs to pursue. It is also valuable on four other levels:

- for those who are not strong on finance, to improve their understanding;
- to enable executives to explain the company's financial performance to their own staff and to help motivate them to achieve new targets;
- if companies want to structure their organization into small cell or unit profit centers;
- to identify short-term action plans for the company.

The accounts used as an example are those of Franks Manufacturing Company Inc. The income statement and balance sheet are included here, although when reading accounts look carefully at all the sections included in the accounts, often the most interesting information is in the notes to the accounts rather than just the balance sheet and profit and loss. In this chapter all money is US dollars.

	2000 (in $)		1999 (in $)	
Net Sales		15,297,462		16,962,824
Cost of Sales		11,910,635		13,135,231
Gross Profit		**3,386,827**		**3,827,593**
Distribution Costs	268,390		457,968	
Administrative Expenses	2,890,201		2,702,983	
		3,158,591		3,160,951
		228,236		666,642
Other Operating Income	108,058		26,341	
Income from Investments	330		1,945	
Interest Payable	(26,985)		(43,194)	
		81,403		14,908
Profit on Ordinary Activities		**309,639**		**651,734**
Federal Income Tax		(96,161)		(194,362)
Profit After Tax		**213,478**		**457,372**
Dividends	(100,902)		(100,902)	
Transfer to General Reserve			(500,000)	
		(100,902)		(600,902)
		112,576		**143,530**
Retained Profit Brought Fwd		1,245,268		1,388,786
Retained Profit Carried Fwd		**1,357,844**		**1,245,256**

Figure 20.1 Franks Manufacturing Co, income statement

	2000 (in $)		1999 (in $)	
Fixed assets				
Tangible assets		1,051,253		970,572
Investments at cost		2,015		45,045
		1,053,268		1,015,617
Current assets				
Inventory	4,436,671		3,687,774	
Accounts receivable	3,140,708		2,625,140	
Cash at bank	41,935		252,571	
	7,619,314		6,565,485	
Creditors				
Amounts falling due within				
1 year	(3,432,135)		(2,440,604)	
Net current assets		4,187,179		4,124,881
Total assets less current				
liabilities		5,240,447		5,140,498
Provision for liabilities and				
charges		(69,247)		(81,886)
		5,171,200		5,058,612
Capital and reserves				
Called up share capital		629,254		629,254
Other reserves		3,184,102		3,184,102
Income account		1,357,844		1,245,256
		5,171,200		5,058,612

Figure 20.2 Franks Manufacturing Co, balance sheet

ANALYSIS OF ASSETS AND LIABILITIES

Lay out the analysis as shown in Figures 20.3 and 20.4. Start with the 2000 figures. Franks Manufacturing revenue for 2000 is $15,297,462 (taken from the income statement). A number of other figures are going to be quoted in terms of their percentage of the revenue figure and this obviously represents 100 per cent.

Analysis of assets and liabilities

	2000 $	%	Days	1999 $	%	Days
Net sales	15,297,462	100		16,962,824	100	
Inventory	4,436,671	29	136	3,687,774	22	102
Accounts receivable	3,140,708	21	75	2,625,140	15	56
Gross current assets	7,577,379	50		6,312,914	37	
Creditors	(3,432,135)	−22	−105	(2,440,604)	−14	−68
Net current assets (excl. cash)	4,145,244	27		3,872,310	23	

Figure 20.3 Franks Manufacturing Co, analysis of assets and liabilities

The next three numbers are taken from the balance sheet. First calculate the value of inventory as a percentage of revenue. Inventory is part of the current assets.

$4,436,671 \times 100 / \$15,297,462 = 29\%$

The same calculation is done with accounts receivable:

$3,140,708 \times 100 / \$15,297,462 = 21\%$

Adding together these two items gives gross current assets of $7,577,379, which is 50 per cent of revenue. Just think about this for a moment. It means that without taking any more credit from suppliers, for every extra $1 billion of revenue the business will need $500,000 of working capital. But of course companies do take credit from suppliers and that is shown on the balance sheet under 'creditors'. Again, calculate this as a percentage of revenue:

$3,432,135 \times 100 / \$15,297,462 = 22\%$

It is often more meaningful to use the trade creditors figure from the creditors analysis shown in the trading accounts or notes to the accounts. This will show just how hard the firm is leaning on its trade suppliers. Subtracting the creditors figure from the gross current assets leaves net current assets of $4,145,244, which is 27 per cent of $15,297,462.

After calculating the percentages, calculate the 'days' figures. These show that the value of inventory being held in the company is equivalent to 136 days of sales, that debtors are, on average, taking 75 days to pay and that the company is paying its creditors in 105 days. The method of calculating days is shown at the end of the chapter. On the Franks Manufacturing example the 'days' figures are already included.

Internally businesses will have the information available to check these monthly, but in reviewing competitors they can only check them every quarter or year.

Is Franks Manufacturing doing better in 2000 than it was in 1999? No: profit after tax has halved, from just under $457,372 to just over $213,478. Worse than that, looking at this analysis, inventory has increased from 102 days to 136 days, accounts receivable have increased from 56 days to 75 days and creditors, who are financing all this, have increased from 68 days to 105 days. This company is relying on its creditors for survival and soon it will have a major problem.

Owing money to creditors can be great, it is free money for the company to use, as we shall discuss later. The caveat for this is that suppliers are willing to extend credit for an extended period because they want the business. This is strength. But just to take the time over the agreed credit period, not from strength but because there is no ability to pay them, is dangerous and leads to supplies being delayed or suspended.

This really brings us to the whole issue of assets and liabilities. Consider for a moment the whole issue of inventory. It is shown on every company balance sheet as an asset. Is it really an asset, or a liability? Depending on the situation of the company, it can be both. Keeping stocks for a long period of time costs money in storage space, tied-up capital and insurance. Large, slow-moving stocks drain cash from the business and become a liability on the business, often being disposed of for virtually nothing. Accounts receivable are shown as an asset, but if customers take a long time to pay, and yet they continue to be supplied without interest charges, this represents a comparative weakness in the supplier to customer relationship.

In Franks Manufacturing increasing inventory and accounts receivable shows weakness. The company is weak, it is losing sales and obviously does not want to put pressure on customers to pay nor lay off its work force to reduce inventory. It is a difficult situation but one that will not be corrected by management inaction.

Franks is a real company that did survive through tough management action. Its first problem was in understanding the situation it was in.

Service companies

In times of economic boom companies in the service sector encounter problems in recruiting staff of the right caliber. Unless the organization has a sensible business model, recruitment and training costs are incurred on new staff long before revenue is generated by them. Often the approach is to try to expand sales in the hope that they can handle extra business with the current staff levels and hence without higher fixed costs. Usually this fails to work and new sales generally result in an increase in cash outflow. This approach can also lead to a reduction in customer service and damage to the company's reputation.

ANALYSIS OF PERFORMANCE

This analysis examines the performance of the company in terms of the financial figures. The strength of the approach lies in its simplicity and its focus on key figures. Figure 20.4 shows how the analysis is laid out.

Analysis of performance (in $)

	2000	1999
Net sales	15,297,462	16,962,824
Cost of sales	11,910,635	13,135,231
Distribution costs	268,390	457,968
Total variable costs	12,179,025	13,593,199
Gross profit	3,118,437	3,369,625
Gross margin percentage	20.4%	19.9%
Sales, general and administration	2,890,201	2,702,983
Break-even point (SG&A/GM%)	14,177,853	13,606,922

Figure 20.4 Franks Manufacturing Co, analysis of performance

Gross margin

The gross margin percentage is one of the key figures in understanding business performance. It is vital that everyone in the company understands what it means and the target that the company is budgeting to achieve.

A very simple example, a pencil, will illustrate how to calculate and use gross margin percentage. This is a useful story for explaining the concept to the company sales force.

The pencil sells for $1.00. It costs $0.90 per unit in direct costs to manufacture. The gross margin per unit is $0.10 or 10 per cent. If 10,000 are sold then the gross margin is $1,000. If the price is increased by 10 per cent the unit selling price becomes $1.10. The manufacturing cost remains at $0.90 and gross margin per unit is $0.20. If 10,000 are sold then the gross margin is $2,000.

A 10 per cent increase in price has caused a 100 per cent increase in gross margin or profit.

But as the price is increased, sales may drop. How much can they go down and yet still produce the same $1,000 profit as before? The answer is they can drop by half, 50 per cent. With half the production the amount of working capital required to finance stocks and debtors will also decrease by half. The overdraft will diminish and so will interest costs. The factory will not always be working at full speed to meet the shipping date, so overtime costs and weekend maintenance could disappear. The fixed overheads might be reduced. So in fact after increasing prices by 10 per cent and losing half the sales, net profits could still increase.

Gross margin percentage is one of the key figures to monitor in business. Ignoring service businesses such as banks and supermarkets, it has been suggested that if gross margin is:

- 25 percent or less, the business will fail sooner or later;
- 40 per cent, there is real strength, with good cash flow and financial durability;
- 60 per cent and more, you have a high-flying company.

Many leadership teams will argue against these figures and say that it is just not possible to obtain 25 per cent gross margin in their industry. From my consultancy work with many low margin companies we have managed to increase the gross margin more than the leadership team originally thought possible. Often the first step is the determination to improve it.

One of my clients is a business involved in the healthcare industry. Quoted on NASDAQ the company had a p/e ratio in the upper 60s and a $4 billion market capitalization. Its strategy consisted of developing more specialist units to meet particular sectors of the market, a viable strategy but one with a high operating cost. At the same time it demanded growth of some 35 per cent per annum from those operations. This often meant they reduced prices in order to win business. The result was that margins were minimal. Over dinner one evening I pointed out to the chairman that there was a dichotomy in the strategy and that instead of focusing on revenue growth we should focus on profit growth. 'Clive', he said, 'if we double profits and only grow at 25 per cent the stock price will halve'. Not long after the stock price dropped by 75 per cent. This was before the collapse of the NASDAQ, in fact during the period when the index was soaring. In the long run, without profits, stock prices will crumble. The key is often to worry less about revenue growth and more about profit growth.

Break-even point

Returning to the pencil example, consider another scenario. Orders are difficult to obtain, so salespeople start offering 5 per cent discounts. The unit selling price is now $0.95. Manufacturing cost remains at $0.90. Gross margin per unit is $0.05. Now 20,000 pencils have to be sold to make the same profit. The working capital requirement will double. The factory will be chaotic and overtime will increase. The total cost will probably not even be covered. The break-even point (see below) will be so much higher that the company almost certainly will not make a profit. And before that happens 20,000 pencils still have to be sold.

The break-even point (BEP) is the level of sales at which all the costs of running the business are covered. It can be illustrated as in Figure 20.5.

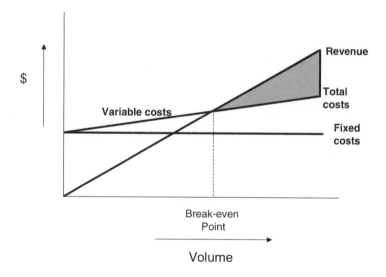

Figure 20.5 Break-even point

Fixed costs are those that are incurred even if there is no production. These would include rent, rates, heat, light, insurance and most salary and wage costs.

Variable costs are those related to the product or service. These could include materials, distribution, commissions, production bonuses and so on.

By drawing the fixed costs on the graph as a straight line, drawing the variable costs as building up from the fixed costs and the sales revenue increasing with sales volume, the break-even point is determined where the sales line intersects with the variable costs line.

BEP is easy to calculate:

BEP = Fixed costs/gross margin percentage

USING THE ANALYSIS TO COMPARE TWO COMPANIES

The analysis can be used to compare two or more companies, for example, you and your major competitor. To show the impact of the analysis comparison has been drawn between Dell and Compaq for the second quarter of 1999.

The analysis clearly shows that Dell is far more efficient in its management of operations than Compaq. The lower the cash conversion cycle, the more efficient the business use of cash and resources. Operational cash per $1 billion of revenue, defined as inventory + accounts receivable – accounts payable divided by the revenue shows that Dell is generating $40 million per billion of sales which can go directly to fund R&D, marketing, improved administration or facilities. It means that as long as Dell maintains or improves on this performance, extra revenue is throwing off cash at the operating level.

In contrast Compaq requires $491 million of operating cash to fund each $1 billion of additional revenue. At the operating level Compaq, on this quarter's numbers, requires nearly $1 of funding for each $2 of revenue generated. In terms of moving forward it is easy to see why Dell finds one aspect of growth so easy, and appealing, whereas for Compaq life is very difficult.

Much of Dell's efficiency comes from Michael Dell's original concept of eliminating the distributor function from the buying process. This enabled Dell to compete with Compaq and IBM during the early part of its corporate life by selling comparable computers at prices 15 per cent below Compaq's.

($ millions)

	Dell		Compaq	
	Qtr to	Qtr to	Qtr to	Qtr to
	7/30/1999	8/2/1998	6/30/1999	6/30/1998
Revenue	6,142	4,331	9,420	5,832
Growth %	42%		62%	
Cost of goods sold	4,788	3,346	7,484	4,722
Gross margin	1,354	985	1,936	1,110
Gross margin %	22%	23%	21%	19%
Administration & fixed cost	660	502	2,198	1,300
Break-even-point	2,994	2,207	10,695	6,830
Admin cost as a % of revenue	11%	12%	23%	22%

	Balance Sheet At 7/30/99			Balance Sheet At 6/30/99		
		% of Rev	Days		% of Rev	Days
Inventory (1)	336	5%	6	2,224	24%	27
Accounts receivable (2)	2,424	39%	36	6,556	70%	63
Accounts payable (3)	(3,007)	49%	57	(4,152)	44%	50
Net current assets (excl cash)	(247)	−4%		4,628	49%	
Cash conversion cycle			−15			39
Operational cash			(247)			4,628
Operational cash per $billion of revenue			($40)			$491

Figure 20.6 Comparison of Dell and Compaq

Dell did not stop driving efficiency, and in the period beginning around 1996 it changed the business model again by dramatically reducing the inventory of parts and moved to assembling computers after they were ordered. This also enabled them to customize computers to the requirements of the buyer.

In the current phase Dell is changing the selling process to Web-based ordering. Already more than $35 million per day is generated over the Web, some 43 per cent of total revenues. This is allowing Dell to reduce the number of sales representatives and helping customers to make better decisions about what to buy. It is also setting up special sites for corporate buyers that integrate with each company's purchasing system.

Physical distribution is through UPS, FedEx and other carriers that are at a cost that is lower than ever for Dell.

Because of Dell's efficient use of funds it can charge lower prices for its computers and still achieve reasonable profits. In fact the gross margin declined from 33 per cent in 1990 to 22 per cent in 1999. Selling, general and administrative expenses declined from 20.9 per cent to 9.2 per cent and operating income increased from 8 per cent to 11.2 per cent. In 1999 Dell was a $25 billion annual revenue company, growing at 40 per cent. In the tough personal computer business this is a fantastic performance. It is driven by excellent products, service, innovation and efficiency. When most competitors are losing money, Dell is still profitable. The gross margin might decline further, but allowing for the volatility in chip supplies, laptop screens and other problems this is a company that has the fundamentals right, and it shows through in all the figures.

This brings me to two earlier points. One is about leaning on creditors. Dell is not leaning on creditors, it is negotiating tough settlement terms with suppliers to which they are willing to agree. It is not late in paying invoices.

Secondly, the rule about companies having less than 25 per cent gross margin failing sooner or later. Generally it is a good rule. Leadership teams should aspire to achieve high margins. However, a business has to be viewed in terms of its total performance. In a fiercely competitive business Dell is winning and improving bottom line figures and percentages. The management recognizes margins have to improve and is changing the product mix to higher margin items, but also they know what is possible in the market. In the age of the Internet, efficiency will become crucial for many – perhaps most – businesses in a way that has never been true before. With comparison between products and price so easy and quick to make, margins will almost inevitably fall over a whole range of products and services. Differentiation is important, but as we discussed before, with mass customization the consumer will become his own differentiator. The whole approach to business will change.

In fairness it must be mentioned that Compaq had acquired Digital Equipment Corporation in June 1998 and through 1999 was still in the digesting process. Even allowing for this the operating efficiency of Dell is of a different order to that of Compaq.

TRADITIONAL COST ACCOUNTING

Some years ago someone had the brilliant idea of allocating overheads in line with direct labor costs. At that time indirect costs were perhaps 5 per cent or 10 per cent of direct costs, so the system was roughly correct. Today, the number of indirect workers exceeds that of direct workers by up to ten times, and it is possible to have an overhead burden of 1,000 per cent. On average, direct labor costs are now 15 per cent of the total cost of most manufactured goods, and that percentage is falling. Hence if a manager can cut one hour of direct cost, he or she is credited with up to ten hours of cost savings.

Looking at an absurd (although unfortunately true) situation, the new CEO of a major corporation had the managers obtain quotations for purchasing all production parts from outside sources. Wherever the cost from outside was lower, the production was sent out. The first run of this exercise resulted in 30 per cent of parts being sent out for manufacture. Factories closed, employees were sacked. The overhead did not decrease by much, but now each direct labor hour carried a larger overhead burden. Again all production was compared to outside quotations, and some more parts made outside. The overhead cost per direct hour went up again. Eventually the stupidity of the situation was seen, the CEO had all factories running flat out, parts were piled into stock, profits increased rapidly through efficiency gains and spread of overhead across high production. The CEO was awarded a large performance bonus, left the company, and another CEO had to save it from extinction.

This sounds ludicrous, but this is what some cost accounting systems have led to. The examples are legion: shipyard managers were measured by return on capital employed (RoCE), buildings are assets, so relocating staff out of buildings and then demolishing them improved the managers' RoCE. The inefficiency of having staff in crowded offices, when it produced no real cost saving, was not captured by the accounting system.

The other big problem with this type of cost accounting is that it can lead to promising new products being killed off. When a product is first produced, as the production workers begin to climb the learning curve, the direct hours are relatively high; with experience they will decrease. But these direct hours attract the indirect overhead, when in fact the amount of overhead time they are using in the offices, computer, secretarial, personnel, accounting, is often only proportional to their volume of production, which is small, not to the labor hours, which are comparatively high.

The same thinking applies to new service products, which when they are first introduced take time to 'shake down'. This increases direct costs and also attracts higher overhead charges. Hence the service looks unprofitable and might be scaled back before it has the chance to become really established.

ACTIVITY-BASED COSTING

From the data collection chapter you will remember that activity-based costing can uncover hidden costs and profits. This book is not about costing as such, but understanding costing systems is crucial to improving company profits.

There are four fundamental concepts that need to be understood in activity-based costing:

- Objects are the things we want to allocate costs to. They can be products, services, customers or markets.
- Resources represent the effort required either to produce an object or carry out a service. They create the costs involved in supplying the effort. People, machinery, buildings and computer systems are prime examples of resources.
- Activities are the work performed by the resources. These would include selling products, operating the management accounting system, developing a new computer system, setting up a machine, and purchasing components. In general activities refer to human actions, but they can also include various types of equipment usage.
- Cost drivers link the activities with the objects being costed. Cost drivers must be measurable, controllable and acceptable to the people in an organization. A cost driver for maintenance might be the number of machines in a department and the frequency with which they break down. If one new high-speed machine replaces all the existing machines and it requires less maintenance, then the cost driver is reduced. Identifying cost drivers is one of the most productive aspects of activity-based costing.

Because of the discipline it imposes, activity-based costing will give a sharper focus to determining customer and product profitability, competing in high-volume markets, controlling overheads and making more profitable investment decisions.

In BKT Strategy we use a simple workshop structure to identify high-cost customers who might not appear as such on the accounting ledgers. Normally we work with three separate groups: sales, warehousing (especially where warehousing also receives returned goods) and accounts receivable. The same approach is used with each group.

A list of customers is put up on a flipchart or overhead. It starts with the biggest in revenue terms and will usually cover the A and B customer segments and sometimes the C as well. A group of staff from the department, if possible all the staff in the department, are asked three questions for each customer:

1. Is this customer pleasant and easy to deal with or are they aggressive, querying everything and unwilling to discuss problems that may be of their causing. Give a mark of 1 to 5 with 1 being pleasant and 5 being aggressive.
2. Do you have a lot of contact with this customer? Do they take up more time than most customers? Give a 1 for less contact, 3 for average and 5 for more than average. (Make allowance for the size of the customer. Comparing two companies with the same purchasing level can be useful).
3. Do they always push for the maximum benefit they can obtain, delay payments on any pretext, return goods on any pretext and always blame your company for problems? Mark 1 to 5 with 1 being a normal business relationship and 5 being a company always looking for credits and reasons to delay payments.

The purpose of these questions is to identify customers who are eating away at margins in ways that might not show on traditional reports. Any customer with a score over 11 needs reviewing.

This (admittedly crude) approach identifies problem customers quickly and enables management to understand how they are 'stealing margin' and seek a solution, just as the HMO did with the industrial giant referred to in Chapter 21.

THE 10 PER CENT RULES

This very simple technique is tremendous at identifying the impact of opportunities and cost reduction. It is a simple scorecard that delivers great results.

The 10 per cent rules focus on the four means by which profits can be increased. They are illustrated based on the figures already produced for Franks Manufacturing. The four rules are:

1. Increase sales by 10 percent.
2. Decrease cost of sales by 10 per cent.
3. Decrease fixed cost by 10 per cent.
4. Increase price by 10 per cent.

The 10 per cent rules show what it is possible to achieve. But companies cannot usually change by as much as 10 per cent at one time. What the 10 per cent rules indicate is where the effort will have the greatest impact. This returns to the 80/20 rule and to looking for those actions that will have the most impact on profit performance. This analysis is at the heart of rapid profit improvement that is often, though not always, possible in a company.

In Franks Manufacturing the results look like those shown in Figure 20.7.

($000s)	2001	Increase Sales by 10%	Decrease Cost of Sales by 10%	Decrease Fixed Cost by 10%	Increase Sales Price by 10%
	$				
Revenue	15,297,462	16,827,208	15,297,462	15,297,462	16,827,208
Cost of sales	11,910,635	13,101,699	10,719,572	11,910,635	11,910,635
Distribution costs	268,390	295,229	268,390	268,390	268,390
Total variable costs	12,179,025	13,396,928	10,987,962	12,179,025	12,179,025
Operating income	3,118,437	3,430,281	4,309,501	3,118,437	4,648,183
Gross margin percentage	20.4%	20.4%	28.2%	20.4%	27.6%
Administration & fixed cost	2,890,201	2,890,201	2,890,201	2,601,181	2,890,201
Income before tax	228,236	540,080	1,419,300	517,256	1,757,982
Break-even point	14,177,853	14,177,853	10,259,365	12,760,067	10,463,016

Figure 20.7 The 10% rules

In a business with a low gross margin percentage, rapid improvement will usually come through cost reduction and price increases. Therefore, the first two items to look at are the decrease in cost of sales by 10 per cent and the increase in price by 10 per cent. Taking the first of these, have a look at the management accounts and at the largest elements in the cost of sales. Then brainstorm how these can be reduced using charts similar to Figures 20.8 and 20.9.

In improvement by incremental percentage we work with teams throughout the business to establish areas where we can generate either increased sales or higher sales price, or decrease cost of sales or fixed cost. Each change is evaluated and added to the scorecard so they can see the impact on the business. The most promising ideas are evaluated and developed into performance targets.

	2001 $	Increase Sales by 3% $	Decrease Cost of Sales by 5% $	Decrease Fixed Cost by 1% $	Increase Sales Price by 2% $
Revenue	15,297,462	15,756,386	15,756,386	15,756,386	16,071,514
Cost of sales	11,910,635	12,267,954	11,654,556	11,654,556	11,654,556
Distribution costs	268,390	276,442	276,442	276,442	276,442
Total variable costs	12,179,025	12,544,396	11,930,998	11,930,998	11,930,998
Operating income	3,118,437	3,211,990	3,825,388	3,825,388	4,140,516
Gross margin percentage	20.4%	20.4%	24.3%	24.3%	25.8%
Administration & fixed cost	2,890,201	2,890,201	2,890,201	2,861,299	2,861,299
Income before tax	228,236	321,789	935,187	964,089	1,279,217
Break-even point	14,177,853	14,177,853	11,904,446	11,785,401	11,106,203

Each percentage change is justified using the Table 20.9.

Figure 20.8 Improvement by incremental percentage

Using the 10% rules and charts

In one company the cost of sales had to be reduced. Reject rates were running at 7 per cent. A very simple and low-cost change in the manufacturing process reduced these to less than 3 per cent. The result was a dramatic increase in profit. We then found ways to improve production scheduling, reduce set-up times, especially on bottleneck processes and machines. It really is no more than the Toyota system where activities and processes are continuously being pushed to a higher level of performance. The scorecard just lets participants know what effect achieving the initiatives will have on bottom line performance. Knowing the impact increases the effort to achieve the result, especially where the team has developed the program.

The same approach applies to fixed costs. Review the key processes in administration and sales, look for where the large sums are being spent. Challenge any sacred cows on fixed cost; see if they can be made into variable cost.

At this stage, referring back to the analysis of products by volume and profit contribution and the customer analysis can help managers begin to discover a far more creative approach to reducing costs and improving service. It is possible to produce a list of the areas of potential saving but usually managers, with a little prompting, know where to start looking. This approach is far more productive than going through a checklist.

Each percentage is justified, as each column is completed, by writing out how this change is achieved. This is done whether the change is positive or negative

Achieved by:

Increase sales by % through –

Decrease COS by % through –

Decrease distribution costs by % through –

Decrease fixed costs by % through –

Increase sales price by % through –

Figure 20.9 Change justification chart

Improving sales and margins is an inherent part of the strategy development and will be looked at many times. At this stage, other than looking at obvious things, such as focusing the sales force on more attractive customers and trying selected price increases, there is probably a limited amount that should be done. The other vital action is to make sure that all the executives and managers understand the importance of the gross margin percentage and work at how to increase it, rather than win business at low prices or with added features that are not charged for.

The 10 per cent rules change from business to business. They apply equally to service or manufacturing companies, as do all the analyses used. Perhaps finally we can do a quick 10 per cent rules analysis on Compaq.

Following on from this are some hypothetical numbers on what performance improvement may be possible.

Because distribution is such a key element in driving efficiency, and is critical to the business model, that row is included though the figure is not readily available. Compaq will also certainly face price erosion, even if that only means selling more powerful computers at the same price. It must increase sales, which should be helped by the price reduction and slash variable and fixed costs. The real actions are much more complicated than this model, but a slightly more complex version of this model would help to keep everyone focused on what has to be achieved.

Many small and medium-sized companies will be driven by the Internet to evaluate their efficiency. Often there is no clear framework to structure any discussion about them. This model used at the

($000s)	Current Performance $	Increase Sales by 10% $	Decrease Cost of Sales by 10% $	Decrease Fixed Cost by 10% $	Increase Sales Price by 10% $
Revenue	9,420	10,362	9,420	9,420	10,362
Cost of Sales	7,484	8,232	6,736	7,484	7,484
Distribution Costs	0	0	0	0	0
Total Variable Costs	**7,484**	**8,232**	**6,736**	**7,484**	**7,484**
Operating Income	1,936	2,130	2,684	1,936	2,878
Gross Margin Percentage	21%	21%	28%	21%	28%
Administration & Fixed Cost	2,198	2,198	2,198	1,978	2,198
Income Before Tax	(262)	(68)	486	(42)	680
Break Even Point	10,695	10,695	7,713	9,625	7,914

Figure 20.10 The 10% rules applied to Compaq

($000s)	Current Performance $	Increase Sales 15% $	Decrease Cost of Sales 8% $	Decrease Fixed Cost 5% $	Increase Sales Price -6% $
Revenue	9,420	10,833	10,833	10,833	10,183
Cost of Sales	7,484	8,607	7,918	7,918	7,918
Distribution Costs	0	0	0	0	0
Total Variable Costs	**7,484**	**8,607**	**7,918**	**7,918**	**7,918**
Operating Income	1,936	2,226	2,915	2,915	2,265
Gross Margin Percentage	21%	21%	27%	27%	22%
Administration & Fixed Cost	2,198	2,198	2,198	2,088	2,088
Income Before Tax	(262)	28	717	827	177
Break Even Point	10,695	10,695	8,169	7,760	9,388

Figure 20.11 Margin performance improvement at Compaq

operational level of the company helps everyone to see the impact of the actions they propose and how they must achieve given targets, whether in revenue increase or cost reduction, to generate the performance required.

This analysis should not only be completed on competitors, but also on major customers and suppliers. The insights it reveals about their business, and also your company's position in the value chain, are often of major strategic importance.

BUSINESS UNIT CELLS AND MARKET/PRODUCT UNITS

For many years there has been a trend to structure organizations as small business units, based either on product cells or distinct market/ product units. One of the keys to making these small business units into successful profit centers is to provide them with simple, easily understood reports on the key financial issues that highlight the performance of their unit.

The analysis of assets and liabilities discussed above will ensure that such units carefully monitor their cash position and it can be seen how they are utilizing assets. The analysis of performance ensures that they are aware of costs and margins.

This form of budgeting and financial analysis enables them continually to review how they can improve their performance and results.

MONTHLY MANAGEMENT PERFORMANCE SUMMARY

Some years ago I went to a lunch in London where Sir Kenneth Cork was a guest speaker. He was the most famous UK insolvency practitioner. De Lorean cars was one of his assignments.

He said that when he was appointed as either receiver or liquidator of a company, he would ask for information. Sure enough, someone would go and dig out a computer report and give him the information. 'What', he would ask, 'is the use of information that no one is acting on?'

He went on to say that every manager ought to be able to leave the office and, without having any papers, be able to plan the basic strategy for the firm or department from the knowledge carried in his or her head. It is this ability to think strategically on information that is carried in the head that needs to be inculcated in all leadership team members.

Many leading captains of industry receive key figures daily, and in certain industries this is the right approach. For many businesses daily is perhaps too often, but the key figures must always be available at least on a monthly basis.

Some monthly management reports, however, are a tribute to the ingenuity of accountants. Every detail is there, but most managers cannot understand what the report means. Some executives can absorb and understand a large volume of data. One managing director of a substantial company can read a 40-page management report, absolutely packed with figures, and can discuss it in detail with each individual director afterwards; but in my experience he is the exception.

Most executives read through the report, pick out sections that mean something to them and make comments on those, but very little is done in the way of strategic decision-making.

Every leadership team should decide which are the key figures for their company. My view is that there should be no more than seven key figures. There is a rule called the 'magical number seven', which says that the number of pieces of information that most people can retain in their short-term memory is seven, plus or minus two. I have met a large number of people who can only remember five and from choice that is the number to stop at if possible. Figure 20.12 suggests some key figures that you might want to choose from, although there may be some additional ones that are far more important for your business. You will notice that there is a mixture of financial and operational information.

If any one of these measures is moving out of line or over budget, then supporting data will track exactly what is happening. The key thing is that the information is acted on. If a performance figure is in line with expectations, the decision may be made that at this time no improvement in that performance will be looked for, perhaps because the impact of any improvement would not be as strong as other actions that could be taken. If performance is out of line or not up to budget, the action is to work through the supporting data to pinpoint why this is happening and what can be done about it. If the management performance summary does not result in action, it is a waste of time.

It is vital that the information chosen for this summary is key information. Even if it also appears in, say, the sales or production reports, if it is important to the overall performance of the firm, then include it in the monthly summary.

Deciding what is the key information is a major input into strategy formulation. The best approach is to decide what the key measures are now, and then, when the strategic options are decided, determine what the key measures will be in the future.

Sales:	$ _____
BEP:	$ _____
Gross margin %	_____%
Net cash in (out)	
this month	$ _____
next month	$ _____
Debtor days	_____
Inventory days	_____
Creditor days	_____
Cash conversion cycle	_____
Forward orders in hand	
value	$ _____
production period	_____
Stocks (critical items)	_____
Staff numbers (by category)	_____
Absenteeism	_____
Top selling lines:	
1.	$ _____
2.	$ _____
3.	$ _____
Lowest-selling lines:	
1.	$ _____
2.	$ _____
3.	$ _____
Number of customers this month	_____
Number of orders this month	_____
Average order value	$ _____

Figure 20.12 Monthly management performance summary

INCREASING MANAGEMENT IMPACT

Performance summary

Often the objective of these reports is for the leadership team to be able to pick up trends quickly and communicate them to their staff. Graphs will increase the impact of the report. Two pages with three graphs on each page, for example, give a vivid indication of how the firm is doing. Seeing the lines on a graph going where the leadership team wants them to is a powerful performance monitor in its own right. Below are three graphs that are generally useful.

Despite the ease of producing graphs with modern software, too few businesses use them in their reporting. Yet because they show trends they are strategically the most powerful medium.

Sales and cost performance

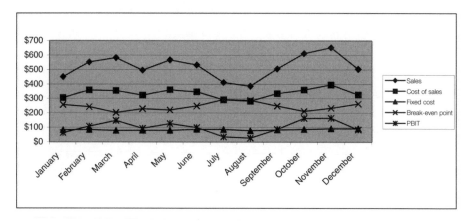

Figure 20.13 Sales and cost performance

Figure 20.13 covers sales, cost of sales, fixed costs and breakeven point. Sometimes it is instructive to mark the profit line (PBIT, profit before interest and tax) along the bottom of the graph, just to make it apparent to everyone how small it is in relation to the other financial figures in the company.

This graph is of particular help in focusing managers on the fact that it is profits that are important. Sales with good margins are vital as a means of increasing profits. Increased revenue for its own sake can cause problems. The saying is: 'Revenue is vanity, profit is sanity.'

Cash performance

On a graph like Figure 20.14 plot net cash flow (NCF), cash in and cash out, with actual figures for this month and forecasts for the next one, two or three months. Generally most companies can plot the next two to three months' cash flow with some accuracy. They know what they have invoiced over the last two months and what they will invoice this month. They have a fair idea of how that cash will flow in from their current debtor days. The cash outflow is known with precision, usually because it can be manipulated over a short time period if necessary.

Sometimes it is useful to plot the corporate borrowing limit on the chart. This concentrates the mind wonderfully.

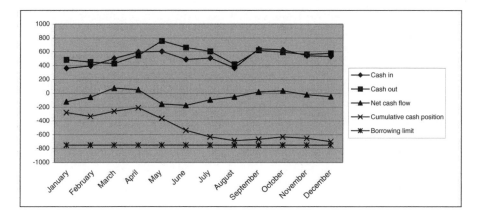

Figure 20.14 Cash performance in $

Performance in days

The other graph that is useful to most businesses is to plot the perform-ance in days (Figure 20.15). This really does indicate if the business is running out of control and to what extent the company is leaning on creditors to fund working capital.

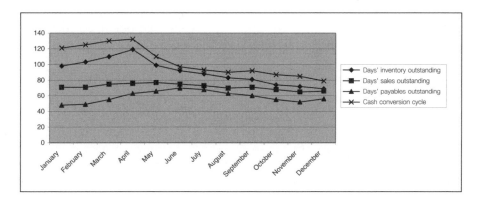

Figure 20.15 Performance in days

DEVELOP FINANCIAL REQUIREMENTS FOR NEXT BUDGET YEAR

In many organizations there are expectations on the financial perform-ance that will be required for the following year. If this is the case in your business it is sometimes worth developing a scenario so that the strategy can be tested against the expectations from time to time in the process. This review will have to occur again at the end of the process to ensure that budget and strategy are in agreement.

By making this rough draft of a budget reasonably detailed it forces the leadership team to consider what has to be delivered by the strategy, and will often encourage them to adopt a more radical or proactive strategy.

It is not always necessary to develop these financial expectations at this stage; a judgment has to be made on when articulating these will produce the best thinking or attitude changes in the leadership team.

ORGANIZING THE FINANCIAL ANALYSIS WORKSHOP

The financial analysis is conducted during the preparation part of the process. The presentation and discussion on the financial analysis is part of the leadership team's first workshop and will usually follow the analysis of the data collection findings.

Start the session by running through the analysis of assets and liabilities. Use figures from the last two or three years. Follow this with the analysis of performance, again for the past two or three so those trends can be clearly seen. Discuss why events happened as they did, with everyone making input. Ask the question 'With hindsight how could we have done better?'

One of the important points to remember here is that not only is past company performance being discussed, but also non-financial executives are being taught some fairly simple financial analysis. Be prepared to take time to explain the terms to those who do not understand them.

From this base, now that there is some common agreement on the company's performance over the last few years, move on to discuss the current situation. Where an analysis has been made of major customers and suppliers, compare their financial performance to your company's and analyze the strongest position in the value chain. This could be a point at which to discuss how your company can strengthen its position in the overall value chain.

Present the performance graphs using both overhead projection and with handouts so participants can draw and make notes on their own copies. Keep the discussion to issues that affect the future; do not let it become an analysis of the past, with recriminations. All the time relate the discussion to performance now, to current conditions and how they are dealt with.

When discussing the graphs, begin with sales and cost performance. The most effective approach is to build up one line at a time, and the previous 12 months is usually a good time-frame. However, if there have been dramatic changes over the last two or three years, split the graph into three-month periods and show those years. It is important to stress where your company is now and where you want its financial performance to be in a year's time.

Next move on to cash performance. Relate cash performance to gross margin, ensuring that everybody understands how the figures relate. In this way the VP sales will begin to understand why it is important not to give discounts, because lowering the gross margin also deprives the company of cash and profits in the medium term. He will also be able to explain this in simple terms to his team.

In finishing with performance days, the objective is to introduce the type of report that will be used in future to indicate performance in these two areas.

Next present any additional graphs that are specific to the company. At this stage use the 10 per cent rules to identify the areas of greatest pay-off. Use the approach outlined in this chapter: first, find out where the greatest pay-off will occur and explore some ideas on performance improvement. Mention that this approach will be part of a workshop held with other members of staff later.

Finally, if this is considered the best time, produce the expectation charts for the next year (see Figure 20.16). Developing these will often help to decide what degree of strategic change is required.

CALCULATIONS

A useful comparison for checking performance on inventory levels, accounts receivable and creditors, is to convert the figures into stock days, debtor days and creditor days. The calculations are given below.

Days inventory outstanding (DIO)

DIO = inventory/cost of sales × 365 days (or the number of days in the report period)

This is an approximate method (accurate to within one to two days). If the cost of goods sold includes the manufacturing overhead then the days figure will only be approximate; it is better to include just materials and labor.

Days sales outstanding (DSO)

DSO = accounts receivable × 365/sales (revenue) (or days in period)

In Europe VAT has to be stripped from the accounts receivable; the calculation is:

accounts receivable excluding VAT = debtors/VAT % (UK VAT rate is 1.175)

Days payables outstanding (DPO)

DPO = accounts payable × 365 /cost of sales

Again, in Europe VAT has to be stripped from the accounts payable figure.

Examples from Franks Manufacturing

DIO = inventory × 365/cost of sales = \$4,436,671 × 365 days/\$11,910,635 = 136 days

DSO = accounts receivable × 365/revenue = \$3,140,708 × 365/ \$15,297,462 = 75 days

DPO = accounts payable × 365/cost of sales (or goods sold) = \$3,432,135 × 365/\$11,910,635 = 105 days

Expectation 1

Sales/profit relationship

	Current Year	Plan Year
Sales		
PBIT		
% PBIT to sales		
Interest		
Taxation		
	————	————
Retained profits	————	————

Quarters 1–4

	1	2	3	4
Sales				
PBIT				
PBIT as % of sales				

Expectation 2

Orders received

	Current Year	Plan Year
Orders received – for delivery in 1 year		
– for delivery beyond 1 year		
	————	————
Total orders received		
Year-end order bank		
– for delivery in 1 year		
– for delivery beyond 1 year		
	————	————
Total year end order bank		

Expectation 3

Income statement ratios

	Current Year	Plan Year
Break-even sales value		
Materials as a % of sales		

Figure 20.16 Expectation charts

Labor as a % of sales
Overheads as a % of sales

Gross margin %
Net margin %
R&D expenditure as a % of sales

Expectation 4

Cash flow

	Current Year	Plan Year
Operating cash flow (pre interest)		
Excess/deficit of operating cash flow over PBIT		

Expectation 5

Employees

	Current Year	Plan Year
Average number of employees		
Sales per employee		
Average cost per employee		
Average added value per employee		

Expectation 6

Balance sheet ratios

	Current Year	Plan Year
Total sales/average net assets employed		
Return on average net assets employed		
Capital approvals/depreciation ratio		

Quarterly averages

	1	2	3	4
Trade working capital percentage of sales				
Average days sales in accounts receivable				
Average days cost in inventories				
Average days cost in accounts payable				

Figure 20.16 (Continued)

21

Business analysis

INTRODUCTION

Many of the techniques included in this section are well known and well established. There is no apology for this. Most businesses do not need more new analysis techniques; the effective application of those that already exist is sufficient. There are huge numbers of businesses, including very big ones, that have nothing but the most superficial analysis of their business. These techniques will take them a long way to improving their business performance.

A start has already been made on analyzing the company and its current performance. In the data collection stage some of the data was analyzed by presenting it in formats that made it easier to understand. The past financial performance of the company has been examined in some depth and the 10 per cent rules have indicated where efforts should be concentrated to improve performance in the future. The leadership team has provided some ideas on how they see the business developing in the personal vision forms.

The next part of the analysis uses techniques that enhance the leadership team's understanding of the business and the direction it may take in the future.

Particular techniques can help to understand the major forces that have an impact on a business and relate these to the company and its goals. However, any technique needs to be used carefully and with some subtlety. The SBP process must not be presented as 'We are now at page 126 and this is what we do'. The underlying process is one of trying to understand the business, where it is and where you want it to go. It is deeply personal and highly important to everyone involved with the company. Techniques applied crudely can make it feel more like an 'off the shelf' strategic business plan, rather than a specific, absolutely unique plan for your company.

ORGANIZATION OF THE BUSINESS ANALYSIS WORKSHOP

Once again, ensure that the important flipcharts, especially those that summarize discussions, are put on the wall. Any actions that need to be taken as a result of the business analysis should be agreed at the end of this session.

THREE-STAGE SIEVE

The SBP approach follows a logical sequence of analysis. It begins by examining some attributes that any company needs if it is to grow and then explores the degree to which these attributes are present or absent in the company. This enables a quick overview of the business to be obtained. The approach is called base analysis and is the first part of the three-stage sieve. The strengths and weaknesses of the company are then brainstormed and refined to produce a key list. The third stage of the analysis is to determine the company's distinctive capability. The process is shown diagrammatically in Figure 21.1.

These three sieves sift out progressively where the real strengths of the business lie and make apparent its weaknesses.

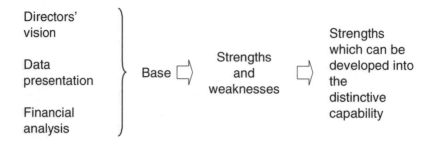

Figure 21.1 The three stage sieve

THE BASE ANALYSIS

The base analysis helps to establish if the foundation blocks of the company are strong enough to enable it to grow, or even survive.

This technique is used in two main situations: in small and medium-sized companies and divisions, where it can be more effective than a strengths and weaknesses analysis; and when management teams want to obtain agreement on the strengths and weaknesses of the business with a structured approach. In this case the key strengths and weaknesses are identified using the base analysis and developed using the Strengths and Weaknesses development charts. The usual approach is to put managers in pairs and ask them to put marks against each item in the columns of the base analysis. A mark of one denotes that they believe the company is weak in this area, a ten denotes that they think it is strong. The results from each pairing are recorded on a flipchart and any differences resolved by discussion. This ensures that the mindsets are aligned before explaining the strategy to the managers.

The base analysis looks at the five attributes that are crucial to maintaining and improving performance:

- the existing resource base;
- the accumulated experience base;
- the control base;
- the leadership base;
- the ideas base.

The outline is shown in Figure 21.2.

The existing resource base

The existing resource base is important because it dictates the ease with which the company can move forward from its current situation into new markets, products and means of doing business. It covers aspects of the company such as:

- Is there adequate current liquidity and availability of finance, either existing or capable of being raised, to fund expansion or new ventures?
- Is the technology up to date and do managers and employees know how to use the technology profitably?

Existing resource base	Accumulated experience base	Control base	Leadership base	Ideas base
Liquidity and availability of finance	Age of company	Adequacy of information and control systems	Common vision	Research and development
Technology	Experience of: • raising capital	Degree of professionalism	Clear role for the leadership team	Number of ideas currently being seriously
Physical assets	• product development	and responsibility of management	Clear operating model for the	considered
Labor: quality/ skills/age/attitude/ flexibility	• different markets • leveraging external agents and resources	team	leadership team Spread of age of leadership team	Degree of development and testing of these ideas
Product range and life	• moving location • managing growth and a bigger	Planning and budgeting systems that allow for growth	Flexible and positive attitude to change	Degree of market planning for these
Managerial resources	company	Degree of delegation to management	Strategic awareness and	ideas
Customer base and loyalty			understanding of environment	

Figure 21.2 Assessing the base potential for growth

- Are there modern and flexible production/operation facilities that provide low-cost throughput and a flexible range of products/ services?
- Are there skilled and adaptable managers and employees with a positive attitude to change and to the future?
- Will the product base continue to produce cash flow and profits in the foreseeable future, without cash outflows for new development or promotion?
- Is the current management strong enough, both in quality and depth, to grow the business?
- Is the customer base impressed with the current service the company provides and willing to accept new products and services from the company?

The accumulated experience base

The accumulated experience base looks at the backgrounds of managers. It considers their knowledge, skill and ability to manage and develop a company in boom times and depressions, to build a layer of effective management under the leadership teams to develop and commercialize new products, to raise finance and negotiate deals. This is that strange mixture of in-depth knowledge of their business and experience of the wider world, of being bright enough to spot the opportunity and sufficiently streetwise not to be taken in. Above all, it means the ability to work as a team, with each member making a contribution but without overlapping too much with other team members.

In 1986 in the United Kingdom there was a management buy-out of an assortment of businesses from Cadbury Schweppes. The management buy-out group formed a company named Premier Brands and raised £92 million from venture capitalists. Initially every member of the buy-out management was a former Cadbury Schweppes management trainee. The financiers involved were unhappy with this and insisted on one extra executive joining the board who had experience from outside the industry, to ensure that the board of directors had at least one member with a different perspective. It is this kind of gap that causes problems with high tech companies when they fail to bring in outside expertise. This kind of gap in experience is what the accumulated experience base analysis is designed to identify, including such aspects as the following:

- Does the leadership team have experience of trading in different markets; using a number of distribution channels; changing the product mix; leading and training a sales force; conducting market research in a number of product areas; extending the life of flagging products and services?
- Does the leadership team have product development experience, especially taking a new idea from conception through to commercialization? Knowing how to manage timescales is one of the major skills required here.
- Has the leadership team worked in organizations of different sizes, some as small as the current business, others much larger? This will give them an appreciation of the different organization structures that are needed at different stages in a company's growth and should avoid them becoming locked into an inappropriate structure.
- Is the leadership team capable of negotiating deals, whether for new premises, finance, acquiring companies or a major sales contract? Negotiation is a skill that must exist within the leadership group. At least one member of the team needs extensive experience of skilful negotiating.
- Finally, does experience exist in the group of using external agents: accountants, solicitors, bankers, advertising agencies, design groups and so on? In his book *The Age of Unreason* (1989) Charles Handy

describes the company of the future as having a core management group who will control the critical functions, surrounded by a number of suppliers who will provide all the services necessary for the company to operate. One of the skills of an organization will be in managing this supplier group.

The control base

The control base must be adequate to meet the needs of the business. This means that the leadership team and budget holders in the company receive the information they need to make decisions and manage their responsibilities.

As described in Chapter 7, the best approach is for monthly reports that consist of a limited number of graphs to give impact to the key financial measures, followed by up to seven key items of data, with supporting information to enable managers to dig deeper into those areas that are moving off track. Areas to examine include:

- Does the information control system ensure that managers are never surprised by an event which someone in the company knew or suspected would happen?
- Is a degree of realism shown by managers in interpreting the financial and management reports?
- Is there evidence that managers plan, budget forward and then manage the company to the budgets? This means they do more than put the budget in a drawer and only look at it every month when the next print-out arrives.
- Which level does the control system extend to in the company? In a manufacturing company, does it reach down to the level of employees, or supervisors or the production manager, and what impact does it have on performance? A control system that supplies information to employees and can affect their performance positively is a real asset to the company. That is why charts on walls that inform employees of their performance, or colored tags on production items which indicate the day of the week on which they are required for shipping, are so effective: it is easy to remember that all blue-tagged items have to be shipped by Thursday and hence they should not be seen in the factory on a Friday.

The leadership base

The leadership base is crucial to the future of the company. We have already looked at how to build a strong top management team. This is the first aspect of creating a leadership base, a united and committed leadership team effectively using their joint resources to direct the company. Under this heading the following questions are considered:

- Is there a common vision of where the company is going among all members of senior management?
- What are the critical aspects of the business that the CEO will concentrate his or her attention on?
- Is there a spread of age in the leadership team?
- Is there a flexible and positive attitude to change?
- Is the management style task- or people-orientated and how appropriate is this style to the future of the business?
- How is ownership vested? Is it through autonomy of decision within specified parameters, through a board of directors dominated by bankers and venture capitalists, or is it vested in an owner/executive group? What effect does this have on the performance needs of the company? In this respect, ratchet arrangements with venture capitalists, whereby each year's profit performance either increases or dilutes the owner's shareholding in the company, focus attention on short-term issues at the expense of longer-term considerations. Involving venture capitalists in the strategic business planning process can encourage them to review this kind of arrangement if it is seen to be beneficial to the overall performance of the company.

The ideas base

The ideas base is the key to the future growth of the company. Unless there are a number of ideas on how to improve the company, through developing new products, penetrating new markets, or changing the method of doing business, then the company has a bleak future. But merely generating ideas is not enough to guarantee that they will be successful.

There are three clear stages in the development of new products/markets/business methods: ideas generation; development of the idea into a product/service/market system that meets a clear customer need, can be delivered at a price the customer will pay and provides a good margin for the company; and commercialization of the idea to be successful in the market. This requires a degree of 'fit' with the company's operations and sales, plus managers who are motivated and believe it will be a success.

When examining the ideas base consider the following:

- How many ideas have been generated over the past year? How many are still at the ideas stage? How many are under active development?
- How many have reached the market?
- Of the ideas that have been launched – product, market or system – how many have achieved their budgeted performance?

This data will be readily available if base data form 10, innovation, has been completed.

Overall, the five bases produce a solid and practical profile of the company's potential for change and development that can be used for assessment. The profile does not, however, indicate how these parameters will mesh together in practice in a dynamic situation. In effect the profile is a 'position audit' of the company at a particular time. As the company faces and copes with change, then almost by definition this base potential will change.

The output from the base analysis is to identify the key areas where the company needs to put in effort and resources to provide a solid base for future growth.

STRENGTHS AND WEAKNESSES ANALYSIS

This second sieve is the first half of a SWOT analysis (strengths, weaknesses, opportunities, threats). Strengths and weaknesses are the internal part of the analysis; opportunities and threats are the external part and are covered in Chapter 22.

The output from a strengths and weaknesses analysis should be the four, five or six key strengths on which the strategy can be based and a similar number of weaknesses which are of critical importance to the future of the company.

Conducting a strengths and weaknesses session

The first phase of the workshop concentrates on identification. This is a brainstorming session in which participants are asked to list the strengths of the business. Write all the words and descriptions suggested on a flipchart. When the impetus of the session gradually dies, do exactly the same with weaknesses.

It is important to remember the ground rules of brainstorming. When ideas are being generated and members of the group are contributing their thoughts, no criticism of any idea is allowed. Each person can only contribute new material, either by building on previous ideas or by offering completely new ideas.

The next stage is grouping. Return to the list of strengths. Group similar strengths together and develop them into simple phrases and sentences so that everyone is sure about their nature and meaning.

Some elements are perceived as both strength and weakness. For instance, if a company sells 50 per cent of its total production to Sears, is that strength or weakness? Sears has very close ties with their suppliers and has a reputation in the main for treating them honestly. The company pays on time, provides reasonable continuity of work and negotiates a fair price. However, it has stopped using some suppliers in the past without a great deal of warning, and in difficult trading times has unilaterally reduced prices paid to suppliers for goods. Therefore it is possible to argue that if Sears represents 50 per cent of a company's sales, this can be viewed as both strength and weakness.

Another strength that is often mentioned is 'our people'. This is followed by a eulogy on their enthusiasm, loyalty and determination to succeed. Companies in similar industries draw their employees from similar sources. The raw working ability resource of most company employees is the same. The critical strength that has to be identified is what it really is about your people and the way they are organized and motivated that gives you strength over and above your competitors. Equally, what are the weaknesses in your people? It may be, for instance, that you cannot employ enough with the right qualifications or attitude to meet the demands of your business.

The real value of the strengths and weaknesses exercise lies in the discussion that arises on the differing perceptions of the management team. Understanding the real strategic strength of the business is critical in developing the distinctive capability.

The third stage of the workshop is refining, continually revising the lists of strengths and weaknesses until there are no more than four of each.

In complex situations, the analysis at the workshop itself is only carried out at a fairly crude and generalized level. Refining and analysis of the results can takes time and it is often better in these cases for it to be done by a small team outside the main workshop. If this is so, the analysis is included in the first draft report and the output discussed at the next workshop. However, in more straightforward situations refining can be done in the workshop. To speed up the process the leadership team can be split into two groups, one to summarize the strengths and the other the weaknesses. Each group then presents its summary to the rest of the team. Based on a wealth of experience of the company, the leadership team can fairly quickly decide what are the key issues.

To refine the list, ask why the strengths *are* strengths. Describe their characteristics and whether they are unique to the company. How can they be used in the strategic development of the business? The same process is followed with weaknesses. Once a maximum of four key strengths and weaknesses has been produced, and there is agreement on the way they are phrased, put the flipchart sheets on the wall of the meeting room to remind the group of what they are.

Figures 21.3 and 21.4 provide a structure to help groups think through the strengths and weaknesses exercise and also to relate the exercise far more clearly to the SBP process. Often this analysis will lead to some fairly immediate actions.

Description of strength	Impact strength has on the company and the competitive advantage conferred	Are you stronger than all competitors in this strength? List those competitors nearest in strength and how they use the strength	How can it be further developed?

Figure 21.3 Strengths

Description of weakness	Criticality to achieving goals/growing the business and improving the profits	Options to correct critical weakness eg outsourcing, functional development, competence development, acquisition	Timescale in which weakness needs to be corrected and realistic achievement timescale

Figure 21.4 Weaknesses

There is an interesting spin-off from this exercise. A rough check can be made on the morale of a company represented by the number of items on the first two attempts at the list of strengths and weaknesses. If the two sides are roughly in balance, or the strengths predominate, it is a reasonable assumption that morale is fairly positive within the workshop group and probably within the company. If, on the other hand, the list of weaknesses is significantly longer than the list of strengths, it could indicate negative attitudes, poor morale or a 'can't do' mentality. This could be the biggest potential weakness in the company, but it may not be mentioned in the list.

There can also be another hidden message in the list of strengths and weaknesses. When the workshop is finished, use the grouped lists and against each strength put down its source. The list of sources might include management, administration, finance, sales, marketing, operations, research and development, personnel, plus any others that are appropriate for the company. Look through the list for one or two departments that seem to feature strongly as a source of strength or any department that does not appear in the list. Repeat this for the weaknesses, highlighting those departments that are seen as a source of weakness and those that do not appear in the list at all.

What is revealed by this departmental analysis has to be used carefully so as not to make winners and losers of those in the group. If the sales department does not appear in the list of strengths and does feature strongly in the list of weaknesses, the sales director is likely to become defensive, especially if he or she feels that the process is a 'set-up'. Hence if the information is presented to the group the facilitator must stress that it is being considered from the viewpoint of the whole company and as part of the planning for taking the company forward. This is not always easy, especially if there is a feeling in the group that one director has not been accomplishing as much as they expected and the results of the strengths and weaknesses session highlight that.

SUMMARY

Four forms of analysis have now been carried out: directors' attitudes, financial, base and strengths and weaknesses. Others will be completed later in the process.

Now is a good time to stop and think where we have reached. In terms of the basis from which the future will be built, is the company sufficiently competent in all five bases? If not, then what action is going to be taken to correct the areas of weakness?

How strong are the strengths, how potentially damaging are the weaknesses? What action needs to be taken? How confident is the leadership team that a real distinctive capability exists in the current strengths that differentiates the company from the competition? How far can we enhance this distinctive capability? What action, if any, needs to be taken now?

22

Some useful techniques

INTRODUCTION

There is a point in strategic planning when there is a need to look at particular areas of the business. The type of analysis used will depend on the situation of the company. Throughout most of the chapters there are specific techniques for developing goals and strategic options. Those described here make up a pot pourri of workshop models I have found useful in developing strategy.

The approach suggested is to read through this chapter, think about the most critical issues in developing a strategic business plan for the company and then use the appropriate technique. The techniques shown here are useful process tools; that is, they can be used for analyzing data, developing understanding, building consensus and making decisions in a strategy workshop. Figure 22.1 shows how the techniques fit together.

Before beginning to describe the techniques, it is worth repeating that SBP is not primarily about techniques, but they do have a role to play. However, using too many techniques hinders progress and my advice to readers is to use these tools sparingly.

PRODUCT/SERVICE ANALYSIS

Product life cycle

The theory of the product life cycle is that all products, brands and industries move through identifiable phases from introduction through

Figure 22.1 Useful techniques map

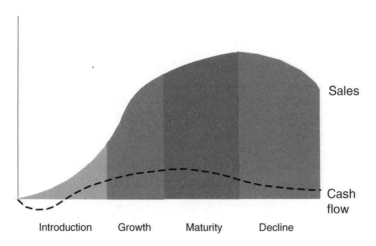

Figure 22.2 Product life cycle

to maturity and decline (see Figure 22.2). Associated with each phase will be changes in the unit margin, the gross margin and the product or brand strategy.

The phases in the product life cycle are:

- introduction – a period of slow sales growth as the product is introduced to the market. Profits are non-existent in this stage because of the heavy expenses of product introduction;
- growth – a period of rapid market acceptance and substantial profit improvement;

- maturity – a period when sales growth slows down because the product has achieved acceptance by most of the potential buyers. Profits stabilize or decline because of increased marketing outlays to defend the product against competition;
- decline – the period when sales show a strong downward drift and profits are eroded.

As with all the techniques that follow, the value of the product life cycle lies in understanding how to use it. Figure 22.3 describes the general characteristics in each phase. Figure 22.4 outlines typical responses in each phase in the product life cycle. The key to using the technique is to decide the phase that products are in and the most attractive option to develop them next. It might be decided that the chart does not describe the situation adequately or correctly for the product or services in this market. That is fine, as long as it encourages the identification of the exact circumstances for the products and services and what needs to be done with them.

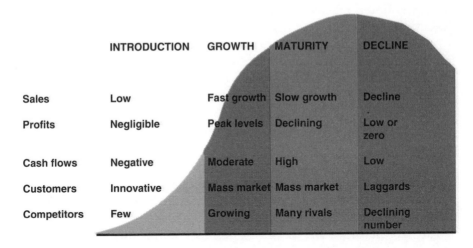

	INTRODUCTION	GROWTH	MATURITY	DECLINE
Sales	Low	Fast growth	Slow growth	Decline
Profits	Negligible	Peak levels	Declining	Low or zero
Cash flows	Negative	Moderate	High	Low
Customers	Innovative	Mass market	Mass market	Laggards
Competitors	Few	Growing	Many rivals	Declining number

Figure 22.3 Implications of the product life cycle – characteristics

One approach to using this technique in a workshop is to explain the concept, draw the product life cycle on a flipchart as shown in Figure 22.2, and then ask the group to locate the various products and services in a segment of the cycle using the characteristics descriptions in Figure 22.3. This is really a simple rearrangement of the product/service list produced in the data collection exercise. Its purpose is to ensure that

	INTRODUCTION	GROWTH	MATURITY	DECLINE
Sales	Expand market	Market penetration	Defend share	Productivity
Marketing Expenditure	High	High (declining %)	Falling	Low
Marketing Emphasis	Product awareness	Brand preference	Brand loyalty	Selective
Distribution	Patchy	Intensive	Intensive	Selective
Price	High	Lower	Lowest	Variable
Product	Basic	Improved	Differentiated	Rationalized

Figure 22.4 Implications of the product life cycle – responses

there is a balance between new products coming on stream through the introduction and growth phases to replace the mature and declining products. Enter sales volumes and gross margin percentages next to the product or service.

If there are uneven distributions – such as no products or services in the introduction phase, perhaps one or two in the growth phase and all others in the maturity or decline phase – then explore whether this is what you want, did you plan for it, how you see the position in two or three years' time. This gives a good visual guide to how the strategy group views the current spread of products or services over the life cycle.

The next step, for the major products or services that currently have high sales volumes or margins or are budgeted to be important in the next two or three years, is to evaluate the strategy towards them in terms of the responses shown in Figure 22.4.

The product life cycle is one of the classic techniques that almost everyone knows, but few seem to use effectively to develop their understanding of their business or their future product/service strategy.

This analysis appears to be a continuation of the current product/service strategy. However, if there are gaps at the early stage of the life cycle this can help lead to the realization that the market or industry is going through significant change and lead to discussion on the need for a more radical strategy.

Boston matrix

In order to dominate a market, a company must normally gain market share during the growth phase of the product life cycle. A mature market is usually stable and it is more difficult and expensive to gain market share. The Boston Consulting Group devised the product portfolio matrix (Figure 22.5) as a means of evaluating a company's range of products in terms of the rate of market growth and its market share. It can also be used as a crude strategy indicator for products in each segment. The terms are defined as follows:

- star: a product (or business) with a high market share in a growing market. The company may be spending heavily to gain that share but the effect of the experience curve will mean that costs are reducing over time and hopefully at a faster rate than the competition. The product should then be self-financing and should, in time, become a cash cow;
- question mark/problem child: also in a growing market but without a high market share. The company may be spending heavily to increase market share but, if they are, it is unlikely that they are getting sufficient cost reductions to offset such investment because the experience gained is less than for a star and costs will be reducing less quickly. Decisions about the future of a product/service group in this segment are the most difficult to make. Should the company spend money to try and turn them into stars, or should they abandon them and write off the costs already incurred?
- cash cow: a product (or business) with a high market share in a mature market. Because growth is low and market conditions more stable, there is less need for heavy marketing. High market share means relatively low costs and the cash cow is thus a cash provider;
- dogs: have low market share in static markets. They are often cash draining, use up a disproportionate amount of resources and usually need to be discontinued.

A modified form of the Boston matrix is usually used in SBP workshops (Figure 22.6). It links closely with the product life cycle approach shown earlier.

The vertical axis in this matrix shows the percentage growth in the market. The example was developed for a materials storage and office partitioning company. At the time this chart was produced inflation was around seven per cent, so an arbitrary cut-off between slow growth

Market share

		High	Low
Market growth rate	High	Star	Question mark (or problem child)
	Low	Cash cow	Dog

Figure 22.5 Boston matrix

and high growth markets was chosen at 10 per cent. This was the growth the company thought it could sustain with what they considered a normal marketing spend on a product. This will depend on the industry, but between 5 and 10 per cent might be considered reasonable growth. Any growth above this line will move a market from low growth to high growth, so to maintain or expand market share in excess of that rate will normally require high investment. On the horizontal axis, 1X represents the smallest of the segment market leaders. If there are three or four companies that dominate the market then they would be located in the quadrants between 1X and 10X. So if this were for the PC market then in the cash cow section would be Dell, Compaq, Gateway, IBM and Macintosh. The rest might arguably be in the dog quadrant. The 1X line needs defining depending on the circumstances, the number of leaders in the segment and the relative difference in their sizes.

The workshop group places the major products or services on the grid. The objective is for the strategy group to decide their own placing and then examine what the results indicate. Marking both products and services together with their sales volume, gross margin percentage and marketing spend makes this chart more valuable. With the company shown in Figure 22.6 the problem is clearly that the company has no cash cow. The result of the process was that the growth of the mezzanine product was deliberately restricted so that it lost market share, but did become a net cash generator. This was more effective than the normal response to cash flow problems, which is to cut marketing expenses across all products. This was a focused and reasoned approach that was facilitated by using the matrix.

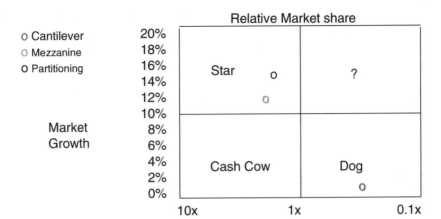

Figure 22.6 Boston matrix development chart

The type of discussion that arises during this analysis covers the definition of the market and the viability of 'me-too' products or services that are not market leaders – there can be some profitable dogs, despite what the classic theory might suggest.

Again, it is the 'hook' that this analysis gives to the process that is valuable. Sometimes, as in the above example, it leads to the insight that the company is always short of cash because it is developing too many stars for tomorrow; or it has no product or service stars for tomorrow, or it fails really to dominate any market and is always having terms dictated to it by the market leader. This is obvious once realized, but often in the daily turmoil of running the business such issues become clouded and confused. The role of analysis in the SBP process is to clarify these issues.

Product/service potential analysis

This technique is useful if you think you have a winning product or service and you want to verify this quickly. It asks questions under four headings to determine if the product stands a chance of success:

- Number of potential buyers: how many people are potential buyers and how much are they prepared to spend for a solution to their problem?
- Homogeneity of potential buyers: do they buy a standard product or does it have to be customized for each buyer?

- Existence of qualified buyers: do the potential buyers know they have a problem, or have they got to be persuaded about the problem first and then sold the solution?
- Existence of qualified providers: are there people to sell the product or provide the service, or is it so complex that only highly skilled (and scarce) personnel can be employed?

The analysis is carried out as shown in Figure 22.7. If there is a reasonably sized market, the chances of success are greater if the product or service scores high on the three factors. Medium or low scores indicate that the product has to have something really special that will enable it to overcome this potential problem.

Number of potential buyers	Average price likely to pay	Annual market value	Market share available to company	Estimated annual sales
1,000,000	£30	£30,000,000	10%	£3,000,000

Success rating	High	Medium	Low
Homogeneity of potential buyers	Standard product	Some customizing required	Is it one market or a number of 'niches'?
Existence of qualified buyers	Know they have a problem, looking for solution	Vaguely aware they might have a problem	Unaware they have a problem
	Advertising and marketing costs are low	Marketing costs may be very high	Market has to be developed before product can be sold. Could be very expensive
Existence of qualified providers	Can be easily recruited or already in company	Difficult to recruit and will need training	Only specialists can do the job

Figure 22.7 Product/service potential analysis

EXTERNAL APPRAISAL

Product/market opportunities

Successful differentiation of a product or service results in customers perceiving a benefit for them in what one company offers over and above competitor companies.

To develop differentiated ideas, brainstorm on a regular basis ideas for new products or services, or methods of doing business. Keep the focus of the brainstorming in line with the selected strategy. For instance, one month you could brainstorm how to improve the response time to customer complaints, another month how to reduce costs in meeting warranty claims.

Use the same brainstorming technique as described for strengths and weaknesses. Generate a list and then refine it until you reach those ideas that appear to have the greatest value. Draw these onto a flipchart in the matrix shown in Figure 22.8.

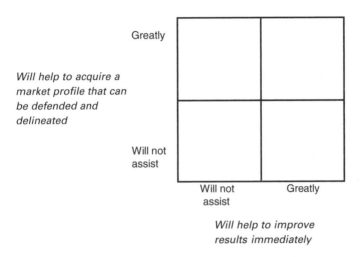

Figure 22.8 Differentiation evaluation

This divides ideas into those that will help to acquire a market profile and those that will help to improve results immediately. All the ideas can be evaluated by discussion and against the criteria shown in Figure 22.9.

This approach can be used to select the best ideas generated in any meeting. It is also particularly useful where a discussion is going round in circles and an approach is needed to break the deadlock, establish the best answer, and move the group forward.

Demographics and near certainties

It is a truism that the rate of change is accelerating so fast that no business can afford to ignore the changes in the environment. Much of what will happen in the future is already predictable. We know what proportion of the population will be aged between 20 and 25 in 2020.

1. **Resulting benefit to customer**
   a. Substantial improvement
   b. Improvement
   c. No change
   d. Reduction
   e. Substantial reduction

4. **Relative market position**
   a. Substantial improvement
   b. Improvement
   c. No change
   d. Reduction
   e. Substantial reduction

2. **Defendable competitive advantage**
   a. Substantial improvement
   b. Improvement
   c. No change
   d. Reduction
   e. Substantial reduction

5. **Risk**
   a. None
   b. Slight
   c. Medium
   d. High
   e. Extremely high

3. **Competitor reaction**
   a. Withdrawal
   b. Partial withdrawal
   c. No change
   d. Reaction
   e. Strong reaction

6. **Utilization of strengths**
   a. Strongly positive
   b. Positive
   c. Neutral
   d. Negative
   e. Strongly negative

Figure 22.9 Evaluation of developed differentiation

The number of university graduates throughout the next 20 years can be estimated with some accuracy. We also know how many there will be in France, Italy, Germany and the United Kingdom. Equally, we know how many will retire on a reasonable pension and, therefore, the spending power those pensioners are likely to have.

Many other factors can also be forecast with a reasonable degree of certainty. For example, the single European market exists with most members having a single currency. It is probable that it will become more integrated over the next ten years and will react to world events as one political entity. It is certain to increase its membership, with Hungary and Poland and other former East European states joining. The only uncertainty is the terms under which they will join.

Companies that are based in Europe, have subsidiaries or significant sales there, need to evaluate the potential impact this will have on them.

Five forces analysis

There are five forces acting on any organization: potential entrants, the bargaining power, respectively, of suppliers and customers, the threat of substitutes and competitive rivalry between players in the industry. This situation is shown diagrammatically in Figure 22.10.

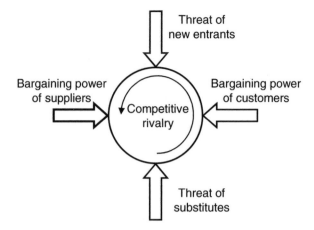

Figure 22.10 The five forces acting on an organization

Sometimes I use this structure in workshops and reports to clarify a company's position. The attached description was used for a real but anonymised manufacturer I have called Plinter Industrial, a company that is in a commodity business.

Potential entrants

For this company in this industry the barriers to entry are provided by the capital-intensive nature of the industry and its current unattractiveness to potential investors. There are few, if any, new entrants to this industry.

Bargaining power of suppliers

The most influential suppliers in this industry are the raw material companies. They tend to be much larger than their customers, typically they are relatively unresponsive to the needs of the industry, and there are indications that they co-operate to create economic conditions favorable to their own objectives. An emerging and concerning trend is for them to integrate forward to protect their volumes. There are indications that the raw material producers who do follow this strategy subsidize their downstream processing operations with low-price finished product.

Bargaining power of customers

The customers in this scenario fall into two categories. Firstly, the service centers and smaller OEMs (original equipment manufacturers): these customers tend to be of a similar size to Plinter or are smaller. In these instances the power between supplier and customer is fairly well balanced with both being relatively inter-dependent.

Secondly, the automotive customers: these are, in most cases, either the relatively large system builders or the huge, global assemblers. These customers can, and do, wield significant power, influencing heavily the price of products and where and how they are manufactured. To compete in this market requires, by definition, well-tuned operations and a drive for zero waste and lowest possible costs.

Threat of substitutes

The Plinter product range has a number of potential substitutes including product made from polymers, aluminum and other alloys. Major drivers are weight and strength, particularly in the automotive industry where there is a strong correlation between vehicle weight and fuel consumption/environmental pollution. It is likely that these replacement materials will, progressively over time, displace the Plinter product range.

However, acting in the opposite direction is a drive to replace other products with Plinter's. Plinter has significant advantages in specific applications. The key issue for Plinter is to accelerate the drive to replace products where we have an advantage and use product improvement/pricing to retain current applications as long as possible.

Competitive rivalry

Two factors serve to limit the competitive rivalry experienced by Plinter. The first is that some of the SBUs (strategic business units) are focused on market niches with few players. There is one significant competitor, Capability, a second, Fredomics, with a relatively weak marketing organization and Fibel who only enter this market opportunistically when their core market, the oil sector, goes into decline.

The second factor is that all players are conscious of the need to avoid a damaging price war. The cumulative effect of the two factors is to limit the amount of competitive rivalry experienced by the industry.

This analysis was driven directly from the five forces model in Figure 22.10.

With another client, the UK leader in the office leasing business, I developed a modified version of the model to explain visually what the forces were doing in their industry as it went through a period of significant change a number of years ago. This is shown in Figure 22.11.

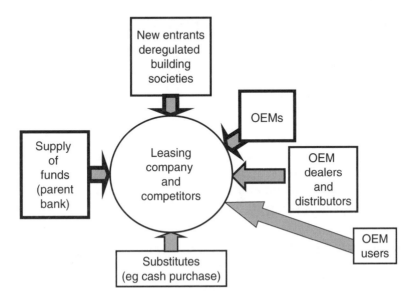

Figure 22.11 Office leasing – industry structure chart

The thickness of the arrow indicates the strength of the force. In this case the supplier of funds was a parent bank, one of the largest in the United Kingdom, so this was a strong relationship. New entrants to the market were seen as being the newly deregulated building societies which had strong funds flow and could gather leasing expertise through acquiring a small to medium-sized leasing company. Because the cost of their funds was low they would be able to offer lower rates in the market to win business. Substitutes, cash purchases or other financial funding were seen as a minor threat at this time. There were effectively three groups of customers, OEMs, who used my client to fund and administer their own lease arrangements. The relationship with this group was strong and would be difficult for a competitor to displace. With OEM dealers and distributors it was not quite as strong, this being a far more numerous group, but it presented a major opportunity for expansion. The end-user market was even more numerous and difficult to penetrate. This was where the small leasing companies were strongest. The approach to this market was to try to ensure that the OEMs offer was stronger, and their sales force better trained in office product leasing, than these local suppliers.

Developing this chart did not take very long and significantly helped in developing the strategy.

An approach to opportunities and threats

A possible structure for approaching opportunities and threats is given below. This is by no means the only approach, nor is it claimed to be exhaustive.

Generation

Start by brainstorming opportunities and threats as previously done for strengths and weaknesses. Refine the lists as before. Use the opportunities and threats analysis forms (Figures 22.12 and 22.13) to evaluate the major opportunities and major threats.

Opportunity	Revenue/profit potential in 12/24 and 36 months	What has to be done to achieve this opportunity?	What are the costs?	Should it be followed-up and if so – when?

Figure 22.12 Opportunity analysis

Ensure that in the discussion that follows the brainstorming all the areas covered below are considered to assess their impact on the company, especially if there is no reference to them in the refined lists.

Threat	What damage could it cause the company?	How can threat be eliminated/ minimized?	Cost of eliminating or minimizing	What is the time scale for the threat and com-pany reaction?

Figure 22.13 Threats Analysis

New business opportunities

The brainstorming should generate a number of business opportunities. These should be prioritized ready for investigation during the development of strategic options. The differentiation evaluation, Figure 22.8, can be used to assist this process.

Political trends

The following areas should be considered:

- Local: restrictions, rates, the attitudes of local politicians;
- National: legislation on trading, pricing, dividends, safety, noise, pollution, tax, employment;
- World: if the company is operating internationally, check the political stability of the countries that form its main markets. Even if covered by default insurance, check the percentage cover this gives (eg 70 per cent of sales invoice), and what the triggers are which cause the insurance to pay out. All companies trading in Europe must keep an eye on the EC and what it is doing and plans to do, which affects the business and trade environment. For instance, new pollution regulations are being introduced by the EC; they will have a major impact on factories in certain industries. The recession has weakened many companies and they will not be able to afford to implement the new regulations. This is a threat to them and an opportunity for their competitors.

Economic trends

The following areas should be considered:

- Local: is the region growing and expanding, or in decay? Is labor of the right quality available at competitive rates? What local financial assistance is available?
- National: economic forecasts are often wide of the mark, but they can indicate trends, although their forecasts of economic turning points are not usually very accurate. For companies with a dominant share of a large market, these forecasts, and their potential impact, can be very important. If retail sales are forecast to grow at three rather than one per cent, this could substantially affect sales volumes. However, for companies with a small market share, a two to three per cent difference in growth on a national scale will only affect their sales by a very small amount. Winning two or three major new contracts, or finding a new niche in the market, can be much more important. Of more value than general national economic forecasts are those for the company's market or market segment. From the ranking of products and customers by sales and profit, as described in Chapter 21 (Data collection), the major customer segments will already have been identified. The economic forecasts for segments can yield valuable data on where to concentrate marketing effort. Look at some of the anomalies that were identified in the product and customer analysis, and the forecasts for those areas. Do they represent potential sizeable new markets?
- World: on the global level, concentrate on large markets, high growth markets and those where the company is exposed to risk.

Social trends

The main significance of social trends concerns the changing values of sections of the population. These include such areas as working hours versus leisure time, private versus public health care, housing, trade unions, retirement and so on.

I have already covered the impact of demographic factors on social change. Totally new markets can be created. For instance, the market for those in their fifties (the 'wrinklies') is now seen as very lucrative. They tend to be well off – they have top earnings, no dependents, and their mortgage is paid. They are potentially looking for goods and services at the top end of the market, where margins are high. If your product or service is appropriate, consider what this group wants and whether you can supply it.

Society adapts slowly, but many indicators of the future are already with us now. Around the fringes of society there are the clues to what the future may hold.

When any move in society is marginal, affecting less than 20 per cent of the population, it can virtually be ignored. Once it exceeds 20 per cent, people inevitably have to take notice of it. One example is divorce. When it affected only one in 10 marriages, the divorcee was a social pariah. As the 20 per cent level was approached, laws, values and language all changed. There are few of us today who, if not divorced ourselves, do not have relatives or friends who are and are accepted as a normal part of society.

One result of this is that the nuclear family, which has been the focus of so much marketing and advertising, is shrinking and other opportunities are opening up. Being aware of the areas where changes in society will lead a group from being a minority who do not have to be taken into account to the 20 per cent level where they become significant is one of the keys to entrepreneurial growth. For instance, from a study that I did recently I believe that the real take-off in health foods is yet to happen. When it does they will not be in their current form and will not be considered as fringe products.

Technology

We all know how technology is changing the world, and how today's technology is obsolete tomorrow. Even if your company's product is technologically advanced today, tomorrow someone will produce one with even more features at a lower price. Today's calculator will sing to you tomorrow and talk to you the day after. That is if you still use a calculator.

However, quality products, such as those supplied by Wedgwood or Waterford, Rolls-Royce or Mercedes, are thought of as brand leaders and this gives them a positioning advantage when they introduce new products.

There is value in a quality branded item whose reputation is built on years of quality products. Imitation and usurpation of that branded position is very hard.

General points

For many small and medium-sized companies, the analysis of the external environment should be restricted to those areas that closely affect the company and about which it has reasonable knowledge. If projections are to be used, then use a range. If the projection still looks viable at the bottom of the range, then that environmental factor has either been sufficiently built into the plan, or it is of no major importance. Large organizations will naturally monitor the environment intensively on a continuous basis, for currency, market and investment exposure. It could be in their interests to keep key suppliers informed of what is happening in these areas.

ORGANIZATION

The restructuring of business

Alongside these environmental changes, there is an increasing shift towards outsourcing operations. This can cause a fundamental change in the way organizations are structured affecting businesses of all sizes. The logic behind this restructuring is that the rapid dissemination of knowledge and information that is now possible, together with the acceleration of technological change and the market's demands for higher service, is shortening product life cycles. To meet these demands, organizations have to be able to react quickly, which might well mean reorganizing the way their resources are deployed. For many companies there is also a strong cost-saving factor. It is estimated that when BP Amoco, the oil giant, outsourced its finance and accounting operations to PricewaterhouseCoopers in 1999 the contract was worth US$1.1 billion over ten years and that it represented in excess of 10 per cent savings.

Companies that have all their human resources in-house, on the payroll, are usually slower at reacting to movements in the market. Managers have to concentrate on running the business as a whole and this, to an extent, distracts them from concentrating on how to take advantage of new opportunities. There also tends to be a large cadre of middle managers, which increases the time between decision-making and implementation. Companies that are leaner, with fewer levels of management between the top and front-line managers, are quicker to react. Similarly, they can only afford to have people on the payroll who will work – productively work – for a minimum of 40 hours a week.

They can no longer afford to have staff who draw a full salary but only effectively contribute to the business for 20 hours a week, or for eight months of the year.

Therefore companies need to define:

- what the critical management areas are for their business;
- what the core areas are that make the company a viable business, that provide the key resources for the company to do business;
- the number of people that need to be employed for these core areas.

All other functions and services that the business still needs, but not on a continuous basis, or that are not central to the company purpose, are bought in from outside service suppliers.

Even though this kind of thinking has existed in a modern form for over 20 years it is still creating a whole new structure and way of doing business. Lessons can be learned from the early pioneers. A good example is the clothing industry in Italy. One region used to have some 700 firms, each employing, on average, 30 workers. Several years later there were some 9,500 firms each employing, on average, five workers. Employment had increased from some 21,000 to 47,500. The interesting point is that the structure had changed. Instead of operating as separate firms, they were subcontractors organized by a coordinating company. This kept to itself the key functions of this particular type of business: design, fabric selection, production scheduling, marketing, brand management, quality control, finance and sales organization. Actual selling was carried out through distributors or sales agents. In other words, this coordinating company kept the critical factors of design and fabric selection under its own direct control and scheduled and managed the overall process through outside contractors. It also funded the operations.

The key lesson is that the coordinating company understood what it had to control centrally and knew how to coordinate all the external suppliers to deliver world-beating products.

The big pharmaceutical companies arguably use outsourcing even for many of their core activities. They buy in new products from the biotech companies who have conducted the original research, they outsource clinical trials to contract research organizations (CROs) and sometimes even rent sales forces from contract sales organizations (CSOs). These are the key activities in the pharmaceutical industry, research, trials to obtain approval and marketing representation. In addition many of them also contract out the 'chore' activities. In practice the pharmaceutical companies maintain full capabilities for their key activities in-house and outsource the excess workload they cannot manage.

If this route continues to be followed, and there is evidence that it will be, then the structure of companies could begin to look more like Figure 22.14. The boxes round the outside of this figure represent advisers, services and suppliers who fulfill the functions other firms have in-house.

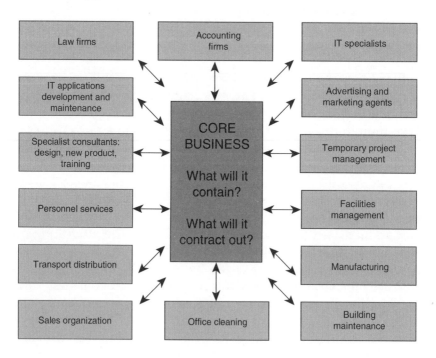

Figure 22.14 New company structure

There is a vital element to making this organizational structure effective. It can be argued that in successful companies the balance between internal marketing, having to sell and implement ideas inside the company, and external marketing, selling to customers, is weighted in favor of the latter. In this new structure, if it is to be successful, the core resources that have to be committed to managing the supplier companies must be less than if those services were provided in-house. The more effectively the supplier relationships are set up the less effort they will require in management from the core and the more successful the organization will be.

Another critical element in outsourcing is in contract flexibility. If the outsourcing contract does not provide the company with substantially more flexibility, to increase and decrease workloads, change the type of work done, change systems and requirements, then it will become a block on change rather than an enabler.

For innovative suppliers this structural change is full of opportunities for creating new services and products. For the core business there are also risks. In particular companies have outsourced their computer operations to application service providers some of whom have gone out of business and left the company without an IT system.

The aim of the supplying companies is to attach themselves so closely to the core business that they are irreplaceable. This could create the very inflexibility that the approach is supposed to avoid.

Such swings in the way companies operate occur from time to time, but this one looks set to continue. Understanding how to work in this new type of environment will be one of the keys to success in the next 20 years.

Organization growth model

This model describes the phases an organization passes through during its corporate growth. It defines the problems that are encountered and the range of actions that are appropriate at each stage.

While this is a theoretical model, it is based on experience and empirical evidence. Its value is as a vehicle for discussion of the organization structure. The new concepts of organization structure, core business, flat management and doing more with less can be evaluated against the model and its historical and conventional approach. Many of the lessons from this model can help in designing successful new organization structures. It is particularly appropriate in companies that are growing, undergoing change and restructuring, where it helps to explain the underlying forces creating the need for change.

Historical forces shape the future growth of organizations. Managers often overlook such critical development questions as:

- Where has the organization been in the past?
- Where is it now?
- What do the answers to these two questions indicate about where we are going in the future?

Managers focus on the market and the environment when looking for growth and ignore the organizational machine that will take them there. The clues to future success lie in their own organization and its stage

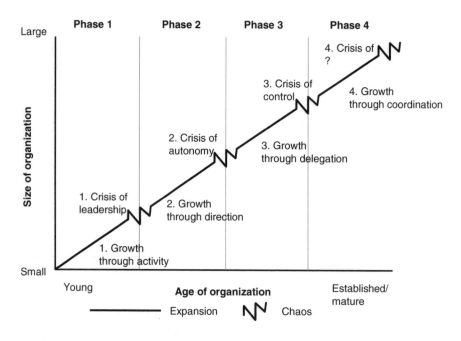

Figure 22.15 Organization growth model

of development. Two terms are used to describe the state of the organization (see Figure 22.15): expansion – prolonged periods of growth where no major upheaval occurs – and chaos – periods of substantial turmoil.

There are four key forces determining the way organizations develop:

- how flexible and controllable the organization is (often related to its age);
- the size of the organization;
- the current stage of organizational development;
- the growth rate of the industry.

A company whose environment is increasingly complex and dynamic, whose market is growing rapidly, which is increasing in size and still relatively young in attitude, will move through the phases of expansion and into the periods of chaos at a quicker rate than a company in a more stable position.

However, once a company has successfully passed through a period of chaos, it usually enjoys between two and six years of continuous growth without another major setback. This is the period of expansion.

Periods of expansion are punctuated with periods of chaos. This is when traditional management practices, which were appropriate for a smaller size company and an earlier time, come under scrutiny by frustrated top managers and disillusioned middle managers. During such periods of crisis a number of companies fail – those unable to abandon past practices and effect major organizational changes will either fold or experience a leveling off in their rate of growth.

The organization growth model dealing with management concerns (Figure 22.16) aims to help managers in each period of chaos to find a new set of practices that will become the basis for managing the next period of evolutionary growth. The solutions are intended as an indication of how to progress to the next stage.

Category	Phase 1	Phase 2	Phase 3	Phase 4
Management focus	Make and sell	Efficiency of operations	Growth and market share	Creation of corporate vision
Organization structure	Informal	Structured	Divisions and SBUs	Corporate leadership team and empowered operations
Top management style	Individualistic and entrepreneurial	Directive	Decisions devolved to lowest level	Encouragement by vision and culture
Control system	Market results	Standards and cost centers	Reports and profit centers	Conformity to agreed SBPs
Management reward emphasis	Ownership	Salary and merit increases	Individual bonus	Profit sharing and stock options

Figure 22.16 Organization growth model – management concerns

Phase 1 – Creativity

When an organization starts up, its emphasis is on creating a product or service and a market: the company's founders are usually entrepreneurs; their energies are focused on making and selling a new product or service and succeeding with their business dream; communication among employees is frequent and informal; control is achieved through feedback from the market and management of the cash flow, particularly the overdraft; management systems, especially the computer systems, focus on the areas of the business that the founders believe are important.

The leadership crisis is caused by the company growing. As the number of employees increases, more emphasis needs to be put on management. The informal systems are no longer able to cope. New employees are not motivated by intense loyalty to the organization or interest in the product. Controls become increasingly important, as market feedback no longer provides timely information for all activities.

The founders find themselves burdened with administrative chores, which they are ill-equipped to handle and which distract them from the technical and entrepreneurial activities that have created the growth. Conflicts between the harried leaders grow more intense.

The crisis of leadership is the onset of the first period of chaos. The founders are often unable to lead the company out of the confusion and provide the managerial expertise the company needs.

They have two options. They may decide that they both can and want to resolve the situation and follow the SBP approach to move the company onto a new and more defined path. Or they can employ a strong manager who has the experience, knowledge and skill to change the organization and introduce new systems and approaches. This second approach, combined with developing a strategic business plan, can be the more successful, although it is not easy for the founders to give up the greater part of their control of the company.

This is the first test, whether they are willing to accept and support a new approach and perhaps a professional manager to pull the organization together. The critical factor is whether the company is big enough, and will be attractive enough, to the right caliber of professional manager. Some owner-managers try to rush this stage because they want to get on with building the organization, and consequently hire the wrong manager, who then damages rather than helps the business.

Phase 2 – Direction

With luck, the new approach will enable the company to enter a period of growth, particularly if combined with a new business manager working in the top management team with the founders jointly developing a SBP, with clear and allocated responsibility for its implementation.

The new predominant style of management will be directive, ensuring that staff, who are increasing in numbers, know what is expected of them, how the tasks are to be performed and to what standard. During the evolutionary period that follows the main characteristics of the organization will be:

- a functional organization structure based on job activities, with increasing specialization;
- development of the accounting function, with emphasis on accurate and meaningful information to help manage the business; which often means revising the computer systems that have been installed in Phase 1;
- the adoption of budgets, incentives and performance standards; the organization structure becomes more rigid, impersonal and formal as the number of new positions increases;
- the SBP document setting the direction of the business, building commitment to the individual roles of the functional managers.

The autonomy crisis occurs when the functional managers find the structure in the expanding organization cumbersome and restrictive. They are growing in confidence and want a bigger role in the company's overall decision-making process, as well as greater freedom to work on their own initiative.

The second period of chaos develops as the senior managers, who believe that their own abilities have been the reason for the company's growth, try to hold on to power. Instead of devolving decision-making to the first line of supervision, which is possible with IT systems that provide information throughout the company, the senior managers hold on to their authority and management information. When they do try to let go it is done too rapidly, with resulting confusion and often the exodus of managers and staff from the company. Provided the move towards delegation and empowerment is carefully planned and executed it is possible to make a relatively smooth transition to the next phase.

Successful organizations plan how to empower their staff, at all levels, ensuring that their managers are trained, that they are clear on the direction of the business, its values and performance standards. Effective financial controls and reporting systems are put in place, along with an open communication approach to ensure that each part of the group is working to the same objective.

Phase 3 – Delegation

The successful implementation of a decentralized organization structure results in the following characteristics:

- greater authority devolved throughout the organization; in particular, managers of plants and market territories are given greater freedom to develop and implement their own plans;
- the use of profit centers and bonuses to stimulate motivation; the top executives at head office concentrate on corporate strategy, managing corporate relations with other organizations, government, finance institutions and involve themselves in operations which are experiencing problems;
- top managers reinforcing the corporate culture.

The delegation stage proves useful for gaining expansion by increasing motivation throughout the organization. It allows the company to penetrate new markets, respond faster to customers and become more innovative.

The control crisis occurs when the top managers sense they are losing control over a highly diversified operation. Autonomous operations managers prefer to run their own organizations without coordinating plans, finance, technology and manpower with the rest of the organization. Head office is viewed as almost a financial holding company. The operations that succeed in obtaining corporate funds are those that can command support among top management. Growth becomes a political exercise, often involving coalitions and reciprocal deals. The crunch comes when the profits level off or start to fall rapidly. Chaos arrives as top managers seek to regain control over the entire company. An attempt to return to centralized management might be made, resulting in the most capable operations managers leaving the organization. Those companies that move ahead do so through a process of coordination.

Phase 4 – Co-ordination

Top managers have to have a clear vision of the organization, which they can sell to each division and business unit. Every senior manager has to know how the business fits together and where it is going as a whole. If parts of the business are interdependent then there must not be barriers between them; there must be no 'over the fence' mentality on handling projects or work (where as one department finishes its part of a project, it metaphorically throws it to the next department and sees it as 'no longer our problem'). The structure of the organization must make sense in terms of its mission statement and the perceived ideas of how the business actually works. Characteristics of this phase are that:

- a corporate 'vision' statement and key corporate goals are established. These are then interpreted and incorporated into the SBP for each business unit or division. All SBP are intensively reviewed and approved at the corporate level;
- the corporate directors are responsible for the overall corporate performance. They do not have line responsibility for divisions or functions within the organization;
- capital expenditure is evaluated according to how far it helps the corporation achieve its goals, not how it helps a division or business unit to realize its individual objectives at the expense of the corporation as a whole;
- stock options and company-wide profit sharing are used to encourage managers to identify with the firm as a whole.

Managers now learn to justify their decisions by thinking through the different options and the likely results. More efficient allocation of funds and a stronger group identity help the organization to continue its expansion.

Summary

With organization change now so rapid, it is difficult to define how organizations develop beyond this co-ordination stage in any meaningful way.

The value of the organization growth model lies in helping managers to recognize where they are in the process and to plan for the next stage within the context of their own business, recognizing that only a narrow range of options may exist. They must also recognize that each new set of solutions brings with it a new set of problems.

Job descriptions

Confusion can be one of the most debilitating diseases in a company. Where confusion really has taken hold, and everyone is fire-fighting, a job description exercise can help to clarify who is responsible for what. However, not every company needs job descriptions and sometimes they can have a negative effect, rather like the rulebook if not handled carefully. My own experience indicates that they should only be used if there really is organizational confusion and they seem the only way of resolving it.

One way job descriptions can be useful is as a position audit, to establish where the company is now, how employees view their current responsibilities and what they believe they are responsible for. Having established this, brief documents can be issued, with the rider that change is constant, that this is only a snapshot of where the company is now and that there is every chance it will have changed in a year from now. This can be done effectively in a workshop.

If you do think job descriptions are useful in your company, make sure they are kept ruthlessly up to date and are built into the appraisal system.

A job description should be no longer than one page, and even then it is difficult to remember all of it. I have seen examples of job descriptions that have 14 areas of accountability, including two with their own subsets of five further sets of accountability. These become meaningless as a motivating or managing tool.

Every statement within the job description needs to be discussed between the manager and the subordinate to ensure absolute clarity and agreement on what each one means. If a job description is given to a subordinate without being discussed carefully it becomes another meaningless list of responsibilities.

The following example of a job description for John Smith is in a format that has proved successful:

Position Description

Job title: Area Manager   Job holder: John Smith

Reports to: Regional Manager   Date: November 23 2001

Purpose: To manage the accounts that constitutes the area for effective cost control and growth in line with the company objective.

Scope: Area includes the following named accounts in Idaho plus any future additions.

Main responsibilities:

Planning: Account improvement. Efficiency improvement. To improve total account turnover by 9 per cent in line with profitability and budget.

Organizing: Customer care calls on a regular cycle. Allocation of operators to meet required volumes.

Evaluation and control (measurement systems):

To achieve results in line with the agreed budget, and to know on a ' real time' basis how the area is performing in terms of sales and costs.

Climate setting: To create a positive working attitude in all dealings with customers and employees.

Operational: To meet key customer-facing personnel at least once every week.

To meet all operators at least once every two weeks.

To ensure that every customer complaint is actioned within 24 hours.

Key relationships:

Reporting up: Regional Manager

Reporting in: Customer Care Department

Liaising: With Other Area Managers

Reporting to: Account Operators

Authority levels:

No authority to spend capital.

No authority to sell assets.

No authority to start new services.

No authority to change wage rates.

CHAPTER SUMMARY

After you have applied the techniques that are relevant to your organization, you should find it possible to complete information under the headings below. Some of this information will be able to be summarized with only a brief statement; other headings will need detailed coverage and will be of vital importance in developing your strategic options. Because of this they will need expanding beyond the outline given here.

Usually this data is not completed until after the first workshop.

New business opportunities

- Potential new products/services.
- Potential new markets.

- Possible acquisitions.
- Possible new approaches to conducting business.

Industry trends and business environment

- Structure of the industry.
- Differences among top three competitors.
- Main competitive thrust.
- Sales/distribution structure.
- Substitution threats where the need satisfied by a product or service can be met by another, different product or service.
- Factors for the most successful companies in the industry.
- Economic forecast for the industry over the next n years.
- Main impacts, cause and effect, expected in industry in the next n years.
- Impact of technology.
- Impact of product innovation.
- Availability of energy, raw materials, labors.

Social factors

- Attitudes towards the industry – customers, political, public.
- Impact on the industry of changes in society – by market.

Economic factors

- Economic forecast for the next n years – by market.
- Possible impact of currency fluctuations.
- Possibility of protectionism in major markets.

Political factors

- Possible impact of a change of political leadership – by market.
- Possible political impact on production/service centers.

$\boxed{23}$

Summary

There are three main reasons why the SBP process is so effective. The first is to do with defining goals. It is the goals that produce the thought and rigor that leads to the production of a plan that will improve company performance.

The goal structure is shown in Figure 23.1.

Distinctive capability	The combination of business processes, attributes and competencies that distinguishes the company and creates competitive advantage. It will also enable it to seize the opportunities that arise in the future that match its strategic direction
Market/ product/service	The focus of application for the skills and competencies of the company
Identity	Communicating a clear positive perception and image of the company to each of the audiences who are important to its future well being
People	Organising the skills and competencies of the company to meet the needs of the customers both now and in the future
Efficiency	Ensuring the business is focused on the correct activities, is run as efficiently as any competitor and fully exploits the potential of e-commerce
Option	Customizing the strategy to meet the special needs of an organisation

Figure 23.1 The goals

The second reason for the effectiveness of SBP is the logical of flow from goals to action program, the information for which is contained on a single page. From the way the plan is presented it is clear how the strategy will be achieved.

The third reason is to do with the process itself, the development of the strategy. The structure of the process, from building the leadership team to implementing organizational change through the system of performance target teams, creates an organization that knows where it is going, has the commitment to take it there and a built-in process to enable it to structure itself to make the change.

THE RULES OF STRATEGY

There are five rules that any strategic process should follow if it is to be successful:

- There should be a formal strategic planning process.
- The strategy team should be championed by the leader of the organization and the top executives.
- The strategy should be communicated to staff and customers.
- The strategy should be continuously probed and tested.
- The strategy should enable managers to think strategically.

The SBP approach clearly encompasses the first four rules. What I want to explain in this summary is how it covers the last point.

STRATEGIC THINKING

To achieve real long-term growth, a company needs a strong leadership team. There may be a dominant leader, but one person cannot run companies of any reasonable size. The leadership team needs to act as one, with common aims and purposes.

The old idea of strategy, as an ivory tower exercise handed down for the managers to implement, just does not work. The leadership team and the managers have to be their own strategists. The practitioners have to be the planners. Therefore they need a system that they can use and follow, that will be comprehensive and exhaustive, yet understandable. They need a model that simplifies the situation, but does not ignore the complexities.

SBP is to do with the mind, both the individual minds and the collective mind of the team. One successful CEO described how he has a mental model of how his company operates, which he calls the 'vehicle'. All the key activities, decisions and outcomes of the business are included in this model. Three things stand out about the 'vehicle':

- It is a conscious idea and he has given it a name.
- It is also subconscious – when he spoke about it to us it was the first time he had discussed it with anyone.
- It defines his role, he uses it to decide his actions; not the actions of his job description, but the operational actions of managing the company.

That is what SBP is, a 'vehicle' for deciding actions, one that every executive, every manager, and every employee has in his or her head. For the leadership team it will be the complete plan, and they will be able to see how outcomes and events either move the plan forward or call for some reappraisal of it. For managers perhaps it is part of the SBP document, but with more detail. The action programs and allocated responsibilities lead directly into day to day management, and give purpose to the work of employees.

The plan itself is simple, and can be recited by those who helped to frame it. It appears almost to be a poor return for all the effort. But the plan is the model that simplifies the complexity. Only by going through the long process of developing common knowledge, understanding and attitudes to the company, does the simplified model become a vehicle for strategically managing the business. The mechanism for developing the common understanding of these factors is the workshop. That is why workshops are so powerful.

When unexpected events affect the company, the managers know what impact they will have on the strategy, and will usually understand the actions that need to be taken. There may be disagreements among the group, but at least there is a common base of communication. Having made their decision, they can all adjust their mental model.

When the SBP process reaches this level, of being a conscious vehicle, then it has truly achieved its aim to become a way of strategic thinking and strategic managing.

Index